Genoa's Freedom

Empires and Entanglements in the Early Modern World

Series Editors
Charles Parker and Ulrike Strasser

An extraordinary pattern of state and empire building across Eurasia and the Atlantic basin in the early modern period inaugurated a new era in world history characterized by ongoing cross-cultural engagement among peoples from around the globe. The monographs and edited collections published in the *Empires and Entanglements in the Early Modern World* series will pursue particular historical themes that illuminate these interactive dimensions in the early modern world. These studies either take a comparative approach to commensurate historical developments in various parts of the world or examine trans-regional patterns and forces that brought together different societies and communities. This series seeks to go beyond essentialist approaches that treat regions and oceans as self-contained, insular cultural spaces to stress interconnectedness in a paramount age of imperial expansion. We therefore welcome proposals and manuscripts on cultural, religious, intellectual, and environmental themes that show connections and conjunctures across territories and oceans or undertake comparisons within particular regions and maritime basins.

Titles in the Series

Genoa's Freedom: Entrepreneurship, Republicanism, and the Spanish Atlantic, by Matteo Salonia

Genoa's Freedom

Entrepreneurship, Republicanism, and the Spanish Atlantic

Matteo Salonia

LEXINGTON BOOKS
Lanham • Boulder • New York • London

Published by Lexington Books
An imprint of The Rowman & Littlefield Publishing Group, Inc.
4501 Forbes Boulevard, Suite 200, Lanham, Maryland 20706
www.rowman.com

Unit A, Whitacre Mews, 26-34 Stannary Street, London SE11 4AB

British Library Cataloguing in Publication Information Available

Library of Congress Cataloging-in-Publication Data Available

ISBN 978-1-4985-3421-5 (cloth : alk. paper)
ISBN 978-1-4985-3422-2 (electronic)

∞™ The paper used in this publication meets the minimum requirements of American National Standard for Information Sciences Permanence of Paper for Printed Library Materials, ANSI/NISO Z39.48-1992.

Printed in the United States of America

For my parents, Gaetano and Veneranda,
and my brother, Leonardo.

Contents

Acknowledgments

I am grateful to many colleagues and friends for their help and encouragement while I was writing this book. *In primis*, I thank Harald E. Braun and Andrew Redden, my PhD supervisors at the University of Liverpool. Their breadth of knowledge and constant support has been invaluable: I shall be forever grateful, and I am honored to call them my friends. I am also indebted to Manuel Herrero Sánchez and Catia Brilli, with whom I have had the pleasure to discuss ideas on the Genoese presence in the Habsburg Empire, and to Sandra Toffolo, whose comments on earlier drafts of this book have been very useful. Needless to say, any shortcomings that a reader may encounter are due to the author alone. Moreover, I want to thank all those who at different stages of my research have offered insights, in particular Şizen Yiacoup, Francisco Bethencourt, William J. Ashworth, and Eugenio Tirelli. Finally, I thank Teng Li and James Duffy for their friendship and companionship, and for the countless, fascinating discussions about medieval civilization during the past four years.

Introduction

Late medieval and early modern Genoa was a city republic with a modest territorial dominion and an urban center of narrow streets and crowded neighborhoods surrounding a bustling port. In this environment (where human action and political ideas were profoundly interwoven), trade and accumulation of capital became socially acceptable, as nobles, merchants, and sailors were involved side by side in an array of economic activities. At the same time, underneath its apparently anarchical political and social life, Genoa preserved for centuries a precise, though relatively unsung, civic philosophy. Thus, this book presents Genoa's market expansion, diplomatic moves, and institutional reforms as the results (and causes) of the Genoese people's entrepreneurial culture, self-perception, and republican ideology. Genoa's economic, political, and intellectual history is here treated within the framework of the Atlantic world, a concept whose historical origins can be traced back to the late medieval Mediterranean city ports—and the Genoese network in particular. In fact, the investigation of Genoa's ubiquitous merchants, captains, and entrepreneurs could well contribute to the redefinition of what we mean by Atlantic world, drawing our attention to the unique role(s) of specific groups in the transfer of colonial techniques and in the exchange of mental capital.

Scholars of early modern Atlantic empires have in the last decades stressed their cultural complexity, entangled nature, and overlapping history. Categories like Spanish, Portuguese, and British "Atlantics" have been scrutinized and found at times wanting, because they are conceptually rigid, unable to capture the common features of the Atlantic experience and the hybrid identity of the people who lived within it.[1] For instance, Jorge Cañizares-Esguerra has invited historians of the Atlantic to move from national narratives to transnational and global frameworks.[2] He has himself offered several examples of historical investigations that center on shared, Atlantic experiences and cultural paradigms, as well as on borderlands, where national identities are challenged, opaque, reshaped.[3] John H. Elliott, in turn, who has proposed a comparative method and hence used more unconcernedly the terms Spanish Atlantic and British Atlantic, seems to accept the notion that in the Atlantic world specific groups and cultures were obfuscated, in the sense that they were absorbed by hybrid historical processes. Only, for Elliott, these processes can be studied and compared in a semi-hemispherical (Spanish; British) rather than hemispherical framework.[4] Therefore, within this lively, fruitful, and sophisticated debate, cosmopolitanism has progressively come to indicate transnationality and overlapping identities—which are admittedly essential ideas to grasp the reality of Atlantic empires. As a consequence, the widely known fact that foreign economic actors were part of the fabric of virtually every colonial society[5] has been either employed to disprove and deconstruct any idea of a cohesive national Atlantic (be it British, Spanish, or Portuguese), or to carefully investigate the social and economic history of a certain colonial city port or region inasmuch as it fit in broader narratives of a national, semi-hemispherical Atlantic to be perhaps subsequently compared with others.

In this context, it appears legitimate to wonder whether the study of specific groups of foreigners within Atlantic empires can proceed in a different way: considering and characterizing each of the groups in question, following them through different regions and in different historical periods. This means that we can detect and describe their unique contributions to the Atlantic world, especially in terms of mental capital, economic praxis, and colonial techniques. While this approach does not deny but rather integrates the recent scholarship and debate on the Atlantic, on the other hand it represents an alternative to chronologically or geographically limited studies, as it attempts to trace the distinct history of a mature entrepreneurial culture entering and shaping early modern empires in the Atlantic. In other words, blurred imperial borders and shared Atlantic historical phenomena could not and did not render specific cultural backgrounds, unique institutional traditions, and past colonial experiences insignificant. If not all groups entering the Atlantic were equipped with the same entrepreneurial behaviors, then a historical study of the value systems and mercantile strategies of each of these groups—or at least of those among them whose impact on the colonial societies or whose continuous presence within the Atlantic world over time seem more impressive—is necessary in order to color our understanding of Atlantic cosmopolitanism.

Since the beginning of the "Age of Discoveries," the Genoese were among the Europeans exploring, traveling, and settling the Atlantic. Genoa, a city in the heart of the Mediterranean, with its far-reaching merchants and businessmen soon became one of the most important commercial and financial hubs of this relational—non-geographical—concept that we call Atlantic world. Since the thirteenth and fourteenth centuries, the Genoese had established trading colonies along the coasts of Catalonia and Andalusia, and they artfully inserted themselves into the Spanish Atlantic in various ways, becoming arguably the most omnipresent and powerful foreigners within it. After the ground-breaking studies of historians such as Robert S. Lopez, Charles Verlinden, and Ruth Pike in the first three quarters of the twentieth century,[6] more recent works have revived the interest in the history of Genoese commerce in the Atlantic.[7] These recent investigations of the Genoese presence in the Spanish kingdoms and, later, in the political entities arising in the aftermath of the Spanish-American Wars of Independence have surely given us a better picture of some Genoese communities in Spain and in the Americas. Research undertaken by both Spanish and Italian historians has produced detailed analyses of local realities. These studies have also assessed the significance of Genoese bankers for the Spanish Crown and quantitatively mapped the specific responses of Genoese businessmen to sudden and profound changes in the geopolitical landscape.[8] However, Charles Verlinden's original focus on colonial techniques and economic skills emerging during extended historical periods has long been abandoned. Consequently, the recent scholarship on the Genoese in the Iberian Atlantic seems unable to answer key, broad, historical questions, which cannot be addressed by chronologically narrow or geographically limited studies. Verlinden's intuition that the modern, Atlantic process of empire-building can be fully explained only uncovering its Mediterranean and medieval origins should be revived and expanded if we wish to tackle some crucial and fascinating historical problems. Why were the Genoese more successful than their Venetian rivals in reorienting their Levantine trades and entering the Spanish Atlantic? What is the relationship between Genoa's constitutional order and Genoese entrepreneurship? Did Hispanic-Genoese diplomatic relations and Spain's perception of Genoa have any impact on the development of the Spanish empire? These questions are not only important for a history of Genoa and of the Genoese people. They are also essential in order to identify the historical roots of some key institutions and cultural attitudes that made it possible for the hybrid, cosmopolitan world recently discussed by scholars of the Atlantic to emerge. Similarly, the study of late medieval and early modern Genoa can contribute to revive and reorient the debate on the so-called "European miracle,"[9] which continues to focus on historical processes taking place in Northwestern Europe during the seventeenth and eighteenth centuries.[10] My research suggests that key institutional developments and changes in value systems were already under way in some areas of the Mediterranean as early as the last centuries of the Middle Ages.

A CITY APART: GENOA'S ECONOMIC CULTURE, INSTITUTIONS, AND REPUBLICAN CONSERVATISM

Because the colonial institutions and the entrepreneurial culture developed by Ligurian[11] merchants during the late Middle Ages are fundamental to understand the Genoese presence in the Atlantic, this book begins with the analysis of documents that were produced in Genoa's commercial network. Chapter 1 uncovers the modus operandi of Genoese medieval colonialism as well as the everyday life in remote trading hubs throughout the Mediterranean (and beyond). Particular case studies are used to depict the economic culture that Genoese businessmen were developing at different times and in different regions. The character of Genoa's market expansion is then briefly compared with Venice's centralized empire and martial rhetoric. This comparison is pivotal to contextualize and assess the significance of the case studies of Genoese colonists in late medieval hubs, as Venice was the historical rival of Genoa in the Mediterranean and Levantine markets. Therefore, while the movement East-West and the transfer of colonial techniques as presented by Verlinden regarded all the various groups of Italians trading in the Levant, my research fleshes out the peculiarities of Genoese intercontinental businesses. This point is of great importance. Historians have usually overlooked Genoa because, searching exclusively for "state-centered" forms of economic expansion, they consider it as a declining force in the Mediterranean after the fourteenth century.[12] Yet, this interpretation tells only a small part of the story, and not by chance it seems inadequate to explain the longevity of the Genoese presence on the international stage and the success of the Genoese participation in the Atlantic economy. If the Genoese lost the clash of economic interests with Venice and since then were unable to compete, then why was a Genoese private fleet of galleys, and not the Venetian maritime forces, to arguably decide the fate of the Italian Wars? Why do we find Genoese, and not Venetians, trading in nineteenth-century Rio de La Plata? My hypothesis is that while the Genoese were retreating from the Levant, they were moving capital and commercial routes towards the expanding west Mediterranean and Atlantic markets. The fact that the Venetians were investing almost all their economic energies in the Middle East and the Levant just before the Ottoman hurricane is not a sign of power, but rather the reason why Venice never conspicuously participated in the transatlantic trade. While Venice was focusing on one, "state-controlled" commercial outlet, Genoa was continuing to pursue its apparently disordered but indeed winning strategy of business diversification and geographical dispersion. These reflections stimulated in chapter 1 by the study of a diverse group of sources are tested and further elaborated in chapter 2, where I focus on the business network and the diversified investments of the Genoese merchant Giovanni da Pontremoli. Pontremoli's file of letters shows that, in the context of a private, relatively unhampered market expansion,[13] new directions of trade and investments depended virtually entirely on the Ligurian entrepreneurs' economic calculation, a fact that contributes to explain the Genoese network's adaptability, geographical fluidity, and longevity. Evidently, the study of Genoa and its people brings together a variety of themes that lay at the heart of the Atlantic world's economic origins and intellectual history. Tracing the cultural roots of the Genoese presence in the Atlantic is, then, an indispensable endeavor to illuminate the historical reality behind the idea of cosmopolitanism that so often has been used to describe the early modern Atlantic world.

Crucially, to understand what kind of regime could favor Pontremoli's economic culture and commercial activities, we need to consider the political history of the metropolis. So the second half of chapter 2 is dedicated to the institutions and constitutional framework developed in late medieval Genoa. In fact, Genoa's entrepreneurial culture also challenges us to revise the way in which we investigate the political life of this city republic. Historians of different schools and generations have argued that the conflict between *nobili* and *popolari* is pivotal in order to tell the history of the Genoese polity. For instance, in the 1950s, Paul Coles went as far as using a rigidly Marxist vocabulary and historical framework when describing Genoa's restless political life.[14] More recently, Andrea Zorzi has applied the narrative of fourteenth-century popular revolts to Genoa, seeing in the events of 1340 and in the establishment of the dogeship a victory of the *popolari*.[15] While these works partly explain the factionalism so famously defining Genoa's political history, their idea of monolithic social classes simply does not fit into the civic life and the vibrant economic activities of the Genoese. Even the innovative framework proposed by Alma Poloni, who interprets the political history of several Italian communes in the fourteenth century by focusing on the emergence of urban textile industries, does not work in the case of Genoa.[16]

That the aristocracy vs. guilds or the textile entrepreneurs vs. wool workers dichotomies—which may perhaps appear more viable when considering the history of other cities, like Florence or Siena—are not applicable to the Ligurian capital has already been observed, more or less deliberately, in writings by scholars such as Diane Owen Hughes, Carlo Bitossi, and Thomas Kirk. In Genoa, some of the *popolari* claimed to be noble themselves. Moreover, the *nobili* were not allowed to become doge; therefore, all the fiscal reforms that (as I aim to show) during the fourteenth and the fifteenth centuries limited discretionary spending and moved revenues from the commune to the Bank of St. George were done to the detriment of *popolari* doges (not of the *nobili*). In other words, in medieval and Renaissance Genoa, a *popolare* could be an aristocrat, whose family had once taken part in the "first government" of the commune and had later abandoned the *nobili*.[17] On the other hand, a *nobile* (such as a Cattaneo or a Spinola) could be involved in entrepreneurial activities side by side (or even in association) with men like Giovanni da Pontremoli, thus sharing the economic culture and partly the political agenda of the Genoese merchants. Kirk has therefore quite rightly stated that "the terminology used to distinguish the two groups is misleading; the division between *nobili* and *popolari* is not a simple horizontal division running across the social pyramid, dividing the feudal nobility from the urban patriciate, the *popolo grasso* of the other cities."[18] Or, as put by Hughes, "Genoa far more than Florence was a merchant city. . . . Its aristocracy [was] active in trade in partnership with lesser men from the very foundation of the medieval commune."[19] All this unavoidably means that in the case of Genoa we have to acknowledge the interaction between, on the one hand, the socioeconomic mobility and the accumulation of private capital rendered possible by the continuous prominence of commerce and banking (rather than textile industry), and, on the other hand, cosmopolitan self-perception and republican philosophy.[20]

Tracing the constitutional tools and the institutions used by the Genoese to limit the power of the doge and to protect the capital market is fundamental in order to grasp the rationale and the objectives of one of the most famous banks in the history of Europe: the Bank of St. George. In chapter 2, this association of creditors is presented as the continuation of a process of institutional change aimed at preserving a traditional, medieval understanding of the commune. Through this bank, Genoese investors coming from a diverse array of economic and social backgrounds aimed to both safeguard the monetary returns of their bonds, and prevent the commune from spending money to embark on military adventures that could usher in a tyrannical *signoria* or jeopardize commercial interests. In an attempt to draw out the rare literary works with which Genoese citizens openly expressed their value system and how they perceived themselves in the Mediterranean landscape, chapter 3 moves from political and institutional developments to literary expressions of identity. In particular, I take into consideration patriotic poems and descriptions of the city port that uncover Genoa's republican conservatism and a civic rhetoric celebrating private wealth.[21]

Italian scholars have produced excellent studies on medieval and early modern Genoa. Historiographical frameworks elaborated primarily by Edoardo Grendi, Carlo Bitossi, and Arturo Pacini have helped other authors (such as Giovanna Petti Balbi and Carlo Taviani) to develop the research on Genoa and Liguria in different directions, focusing on more specific characters or issues.[22] Yet, the link between Genoa's medieval entrepreneurship and communal institutions on the one hand, and the increasing Ligurian presence in the Spanish system on the other remains hidden. In Anglophone scholarship, the Ligurian city republic is usually ignored altogether, as Florentine-centric narratives have diverted the attention of most scholars of humanist civic philosophy and Renaissance republicanism towards Florence.[23] This is particularly unfortunate because the history of Genoa completely undermines the very assumption that in fifteenth-century Northern Italy there was only one stream of republicanism and that this was necessarily bound to develop in the direction of the modern, territorial state. Such an assumption is detectable even in the work of an eminent and gifted historian like Maurizio Viroli. His book *From Politics to Reason of State* masterfully opens with two chapters dedicated to the intensity and complexity of late medieval political discussions.[24] Viroli then explains the gradual definition of a civic language typical of the *vita politica* in free republics, as well as the subsequent emergence of alternative discourses and political vocabularies, which accompanied the crisis of the city-states and eventually developed into the rhetoric and ideology of reason of state. Such a framework has many merits, among them the audacity to look at long intellectual processes and refined value systems. Viroli argues that, from the end of the fourteenth to the beginning of the sixteenth century, radical institutional changes occurred in Northern Italy together with a key ideological shift in political language; and indeed this same idea resonates throughout the pages of my work.

However, at least one city in Northern Italy elaborated and maintained a stream of republicanism that, resisting the said ideological shift, differed substantially from the Florentine one. As I discuss here, this alternative republicanism (born in part from a more dramatic enfranchisement of entrepreneurial activities) was opposed to the creation of standing armies (and/or public fleets), cherished private wealth, and placed at the center of republican ideology property rights and economic prosperity—not political participation or sovereignty. This does not diminish the value of Viroli's investigation into the medieval and early modern political culture of Florence. The fact that Florentine intellectuals were more prolific than others (especially the Genoese) in the literary endeavors with which they debated political philosophy remains undeniable. Nonetheless, as I aim to show in this book, conflicting ideas of republicanism did face and challenge each other: and they did so ever more dramatically after the French invasion of the peninsula in 1494. Hence, because the study of Genoa uncovers such problems in the historiography of Renaissance Italy, my book is relevant to debates and fields that go well beyond Ligurian culture and Atlantic cosmopolitanism. Chapter 5 especially aims to show (among other things) that the territorialization and militarization of the state prescribed by Machiavelli were utterly incompatible with Genoa's republican tradition. While explaining the peculiarity of Genoa's civic tenets, I suggest that behind the curtains of a traditional language, Machiavelli proposed a set of radical political prescriptions. Because Viroli (following the "Cambridge School") uses language as a virtually exclusive methodological tool of textual analysis, what he detects in Machiavelli's political writings is mainly continuity, as the Florentine secretary respected and replicated the traditional, late medieval, and humanist separation between the "art of the state" and the "language of politics."[25] Yet, as aptly observed by Mark Jurdjevic, "[o]nly by privileging certain sources at the expense of others can one conclude, as Skinner and Viroli have done, that Machiavelli was reiterating traditional Florentine assumptions, in spite of what nearly all of his sixteenth-century readers thought."[26] Viroli's conclusions need to be integrated if we want to fully appreciate the practical (if not linguistic) novelty of the political tenets elaborated (and practiced) by Machiavelli, especially with regard to the conception of the state. Interestingly, Viroli himself illuminates the way out of this historiographical impasse, when he rightly suggests that "[Machiavelli's] position on war and expansion was that a republic (like *any* state) must attain an appropriate size and be capable of fighting, if its liberty has to be preserved."[27] My research expands and integrates this intuition. The militarized, territorial state—not a language or any particular constitutional arrangement—is at the heart of Machiavelli's thought.[28] This is precisely why, as we shall see in the second part of chapter 5, a Genoese who accepted and sponsored Machiavellian ideas was considered in Genoa a dissident with bizarre political views. Hence, by presenting the case of a city republic that rejected the ideological shift from medieval commune to modern state, I indirectly redefine Machiavelli's position and intellectual role with regard to such a shift. Genoa remained sceptical of public fleets, military expansionism and centralization even after 1494 and chose to continue to see itself as a community of private citizens.

Understandably, Genoa is usually given little space and attention by scholars who attempt to propose all-encompassing interpretative frameworks for Renaissance republicanism in Italy. For instance, Fabrizio Ricciardelli's otherwise brilliant work on this subject does not even mention Genoa in the section entitled "Towards the Modern State."[29] The reason is that Genoa simply does not fit into any interpretative framework that aims to explain at once the political history of polities as different as Genoa, Venice, and Florence and that assumes that the modern state is a necessary stage in the progressive unveiling and protection of human liberty. Once this assumption is almost unconsciously made, Genoa's stubbornness in rejecting the monopolization of violence and the territorialization of the state becomes an unsolvable (and uncomfortable) puzzle, even for exceptional historians like Viroli and Ricciardelli.[30] Similarly, spontaneous nongovernmental associations like the Bank of St. George represent an alternative to—rather than a step towards—the modern state. This is a powerful indication of the fact that the rise of the modern state was actually *not* inevitable, and I intend to follow this line of inquiry as formulated by Elliott.[31] That by the fifteenth century communal self-government and republican *libertà* were envisaged by large sectors of the Genoese society in a profoundly different way than in Florence or Venice has indeed been sporadically noted by other scholars, like Osvaldo

Raggio.[32] One of the questions that I attempt to answer in this book then is why Genoa resisted the creation of a centralized state; and to answer this question, it is pivotal to understand on what definition of *libertà* was the Genoese *civitas* built.

The term *libertà* in the context of late medieval and early modern Liguria is potentially problematic, mainly because we can easily miss its economic tone. The peculiar, though often unspoken meaning acquired by this key concept in a local environment characterized by entrepreneurial activities and the celebration of private wealth challenges categories and definitions often used to write the history of Florence. Christine Shaw has well summarized some of the reasons why Genoa's freedom cannot be seen as an idea intrinsically linked to independence and political participation. In Genoa, *libertà* was foremost intended as the freedom to do business.[33] While I largely follow this approach, I stress here (in chapters 3 and 5, but also throughout the entire book) that Genoa's Renaissance republicanism was the result of a long history of entangled, mutual influences between the economic life of the city (and its colonies) and its institutional and constitutional history. The conviction that Genoa's civic cosmology (and, hence, Genoa's *libertà*) can be deciphered only when looking at cultural and economic processes starting well before the Renaissance period brings me, in a sense, close to the method of a key essay written by Riccardo Ferrante on the relationship between law and republicanism in late medieval Genoa.[34] Moreover, contrary to Shaw's interpretation, I argue that the reforms of 1528 did not change practically anything in the spirit and the structural aims of the Genoese political system. Genoa emerged unconquered from the turbulent decades opening the sixteenth century precisely thanks to (and not in spite of) its private arms and private wealth. Therefore, the Genoese idea of *libertà*—based on the protection of property rights and the impossibility for the doge to accumulate power or easily wage war—survived the crisis brought by the Italian Wars. This fact is an important one also for scholars of the Habsburg intellectual and political world, because it shows that, at the moment in which Charles V welcomed the Ligurians under the umbrella of his polycentric imperial system, they brought within it almost intact a medieval civic philosophy linked to their entrepreneurial culture and preserved since the fourteenth century through constitutional reforms and institutional changes. The French king, Francis I was baffled by Genoa's communal ideology and clumsy in his assessment of Genoese private arms. Charles himself needed a few years to patiently learn how to deal with the Genoese polity, and we can surely see in this a confirmation that Genoa's republican conservatism had by then become quite unique.

A CITY OF TWO WORLDS: GENOA IN THE HABSBURG EMPIRE

When looking at the Genoese presence within the Spanish kingdoms on both sides of the Atlantic, we need to address two pivotal questions. First, when and how did the idea that Genoese ships, investments, and mental capital could bring prosperity to the Spanish kingdoms (while also increasing their revenues) first materialize? And secondly, what roles did Genoese immigrants play during the first phase of empire building in the Castilian Americas? Chapter 4 analyzes Ferdinand the Catholic's letters and policies dealing with Ligurian merchants (and pirates). Aragon's economic crisis and entrepreneurial decline in the fifteenth century should be seen as a crucial moment in the development of Hispanic-Genoese relations, as—notwithstanding the continuing political and military tensions between Genoa and Barcelona—both Castile and Aragon became more integrated into the Genoese commercial and financial network. My research is in this case virtually unprecedented, as in chapter 4 and chapter 5 I aim to identify decisive events that in the course of almost one century progressively changed the way in which the Genoese were perceived by Spanish monarchs and bureaucrats. From 1494, the year that signals the beginning of the Italian Wars, the diplomatic history of Genoa is inextricably linked to external threats, but also to internal political turmoil. The general framework that I use to present the strategies, perceptions, and political deeds of Genoa, Charles V and Francis I in the 1520s is borrowed from the excellent work of Arturo Pacini, and in particular from his invaluable book entitled *La Genova di Andrea Doria nell'Impero di Carlo V*.[35] Pacini vividly portrayed the effects of the two monarchs' military clashes and financial needs on Genoa's institutions and delicate internal affairs; he also reflected on the different approaches of Charles and Francis and on the nature of the Spanish "protection" during Doria's regime. In chapter 5, I follow Pacini's reflections and at the same time attempt to expand his historical reconstruction by identifying the origins of Charles's tactful and successful attitude towards Genoa, its private fleets, and its bankers. In this respect, I argue that, contrary to what has been suggested by Thomas Kirk, private arms and private capital are precisely what kept Genoa from becoming a subject state.[36] Genoa's republican conservatism as well as the developments in Hispanic-Genoese relations are relevant to understand the subsequent Ligurian presence in the Atlantic. In the first section of chapter 6, the conclusions drawn with regard to the new opportunities for Genoese businessmen in the Habsburg overseas kingdoms are also substantiated by a brief study of the relevant Spanish legislation. In a sense, this book integrates in two ways the extraordinary work of Céline Dauverd.[37] While she has uncovered the religious underpinnings of the friendship between Genoese and Habsburgs, my research focuses on the compatibility between Genoa and Spain in terms of governance and political culture; and, while her book focused on the Hispanic-Genoese alliance in southern Italy, I look across the Atlantic Ocean. Both Dauverd and I stress the adaptability of Genoese economic actors, as well as the diversity of entrepreneurial, military, and social roles that they played for the Spanish Crown besides their more famous banking activities.

The final chapter of *Genoa's Freedom* then moves to show that an economic, social, and political entanglement between Genoa and the Castilian Americas existed since as early as the first half of the sixteenth century. Scholars have usually focused on the financial role of the Genoese in Spain,[38] but in chapter 6, the reader will find an extensive treatment of the careers and lives of some of the first Genoese who crossed the ocean and entered the Spanish Americas. Considering a diverse series of documents, I tell the story of Giovanni Battista Pastene, a Genoese captain turned conquistador and *encomendero* at the outskirts of Charles's empire. Then, I present an array of manuscripts illustrating how Genoese immigrants were scattered throughout the Castilian Indies since as early as the phase of conquest and settlement. Evidently, this is significant for the study of Spanish colonial societies, as it suggests that the Genoese were the first (and for many decades the only) group of *extranjeros* to explore and live in certain areas of the Habsburg Empire like Mexico and Chile. This final chapter is also methodologically and conceptually linked to the first two chapters of my work, because I put ideas and human action at the center of my investigation—just as I do for the study of medieval hubs and networks. Ultimately, my work rests on the conviction that complex historical processes can be understood only by looking at value systems and institutional arrangements which develop throughout a long period of time.

NARRATIVE AND THEMES

The themes treated in this book address a variety of questions with regard to the economic development of Western Europe, late medieval and Renaissance republicanism, Habsburg governance, and empire-building in the Atlantic world; but clearly, also historians who work on different areas or periods will find that my research embodies a challenging (if not agreeable) methodological approach. The history of Genoa and its citizen-businessmen offers the opportunity to follow a specific group of people throughout several centuries, as it develops a culture cherishing human action and prosperity. Institutions, political ideologies, and colonial techniques progressively shaped by the Genoese to protect their entrepreneurial activities in turn influenced the way in which this group changed its economic role(s) and adapted to different geopolitical conditions. Reconstructing economic history starting from the ends chosen and the means used by people living in the past can reward us with a neater picture of their intellectual universe.[39] Economic cultures are formed by ideas and value systems that escape graphs, numerical data, and at times even literary expressions.[40] Yet, economic cultures engender and underpin human action, so they remain crucial if we want to answer broad questions in economic history and color our knowledge of complex, entangled and relational historical concepts such as the Mediterranean and the Spanish Atlantic.

NOTES

1. See, for example, John Thornton, *Africa and Africans in the Making of the Atlantic World* (Cambridge: Cambridge University Press, 1998); Nicholas Canny, "Writing Atlantic History; or, Reconfiguring the History of Colonial British America," *Journal of American History* 3 (1999): 1093–114; *The Atlantic in Global History, 1500–2000*, ed. Jorge Cañizares-Esguerra (Upper Saddle River: Pearson Prentice Hall, 2007); Daviken Studnicki-Gizbert, *A Nation upon the Ocean Sea: Portugal's Atlantic Diaspora and the Crisis of the Spanish Empire, 1492–1640* (New York and Oxford: Oxford University Press, 2007); Eliga Gould, "Entangled Histories, Entangled Worlds: The English-Speaking Atlantic as a Spanish Periphery," *American Historical Review* 3 (2007): 764–86; Jim Sidbury and Cañizares-Esguerra, "Mapping Ethnogenesis in the Early Modern Atlantic," *William and Mary Quarterly* 68 (2011): 181–208; and *Theorising the Ibero-American Atlantic*, ed. Harald E. Braun and Lisa Vollendorf (Boston: Brill, 2013), where the chapter written by Eliga Gould questions the very existence of categories like a "Spanish Atlantic." Yet, this historiographical discussion had perhaps already started with Nicholas Canny and Anthony Pagden, *Colonial Identity in the Atlantic World, 1500–1800* (Princeton, NJ: Princeton University Press, 1989).

2. See his and Erik R. Seeman's introduction in the already cited volume *The Atlantic in Global History*.

3. Jorge Cañizares-Esguerra, "The Devil in the New World: a Transnational Perspective," in *The Atlantic in Global History*, 21–37; and idem, *Puritan Conquistadors: Iberianizing the Atlantic, 1550–1700* (Stanford: Stanford University Press, 2006). See also his interesting considerations in "Entangled Histories: Borderland Historiographies in New Clothes?," *American Historical Review* 112 (2007): 787–799.

4. John H. Elliott, *Empires of the Atlantic World: Britain and Spain in America 1492–1830* (New Haven: Yale University Press, 2006).

5. The literature on this is rich in studies focusing on specific regions, trades, or groups of foreigners (in specific periods). See, for instance, Guadalupe J. Codinach, "Veracruz, almacén de plata en el Atlántico: la Casa Gordon y Murphy, 1805 1824," *Historia Mexicana* 2 (1988): 325–53; Maria Christina Chatziioannou, "Mediterranean Pathways of Greek Merchants to Victorian England," *Historical Review* 7 (2010): 213–35; Alex Borucki, "Trans-Imperial History in the Making of the Slave Trade to Venezuela, 1526–1811," *Itinerario* 2 (2012): 29–54. For a collection of essays with a broader approach, see *Extranjeros y enemigos en Iberoamérica: la visión del otro: del Imperio español a la Guerra de la Independencia*, ed. David González Cruz (Madrid: Sílex, 2010).

6. Robert S. Lopez, "Il predominio economico dei genovesi nella monarchia spagnola," *Giornale storico e letterario della Liguria* 2 (1936): 65–74; idem, *Storia delle colonie genovesi nel Mediterraneo* (Bologna: Zanichelli, 1938); Charles Verlinden, "Italian Influence in Iberian Colonization," *The Hispanic American Historical Review* 33 (1953): 199–211; idem, *The Beginnings of Modern Colonization* (Ithaca, NY: Cornell University Press, 1970); and Ruth Pike, *Enterprise and Adventure: The Genoese in Seville and the Opening of the New World* (Ithaca, NY: Cornell University Press, 1966).

7. David Igual Luis, Germán Navarro Espinach, "Los genoveses en España en el tránsito del siglo XV al XVI," *Historia. Instituciones. Documentos* 24 (1997): 261–332; Catia Brilli, "Da Cadice a Buenos Aires: crisi e rinascita del commercio ligure nella nuova configurazione

dell'Atlantico iberico (1797–1837)," *Annali della Fondazione Einaudi* XLIII (2009): 143–73; idem, "The Genoese Response to the Collapse of the Spanish Empire in America," *Jahrbuch für Geschichte Lateinamerikas/Anuario de Historia de América Latina (JbLA)* 47 (2010): 247–72; *Génova y la monarquía hispánica (1528–1713)*, ed. Manuel Herrero Sánchez (Genova: SLSP, 2011).

8. On the Genoese bankers working for the Spanish Crown, see Romano Canosa, *Banchieri genovesi e sovrani spagnoli tra Cinquecento e Seicento* (Rome: Sapere, 2000).

9. Eric L. Jones, *The European Miracle: Environments, Economies, and Geopolitics in the History of Europe and Asia* (Cambridge: Cambridge University Press, 1987); Ralph Raico, "The Theory of Economic Development and the 'European Miracle,'" in *The Collapse of Development Planning*, ed. Peter J. Boettke (New York: NYU Press, 1994), 37–58.

10. See, for example, Deirdre N. McCloskey, *The Treasured Bourgeoisie: How Markets and Innovation Became Ethical, 1600–1848, and Then Suspect* (Chicago: Chicago University Press, 2015).

11. Liguria is the narrow coastal region surrounding Genoa, and historically under its political control. The adjective "Ligurian" is used throughout the book interchangeably with Genoese.

12. For instance, according to John A. Marino, "[T]he Venetians and Genoese fought a series of inconclusive wars for over a century between 1257 and 1384; but, by managing to survive intact and tie their eastern trade to the Egyptian/Red Sea route to Asia, the Venetians won the long duel. The Genoese were never able to gain the same kind of state-centered control in their eastern Mediterranean and Black Sea strongholds at Pera, Caffa, Tana, Chios, Cyprus, and Egypt as enjoyed by the Venetians, and Genoa's eastern trade declined to only 20 to 25 percent of that of Venice." John A. Marino, "Economic Encounters and the First Stages of a World Economy," in *A Companion to the Worlds of the Renaissance*, ed. Guido Ruggiero (Oxford: Blackwell, 2002), 282.

13. The nature of Genoa's market expansion is the topic that inspired a brilliant paper published by Lopez in the 1960s. Robert S. Lopez, "Market Expansion: The Case of Genoa," *The Journal of Economic History* 4 (1964): 445–64.

14. Paul Coles, "The Crisis of Renaissance Society Genoa 1488–1507," *Past & Present* 11 (1957): 17–47.

15. Andrea Zorzi, "The Popolo," in *Italy in the Age of the Renaissance: 1300–1550*, ed. John M. Najemy (Oxford: Oxford University Press, 2006), 145–64, in particular 155–56.

16. Alma Poloni, "La mobilità sociale nelle città comunali italiane nel Trecento," in *I comuni di Jean-Claude Maire Vigueur. Percorsi storiografici*, ed. Maria Teresa Caciorgna et al. (Rome: Viella, 2014), 281–304.

17. See Carlo Bitossi, *Il governo dei magnifici. Patriziato e politica a Genova fra Cinque e Seicento* (Genova: ECIG, 1990), especially 33.

18. Thomas A. Kirk, *Genoa and the Sea* (London: Hopkins University Press, 2005), 23.

19. Diane Owen Hughes, "Urban Growth and Family Structure in Medieval Genoa," *Past & Present* 66 (1975): 5.

20. In fourteenth- and fifteenth-century Italy, commerce and banking were significantly more lucrative than industry. Sergio Tognetti, "Attività industriali e commercio di manufatti nelle città toscane del tardo Medioevo (1250 ca.-1530 ca.)," *Archivio storico italiano* 159 (2001): 423–79; especially 424–25.

21. Riccardo Ferrante has described the Genoese political culture as a "republican conservatism with anti-seigniorial connotation." In the Italian text, "conservatorismo repubblicano a connotazione antisignorile." Riccardo Ferrante, "Legge e Repubblica: l'esperienza genovese tra XIV e XVI secolo," in *Politica e cultura nelle repubbliche italiane dal Medioevo all'Età moderna*, ed. Simonetta Adorni Braccesi e Mario Ascheri (Roma: Istituto Storico Italiano per l'Età Moderna e Contemporanea, 2001), 261. This definition can be accepted, as long as we do not attach to conservatism the anachronistic meaning of the modern political philosophy, but rather we intend it here as the continuation of a certain civic culture. For the role played by the law in the limitation of the doge's authority and in the division of political power, see chapter 2 of this book; and Ferrante, "Legge e Repubblica," 243–49.

22. Edoardo Grendi, *La repubblica aristocratica dei genovesi* (Bologna: Il Mulino, 1987); Carlo Bitossi, *Il governo dei magnifici*; Arturo Pacini, *La tirannia delle fazioni e la repubblica dei ceti: vita politica e istituzioni a Genova tra Quattro e Cinquecento* (Bologna: Il Mulino, 1992). On the importance of Pacini's research see pp. xvi–xvii of this introduction. See also Osvaldo Raggio, *Faide e parentele: lo stato genovese visto dalla Fontanabuona* (Torino: Einaudi, 1990); Giovanna Petti Balbi, *Simon Boccanegra e la Genova del '300* (Genova: Marietti, 1991); idem, *Governare la città. Pratiche sociali e linguaggi politici a Genova in età medievale* (Firenze: Firenze University Press, 2007); and Carlo Taviani, *Superba discordia: guerra, rivolta e pacificazione nella Genova di primo Cinquecento* (Roma: Viella, 2008).

23. A notable exception is Christine Shaw. Christine Shaw, "Concepts of *Libertà* in Renaissance Genoa," in *Communes and Despots in Medieval and Renaissance Italy*, ed. John E. Law and Bernadette Paton (Farnham: Ashgate, 2010), 177–90; and idem, "Genoa," in *The Renaissance State*, ed. Andrea Gamberini and Isabella Lazzarini (Cambridge: Cambridge University Press, 2012), 220–36.

24. Maurizio Viroli, *From Politics to Reason of State* (Cambridge: Cambridge University Press, 2005).

25. Ibid., 154. Viroli also stresses that "Machiavelli was upholding and reinforcing a line of attack against the republican-Ciceronian language of politics that was already rooted in the Florentine political language, as we have seen from the records of the *Pratiche*. His critique of the conventional view of politics was not uncommon or unheard of." Ibid., 147.

26. Mark Jurdjevic, "Machiavelli's Hybrid Republicanism," *The English Historical Review* 122 (2007), 1235.

27. Viroli, *From Politics to Reason of State*, 162.

28. Alissa Ardito has recently highlighted the importance of military conquest and territorial extension in Machiavelli's thought, though unfortunately she still frames her argument within the debate on republicanism, rather than focusing on the issues of state and power. Alissa M. Ardito, *Machiavelli and the Modern State: The Prince, the Discourses on Livy, and the Extended Territorial Republic* (Cambridge: Cambridge University Press, 2015).

29. Fabrizio Ricciardelli, *The Myth of Republicanism in Renaissance Italy* (Turnhout: Brepols, 2015), 28–30.

30. On the formation of the modern state and the monopoly of violence, see the thought-provoking reflections in Luigi Marco Bassani and Carlo Lottieri, "The Problem of Security; Historicity of the State and 'European Realism,'" in *The Myth of National Defense*, ed. Hans-Hermann Hoppe (Auburn, AL: The Ludwig von Mises Institute, 2003), 21–64, especially 34–38.

31. J. H. Elliott, "A Europe of Composite Monarchies," *Past & Present* 137 (1992): 48–71; in particular 51.

32. "The case of the Republic of Genoa does not seem to apply to any of the models of modern state elaborated so far; not even to the model of regional state that, although used for very different territorial entities, has been considered as the most common form of state formation in Italy in the central centuries of the modern age." In the original Italian: "Il caso della Repubblica di Genova non sembra rientrare in nessuno dei modelli di stato moderno fino ad ora elaborati Raggio; neppure in quello dello stato regionale che, sebbene riferito a configurazioni territoriali molto diverse, è stato considerato come la forma di aggregazione statale prevalente in Italia nei secoli centrali dell'età moderna." *Faide e parentele*, xi.

33. Shaw, "Concepts of *Libertà* in Renaissance Genoa."

34. Ferrante, "Legge e Repubblica," 237–65.

35. Arturo Pacini, *La Genova di Andrea Doria nell'Impero di Carlo V* (Florence: Olschki, 1999). See also idem, *I presupposti politici del secolo dei genovesi: la riforma del 1528* (Genova: SLSP, 1990).

36. Kirk, *Genoa and the Sea*, 19.

37. Céline Dauverd, *Imperial Ambitions in the Early Modern Mediterranean* (New York: Cambridge University Press, 2015).

38. See, for instance, Ramón Carande, *Carlos V y sus banqueros* (Barcelona: Critica, 1977); Romano Canosa, *Banchieri genovesi e sovrani spagnoli tra Cinquecento e Seicento* (Sapere:

Roma, 2000); Carlos Álvarez Nogal, "Las compañías bancarias genovesas en Madrid a comienzos del siglo XVII," *Hispania* 65 (2005): 67–90.

39. Although dealing with a different period in Italian history, and although using intellectual rather than economic history as a starting point, Cecilia Carnino has recently proposed a very similar global and interdisciplinary approach. Cecilia Carnino, "Luxury and Consumption in Eighteenth-Century Italy: Intellectual History, Methodological Ideas and Interdisciplinary Research Practice," *History of European Ideas* 40 (2014): 495–515.

40. On the shortcomings of quantitative economic history, see the interesting reflections of Joseph T. Salerno, in his introduction to Murray N. Rothbard, *A History of Money and Banking in the United States: The Colonial Era to World War II* (Auburn, AL: Ludwig von Mises Institute, 2002).

Part I

Entrepreneurship and *Libertà*

Chapter One

Economy, Everyday Life, and the Expansion of Genoa's Colonies

Late medieval Genoese businessmen built a vast, intercontinental network that was able to adapt to geopolitical earthquakes and whose mental and financial capital played an important role in the establishment of the sixteenth-century Hispanic-Genoese alliance. The reason for this continuous economic success was that the Genoese medieval colonies had soon given to the sons of the Ligurian republic an entrepreneurial economic culture, a set of administrative knowledge, and an extraordinary experience in trading and moving within a cosmopolitan world. This economic culture, partly born from the necessities related to the geographical extension of the Ligurian network, was rooted on two main features: adaptability, and institutions protecting property rights. But this commercial revolution involved several other city-republics in Italy and in the Mediterranean. What distinguished the Genoese (as we shall see) was the impact that their colonial experience and mercantile values had on the political organization of the metropolis. In particular, the Genoese maintained for longer (well into the sixteenth-century) a communal, medieval constitution that prevented the centralization of political power and favored economic prosperity. The absence of a public fleet and of a state-centered control over the colonies was, in turn, a key advantage, as the fluidity of the Genoese economic system helps to explain the readiness with which Genoese merchants were able to move capital and adapt to changed conditions.[1] Moreover, the private character of the Genoese colonial world helps to elucidate the fact that the Genoese presence within the Spanish empire was never perceived as a political or military threat.

To recount this story, we should start from the colonies. Charles Verlinden's theory about the transfer of colonial techniques is used here as a broad, flexible framework, but is also problematized and developed in order to grasp the specific features of Ligurian culture and market expansion.[2] In this chapter, it is my objective to show—through a series of particular case studies—that medieval Genoese colonists scattered across the Mediterranean world and beyond successfully faced and overcame the problems related to long-distance business and weak (often nonexistent) military presence of their mother country. An understanding of the economic life in some of the Genoese colonies is pivotal to show Genoese adaptability and explain how Ligurian merchants maintained their presence and quickly changed their role(s) once the Levant was lost and Atlantic powers appeared on the scene. The thirteenth-century notary deeds written in Tunis by Pietro Battifoglio constitute the first group of documents that I am going to study, illustrating how Genoese merchants industriously accumulated, moved, and reinvested capital.

HOW TO COPE WITH DISTANCE: VOICES FROM TUNIS

The Genoese merchants and professionals living in Tunisia had no direct political power in the country, but nonetheless they were given fiscal rights and economic privileges. This happened thanks to a series of official treaties, signed in 1236, 1250, 1272, and 1287. These diplomatic agreements were not conceding a sovereign colony to the Genoese, but they were assuring them a special status and political protection. The last treaty, in 1287, assigned to the Genoese two warehouses (a favorable condition that no other foreign community could boast) and allowed them to be their own tax collectors.[3] But why was the Tunisian king so generous to the Genoese in particular? Why was he glad to allow the Genoese republic to have a share of the tax revenues collected in the harbor? And were the Genoese prepared to take advantage of such a generous agreement? Some interesting answers come from Pietro Battifoglio's notary deeds, especially with regard to the way in which Genoese merchants were perceived and the notary instruments used by them to connect different regions and markets at this early stage.[4]

In Tunis, the Genoese felt a particular need to be constantly represented, because the officials of the Tunisian government were often trying to deny the Genoese privileges as stated in the treaties.[5] On the other hand, the (limited) involvement of the commune in the organization and representation of a colony meant the beginning of legal disputes concerning local offices and powers. For instance, who was entitled to the *scribania* of Tunis, the man chosen in Genoa by the *podesta* and the *capitani*, or the notary named by the consul in Tunis?[6] In this context, lawyers and notaries were greatly needed. Pietro Battifoglio, the author of the file of documents that I shall now examine, was a Genoese notary who came to Tunis in the mid-1280s and worked there until at least 1292 (even though the file stops in June 1289).[7] The meaning of his surname would suggest that his family was involved in the art of laboring gold and silver.[8] Evidently Pietro decided not to become an artisan, and instead he studied law. At the time of his arrival in Tunis, he probably had already worked as notary in the Ligurian territories controlled by Genoa for some years, as it would be unusual for an inexperienced notary to embark in such a challenging adventure as it was to furnish legal representation and support to the Genoese community in the kingdom of Tunisia.

The first document that is important to analyze, dated February 28, 1289, is a significant deed for a variety of reasons.[9] It states that Guglielmo Embriaco, who was representing his relative Bonifacio Embriaco through the legal instrument of *procuratio* (a sort of temporary mandate), had received from Balianno Imbrono 825 bezants. Guglielmo was going to invest the money as he pleased, but he promised to deliver fifty bales (*cantari*) of grease wool to Balianno Imbrono in Susa by the 15th of April. Otherwise, Guglielmo would return the money to Balianno Imbrono in Genoa, by the 1st of July, paying six Genoese coins (*genovini*) for every bezant received. If the first scenario materialized, and the fifty bales of grease wool were delivered in Susa, Guglielmo promised Balianno to let him rent the Embriaco's ships to transport the wool to Genoa paying the same price that another merchant needing to move goods to Genoa (Manuele Tavanno) was also going to pay. The first reason why this document is significant is that it gives us an idea of the nonchalance with which the Genoese were used to moving large amounts of money without necessarily being in Genoa (actually, being in Genoa but doing it through a representative in one of the colonies), in order to reinvest it in businesses which were going to take place in yet another location. In this case, this third place was the Tunisian city of Susa, a fact confirming that Tunis was not the only Tunisian harbor frequently visited by Ligurian vessels. The second reflection stimulated by this deed is that the Genoese commercial empire, though apparently dispersed, was indeed kept together by those same merchants who had built it, and who needed each other to borrow money, obtain cheap transportation, and take valid legal precautions while doing business in foreign countries. Probably, Balianno Imbrono did not have the connections or the time to purchase grease wool; on the other hand, the Embriacos had evidently some experience in the wool trade, but needed a loan for other reasons. By chance, Guglielmo and Balianno met in Tunis, where the Genoese warehouses were a place for negotiations of future deals at least as much as for the realization of the ones already concluded. Moreover, one should note that the Embriacos were a powerful Genoese noble family, so this document is suggestive of an entrepreneurial aristocracy, involved in trade and money-lending side-by-side with lower social groups.[10] Finally, it is legitimate to wonder whether the legal instrument of *procuratio* mentioned in this deed was an exception or a widespread strategy able to reliably tie together the vastness of the Ligurian network; the next documents taken into consideration will clarify this point.

The contract dated February 20, 1289, represents the typical notary deed used within the Genoese community to deal with the problem of legal representation. It states that Giovanni Dachirida appointed a representative in order to collect one hundred bezants from Oberto Magistreto di Castelletto.[11] Interestingly enough, the man hired as representative was once again Guglielmo Embriaco. So, he did not merely conduct some businesses for his relatives, but he also carried out tasks in the name of other countrymen. It is not far-fetched to imagine that Giovanni Dachirida would have preferred to appoint a member of his own family, but because he had no relative in Tunis, and because he wanted to collect his money quickly, he turned to Guglielmo. That the terms of the loan to Oberto Magistreto had expired appears clear from the forceful tone of the deed, which states that Guglielmo was not simply going to ask or solicit the payment (*ad petendum*), but also that he would demand and obtain it (*exigendum et recipiendum*). However, while this deed was empowering the procurator only for a very specific and limited task, the Genoese at times needed to entrust their representatives with more extensive powers, especially when the sum to collect and reinvest was more substantial and coming from more than one debtor, or when the situations that the collector was going to face in distant lands were unforeseeable. Such is the case recorded by another of the notary's documents.

On March 25, 1289, Battifoglio wrote a complex deed, which granted Giorgio de Vedereto extensive powers over the capital of Pietro di Troia. Giorgio was not appointed for a specific task; instead, he was becoming a sort of professional representative, who could collect all Pietro's credits in Tunis, the towns of Barbary and everywhere else (*in tota Barbaria et in Tunexi et extra*). At the same time, Giorgio was entrusted with decision-making powers, so that he could reinvest the capital in other businesses, and was asked to represent Pietro in every pending legal dispute. This powerful and complex institution is still called by Battifoglio *generalem procuratorem*,[12] but it evidently differs from the one seen above. Some Genoese merchants were diversifying their investments, taking advantage of the many markets made reachable by the expansion of the Italian maritime empires. In this context, a merchant could decide to assign to a procurator not just a specific, limited task, but rather the general management of a significant portion of his international investments. Thus, to appreciate the strength of the Genoese network it is crucial to realize the practical applications and the legal variations of medieval (or even ancient) institutions. In the hands of the Genoese notaries, the *procuratio* was not always the same temporary and circumscribed instrument of representation.

That there was a necessity to quickly reinvest capital obtained from debtors is proven by the powers given to many procurators over the money they were sent to collect. A notary deed written by Battifoglio on March 27, 1289, confirms the tendency among businessmen to grant decisional powers to their procurators. In this case, Gilleto de Segnorado appoints his relative Ambrogino de Segnorado as his representative, in order to collect all the credits he has in Genoa and everywhere else (*in Ianua et extra*).[13] The document continues with Gilleto granting Ambrogino the power "to lend money for me and in my name, up to the sum of 300 Genoese lire." Moreover, Gilleto declares that Ambrogino himself "can appoint one or more procurators, as it will appear more appropriate to him, for me and in my name."[14] The newly appointed Ambrogino was thus more than a solicitor: he was a manager. The *procuratio*, in this case, constitutes simply the legal shell for the creation of a completely new legal figure, as Ambrogino is going to collect, control, manage, move, reinvest, and entrust his relative's wealth in every spot of the Genoese mercantile empire. Since the Genoese community used to move highly valuable goods and to connect a myriad of different places through money-lending and commerce, perhaps the Tunisian king had a vested interest in conceding special privileges to this community, so that Tunis could become a cosmopolitan hub and be drawn into a very profitable, far-reaching network even though it did not have a competitive mercantile fleet of its own.

It is important to point out two aspects of Ligurian expansionism. First, the characteristics of the Genoese economic system did not isolate it and make it a sort of coastal entity with no relations with the interior. Second, the Genoese merchants were not keeping their administrative skills and their financial liquidity for themselves, and thus their warehouses were not a mercantilist and exclusive space. Charles Verlinden has already addressed the first point, proving that the Ligurian colonies in the Levant were not simply ports of call or fortresses, and that the Genoese were responsible for the rise of the first plantation economies in the interiors of many of their eastern colonies.[15] Therefore, I am going to briefly focus on the sharing of administrative skills with other businessmen and on the financial interactions with local subjects and rulers. Battifoglio's deed of March 14, 1289, is an agreement concerning taxes signed between Nello Martello, a Pisan citizen, and Francesco de Iulianno, representative of the Venetian citizen Pietro Bauduco. The document clearly states this, designating the two men as *civis Pisannus* and *Veneticus* respectively, and clarifying also that one of the witnesses is a Venetian.[16] On May 20, 1289, Battifoglio wrote another deed for Guglielmo Embriaco, who in this case was acting for his relative Bonifacio, to state that he collected the money that some Florentine merchants had borrowed from Bonifacio; in the document, the debtor is identified as "Raynaldo Maffei, citizen and merchant of Florence," who is acting "in his name and for his associates."[17] Another deed, dated May 9, declared that Icopina di Savignone, widow of Oberto di Chiavari and now wife of Gilleto di Lavagna, had collected all the credits of her deceased husband. Among the debtors listed, there are three Africans: Busaito Ben Naroso, Ablayno Elfo, and Saleme Sachefi.[18] Deeds like these give us a sense of the transnational and entangled nature of the Ligurian economy; Genoese officials were ready to sanction transactions between foreign merchants, while Genoese citizens were lending money to and doing businesses with both foreigners and local subjects of the Tunisian king. Thanks to these documents, it seems even clearer the reason why the king of Tunis was so keen to favor the Genoese presence, which was bringing not only precious goods to his port, but also liquidity to his subjects and to his government.

The fact that the Ligurian community in Tunis, an often neglected ring in the commercial chain composing the Genoese medieval network, was facing and solving already in the thirteenth century the problems of a long-distance trade and an international system of credit is revealing. Obviously, Genoese Tunis was not an "end product" in the process of network building and in the path towards modern colonizing techniques, and the solutions found at the end of the thirteenth century were not definitive. Tellingly, the deed written by Battifoglio for Gilleto and Ambrogino de Segnorado was rescinded on October 3, 1290. Because of the broad nature of Ambrogino's role, which was not confined to the mere execution of a single task, one may reasonably speculate that problems of trust and reliability had arisen. Perhaps, this is an indication that the Ligurian intercontinental system needed a bigger empire to penetrate and to exploit in order to provide the overarching judicial system needed to regulate transactions and to ensure fiscal accountability across large distances. And in the future, what more remote and yet reassuring symbol of legality than the head of the Spanish composite monarchy, the emperor of the Americas and the paternal figure to whom every subject from Florida to Chile could appeal?[19] This issue is an important one, because it helps to explain both the Genoese diplomatic relationship with Byzantium (that is not extensively treated in this book) and the Genoese multiform and thriving activities within the Castilian Atlantic (which I shall investigate in part II).[20] The concept of an empire being exploited by a smaller political entity seems admittedly curious, but the Genoese proved that it was viable.

To say that the Genoese did not find a way to always enforce commercial law throughout their colonies does not mean that they did not lay down the basis for future refinements. Indeed, the Genoese contributed to forge the colonial techniques which were to be applied in the Atlantic world. Charles Verlinden appropriately claimed that "the majority of the techniques of colonization that developed in the Atlantic area in modern times had their origin in the later Middle Ages in the colonies of the eastern Mediterranean."[21] And yet, like any other knowledge, also colonizing strategies were not immediately perfect: their application could cause problems in specific environments, their profitability needed to be improved, and their transfer to newly discovered lands and newly opened markets was never a matter of pure imitation, but rather one of delicate adaptation. In sum, the study of Battifoglio's notary deeds suggests how the Genoese were continuously adapting their administrative skills and their economic strategy. But more importantly, these thirteenth-century documents prove that at a very early stage the Genoese were offering their financial support and the benefits of international maritime trade to foreign rulers. As we shall see, the Genoese progressively penetrated an impressive number of regional economies, profitably weaving together points of supply, ports of call, and distant markets.

A REMOTE LABORATORY FOR ATLANTIC MODELS: SLAVE SOCIETY AND COLONIES AROUND THE BLACK SEA

Besides distance and representation, another problem with which Genoese businessmen had to contend was the legal status of the slaves being traded across their colonial system. Slavery appears with regularity in a file of notary deeds written in another city of the Genoese commercial empire and at a different time than Battifoglio's. In 1360, the Genoese notary Antonio di Ponzò left Genoa to practice law in the colony of Chilia (Kiliya). This city, on the coast of the Black Sea and at the mouth of the Danube, was in an extraordinary strategic position, which makes its absence from the historical debate a serious gap.[22] Chilia offers to the historians' lens a striking example of a colonial laboratory, because here the Genoese were not only accumulating capital, but also building a stable community and creating a forgotten slave market in a place far from the Atlantic.

The notary deed written by Antonio di Ponzò on April 8, 1361, seems to indicate that slaves were an important part of Chilia's society, that they were owned not only by landowners, and that they were not considered something extraordinary but rather an easily obtainable good. In this document, Iarchas de Caffa, who identified himself as a "retailer of wine and honey, resident in Chilia,"[23] stated that he had received from the Genoese citizen Antibo de Opicis de Monelia a certain quantity of silver, and that he was going to repay him with a vase of wax in two months. Antibo had a security, as Iarchas stated that with this deed he was pawning "all his houses and two of his slaves."[24] Iarchas was neither an aristocrat, nor a rich merchant; he was a permanent resident of Chilia, who retailed goods such as wine and honey. If a man like Iarchas owned slaves, and probably used them as labor in his storehouse, it is reasonable to think that many other inhabitants of Chilia were slave-owners. This impression is confirmed by the number of deeds dealing with slaves that we find in the Ponzò file. Even during the winter months, when maritime trade was suspended and the economic transactions were fewer, the purchase of slaves within the little Chilian community continued.[25] This society was not similar to the first plantation-based colonies studied by Verlinden in Palestine, Cyprus, and Crete. Nevertheless, the nonchalance with which the slaves are mentioned in this deed indicates their availability on the market as well as their ordinary use at every social level. Chilia is not a prototype of the Atlantic plantations, but it appears strikingly similar to the Atlantic towns of the Spanish empire.

Very often, the slaves mentioned in the documents are young Tartar girls, sold by their own people. The friendly relations of the Genoese with slave-hunters from the highlands and local slave traders is an important aspect to mention, because even though the Genoese did not organize sugar plantations around the Black Sea (and for obvious climatic reasons), many of the Slavonic and Tartar slaves used in Palestine and the Aegean Sea came from this area. Moreover, the Genoese held a monopoly on the traffic of slaves from Crimea and other Northern regions of the Black Sea to Egypt, where they were used as mercenary soldiers. Chilia was in the periphery of this specific route of international slave trade, and yet Ponzò's deeds clearly delineate a society whose contacts with the Tartars for matters concerning slaves were very frequent. On February 16, 1361, the Genoese notary Bernabò Carpena bought from the Tartar Thoboch the Tartar slave Bayrana, who was 13 years old.[26] Only ten days later, we find Ponzò presiding over the purchase of another Tartar slave, named Ianecotolo, who was brought to Chilia by the Tartar Themir and bought by Francesco di Mezzano for himself and for his brother Oberto.[27] Sometimes, Venetian merchants tried to take advantage of the relatively cheap slave market that the Genoese controlled in the Black Sea; this was the case of Bonsegnorino di Murano, who decided to purchase a slave in Chilia.[28] He could not buy a slave directly from the Tartars, and thus the already mentioned Antibo de Opicis de Monelia gladly mediated, and gained some money selling to him the thirteen year old slave registered by Ponzò with the name Rorach, in the document dated May 4, 1361.[29] Antibo seems to be a rich businessman, but another deed, written just six days later, confirms that owning (and trading) slaves was something common at every social level of the colony. In this case, the seller is Ibraino Avarame, a Genoese *botegarius*, a shopkeeper who lived and worked in the town.[30] It is not too improbable that the man buying the slave, a merchant from Pera named Antonio Gategaro di Voltri, passed by Ibraino's shop to load his vessel with some wax, wine, or honey; there, he saw the twelve-year-old girl and thought that she would be a good investment, possibly to be sold in Constantinople at a higher price. At times, specific problems could rise from the slave trade at this early stage in the East, but the Genoese notaries were experienced and ready to satisfy their clients and to facilitate economic transactions. Thus, on May 12, 1361, Ponzò added a long and peculiar sentence to the contract with which Manoli Offlimi bought the slave Taytana from the Tartar Daoch: "It is established that, if the said slave urinates on herself, the said Daoch has to and must and promises to return the said sum of money to Manoli, and in this case the said Manoli has to and must and promises to return the said slave."[31] A wary buyer with very precise concerns about the condition of the slave was hence reassured through a sort of legal guarantee.

The moral legitimacy of the slave trade was often another problem that the Genoese had to deal with. Certain Christian kings in the region were eager to regulate or limit this trade on their lands. In these cases, the Genoese consuls and ambassadors deployed all their diplomatic talents, working together with local authorities in order to regulate the traffic of human beings and to reassure local religious leaders. For example, in the last decades of the thirteenth century the Genoese entered into negotiations with the kings of Armenia, Leo II and his son Hethum II. As a result, the Republic of Genoa and the Kingdom of Armenia ratified a treaty that at its third clause stipulated: "The slaves that [the Genoese] want to buy and take from this kingdom will not be subject to taxation. However, when [the Genoese] want to buy Christian slaves they have to swear that they will not sell them to the Turks, or to any other slave trader."[32] Armenia was at that time a small but prosperous Christian kingdom that had to cope with a delicate political and military situation in the region. Surrounded by the Byzantines, the Turks, and the Persian Mongols, Armenia needed stable allies, and the Genoese knew it. What the Ligurian merchants could offer was the best fleet in the Mediterranean and fresh capital, which meant that Armenian goods could find consistent buyers and take advantage of far-reaching commercial routes. On the other hand, the Genoese were interested in penetrating the Armenian market (where yet again the Venetians were trying to compete). Moreover, they wanted to safely travel across the territories of Hethum II and to purchase slaves.[33] The fact that the Genoese were able to cope with difficulties and expand their network while testing for the first time a variety of colonial techniques tells us something about their role in the later Middle Ages and at the dawn of modernity. The Genoese were used to solving the legal problems arising from both a slave society and an international system of slave traffic as early as the fourteenth century.

Also in the case of slavery, the solutions found by the Genoese were not definitive, but the acquired experience was enough to place them among the most successful slave traders of the Mediterranean. So much so that two centuries later, after the first contact with the Native Americans, the Genoese (Christopher Columbus and his financial backer Francesco Rivaroli *in primis*) were absolutely comfortable with the idea of enslaving them, having settled the ethical polemic some centuries before.[34] But enslaving a peaceful population was morally problematic to the Catholic monarchs.[35] In 1500, Fernando and Isabel forbade the enslavement of their American subjects, surprising and disappointing the Italian businessmen already involved in human traffic.[36] This sort of moral gap is all the more revealing when we think that the Spanish were anything but trailblazing abolitionists. In fact, throughout the long period during the Middle Ages known as the *Reconquista* they were quite used to enslaving the Moors (as much as the Moors had been enslaving Christians). In other words, the objectification of people was not a concept foreign to the Castilian culture of the time. Nonetheless, already during the conquest of the Canary Islands (1402–1496) the Spanish monarchs had been troubled by the enslavement of innocent people who they considered to have been recently converted to Christianity. Moreover, during the *Reconquista* Moors (and rarely Jews) were sometimes enslaved simply in order to get ransoms; even the few of them who were not ransomed and lived in slavery were often kept in an urban environment.[37] Instead, what Columbus proposed in 1494 was to transform an enslaved labor force into the main source of wealth in the Americas. The notary deeds from Chilia are a key source to understand why Columbus's idea was nothing more than the consequence of the praxis developed in many Genoese colonial hubs during the previous centuries. For the medieval Ligurian merchants and colonists, the slave trade was not an exception, limited to the Crimean-Egyptian route and due to the extraordinary profit one could make in Egypt. On the contrary, slaves were part of the everyday life both in Genoa and in most of its colonies, where they could be employed as domestic servants and warehousemen (like in Chilia), or as serfs in plantations.[38] As the example of Armenia clearly shows, not even the Christian faith of some of their captives could stop some Genoese merchants from trading them as stock. The Genoese were undoubtedly one step ahead towards that "slave society" that has possibly been one of the most striking (and tragic) characteristics of modern Atlantic empires.[39]

Yet, this little town on the mouth of the Danube is not significant only because it tells us something about the institution of slavery in the Genoese Levant. Slavery was only one among the many trades and businesses taking place in this restless corner of the Genoese network. In Chilia, the Genoese had a consul who coordinated the administration of the colony and represented the republic in a politically complicated and fragmented area. With its consular building (*curia*), mill, bakery, and warehouses, the Genoese Chilia was a sort of town within the town; the community was composed of permanent residents (mostly artisans and bankers), seasonal visitors (such as Antonio di Ponzò), and merchants selling and buying goods. The other people living in Chilia were Greeks and Tartars, with also a small group of Jews.[40] It is important to remember that the Genoese of Chilia were not isolated; instead, their community was part of a system of colonies running all around the Black Sea.[41] As they had done in Tunis, the Genoese in the Black Sea were offering administrative assistance and services to other communities living in this region. For instance, on April 27, 1361, Ponzò prepared two contracts where no Genoese citizen was mentioned: these were two deeds regulating the business relation between a Greek and a Venetian.[42] Interestingly enough, in one of these documents, the Venetian man is called "Petrus de Ognibem venecianus, habitator Chili."[43] In this case, the Genoese were doing something more than merely offering administrative skills to local business partners: they were allowing non-Genoese businessmen (subjects of competing political powers) to actively participate in the social and economic life of one of their most strategic colonies. To be sure, this does not mean that the Genoese merchants did not like monopolies and privileges; nevertheless, the private, mostly uncoordinated character of the Genoese commercial expansion favored the creation of a fluid and open structure, which could benefit from the participation of non-Genoese economic forces.

The Genoese had revitalized the economy of the Black Sea since the beginning of their penetration there at the end of the thirteenth century (Treaty of Nymphaeum, 1261), and Ponzò's deeds are an invaluable instrument to understand how the Genoese were taking advantage of their fleet to link the movement of some goods to the arrival of others, making Constantinople dependent on them and almost transforming the Black Sea into a Ligurian lake.[44] There is enough evidence to suggest that the economy of the Black Sea depicted in Antonio di Ponzò's notary deeds was at a turning point in its history. Until the 1330s, the Mongolian empire had been able to guarantee stable communications and relatively safe land routes connecting eastern Europe and the Middle East to central Asia and China. To be precise, what the Mongols were holding together was not a monolithic political entity, but rather a weak federation of four Khanates. Not infrequently some of the Khans were even at war against each other. However, in the decades preceding Ponzò's stay in Chilia, this vast empire started to collapse, with the Persian Khan dying with no heir as early as 1335, and the Golden Horde beginning its long phase of decline in the 1350s. The Genoese merchants had greatly benefited from the Mongolian stability, traveling across Asia and receiving in the ports of the Black Sea spices and silk. Some of the documents penned in Chilia by Ponzò have a great historical value precisely because they suggest what happened after the 1350s in the Ligurian Levant, and more specifically how the Genoese around the Black Sea reacted to the disintegration of the Mongolian empire.

On April 5, 1361, Ponzò wrote two contracts concerning wheat. With the first, the banker Francesco Bustarino declared that he had invested the forty *sommi* of silver received from Giovanni Torniello, a merchant from Pera, in September. The investment chosen by the banker was 270 *moggi* of wheat, which had already arrived and had been stored in the warehouse of Sava, the smith.[45] Later on the same day, Ponzò wrote another deed, with which the merchant Michele di Recco, owner of the ship San Nicola, stated that he had loaded seventy *moggia* of wheat owned by Teodoro Osgoragi and 25.5 *mog-*

gia of wheat owned by Teodoro Canavori. Michele was going to transport the wheat to Constantinople, where the other two merchants were then going to pay him after the delivery.[46] In both these deeds, wheat is the product traded by the Genoese; and in both cases Constantinople, not Chilia, appears as the final destination.[47] The rest of Ponzò's file confirms that in Chilia grain was one of the most important goods to trade. Thanks to a deed written on April 10, 1361, we know that even the consul of the city, Bernabò di Carpena, was involved in the transport of wheat.[48] Two days later, another contract attests that the Genoese brothers Brancaleone and Cristiano de Guisulfis, owners of the vessel San Giovanni, were going to use the money borrowed from Ianino di Focea to buy wheat in Bruscaviza, a place probably close to the Romanian town called Mahmudia; then, they were going to head for Constantinople, where the grain was to be sold and the debt to Ianino paid.[49] Interestingly enough, Ianino himself wanted to buy wheat in Bruscaviza to sell it in Constantinople, thus Brancaleone and Cristiano promised to load six *moggia* of Ianino's wheat on the vessel for free.[50] These documents seem to suggest that Genoese merchants quickly adapted to the new political conditions, as with the end of the Mongol *Pax* they shifted their investments from silk and spices to wheat, making Constantinople dependent on their shipments. But how could the Genoese think to reorient their investments and activities so quickly?

Two deeds prepared by Ponzò on May 5 can answer this question in particular. The first document is a contract with which a man called Carlo Iane di Mesembria rented the ship San Gregorio, owned by the Genoese Antonio di Finale. Carlo Iane, who would have paid one *perpero* and thirteen carats of gold for the service, needed the ship to transport 157 *moggia* of wheat from Chilia to another town of the Black Sea.[51] Thanks to the second document, we learn a good deal of details about the business relationship between these two men. The same Carlo Iane who in the first document was renting the ship of a Genoese merchant to transport wheat from Chilia to some Byzantine town had been able to buy his cargo only thanks to a loan, offered once again by that same Genoese man.[52] Moreover, from this second document we learn that Carlo Iane was a Greek (*grechus*), and that the connection between the money he borrowed and his wheat trade is absolutely clear as he promises to pay back the debt "by nine days after the arrival of the ship in one [of the ports],"[53] which means that he assumed he would sell the wheat in nine days. As these two documents suggest, the Genoese were able to swiftly adapt their commerce to the new political conditions of the region thanks to their capital and their naval superiority. The Tartars had never competed in maritime trade. The Venetians had been relegated to some corners of the Black Sea. And the Greeks could not resist the rapid rise of a new Genoese monopoly because they lacked an adequate fleet and even the money to invest in the purchase of grain. Now that the land routes around the

Black Sea had become dangerous, they had to buy at least part of the necessary food supply from Genoese merchants, at a higher price. Otherwise, the Greeks could borrow money from the Genoese, rent their vessels, and bring the wheat to their own towns. Yet, this complicated investment, as well demonstrated by the two deeds just analyzed, was once again allowing the Genoese to gain money at the expense of the Byzantines.

But this new situation was not exclusively detrimental to the Greeks. The growing importance of maritime transportation for regional commerce brought more Genoese shipowners to the coasts of the Black Sea. Admittedly, many of these merchants had already the means to purchase wheat; and those among them who did not were often able to borrow money from Genoese bankers in Pera or Caffa.[54] Yet, the money-lending market undoubtedly expanded enough to give opportunities also to those Greeks who had no experience in maritime trade, but possessed some capital to invest. We see here an unexpected economic relation, with the Greeks furnishing financial resources. Traces of this kind of business operations, where Genoese arriving in the Black Sea decided to borrow silver from Greeks, are present in Ponzò's documents. For example, in Chilia, on May 6, 1361, the two Greek associates Carlo Iane Francopolo and Carlo Iane Vassilico lent silver first to the owners of the Genoese ship San Demetrio, and later on the same day to the owners of the vessel San Giovanni e Santa Caterina.[55] While these cases may be seen as exceptions, they are meaningful because they show the complex relations between Genoese and local economic actors; moreover, they exemplify the economic growth sustained by the Genoese model, precisely at a time when the previous commercial system in the Black Sea was being dramatically challenged by the fragmentation of the political landscape and the interruption of stable contacts with central Asia and China.

However, appearance is often misleading, and it would be wrong to simplify the Genoese economic adaptation that followed the collapse of the Mongol empires. To say that the process was swift does not mean that it was easy. In fact, in spite of the readiness with which the Genoese seem to have replaced their trade in spices and silk with a flourishing commerce of wheat and wax, an economic change of these proportions had inevitable and more complex consequences. First, the implosion of the Persian Ilkhanate and the impossibility of purchasing Chinese goods provoked an adjustment in the financial geography of the Genoese Black Sea. The harbors of the southern coast probably entered a phase of decline, while Ligurian merchants moved their investments toward the heart of their regional network, Caffa, and other northern places (such as Chilia). Not by chance, the delicate balance of power with Tartars and local rulers was jeopardized, with the Genoese presence on the northern and eastern shores of the Black Sea increasing and becoming more aggressive.[56] The second consequence of the process was the need for new goods to exchange with the hinterland regions of Romania,

Bulgaria, and Moldavia, where grain and wax were being produced. After studying the notary deeds written in Chilia, I would suggest that by 1360 the Genoese were using silver not only as a means of banking and money-lending, but also to barter for wheat. This is noteworthy, because until then those Genoese who wanted to buy some grain in the northern shores had done so by bartering small parts of their cargoes of silks and spices.[57]

Finally, a third consequence of the growing importance of wheat, wax, and other goods was the necessity for the Genoese to penetrate the highlands. In fact, they expanded their influence through an aggressive military policy, consisting in building fortresses, citadels, and castles with the aim of protecting the roads connecting the agricultural areas to their ports. This peculiar and pivotal page in the history of the Genoese empire has been so far completely ignored, partly because of the lack of archeological investigations. However, ethnologists, geologists, travelers, and diplomats visiting Bulgaria, Ukraine, and Circassia in the nineteenth century have witnessed the presence of Genoese ruins deep in the countryside of these areas. For example, the English diplomat James Stanislaus Bell, who traveled across Circassia in the 1830s, reported in his journal an accidental but revealing discovery:

> On Friday evening I took a ride with him [one of the leaders of the Circassian resistance against the Russians] to see the site of a famed ancient fortress. I found it situated on the top of one of the highest and steepest hills, and it seems to me probable that the situation had been chosen by the Genoese (for our host attributed the fort to the Franks or "Genoese") as commanding a road through the hills from the plains of the Kuban to Suguljak and Ghelenjik—the best places for shipment. Towards the upper part of the hill two ridges were shown me, as having been walls with gates in them; and on the summit, where an excellent well is said to have existed (not long since), I found a pretty large space surrounded by a mound, but of what the mound was composed I had no means of ascertaining, for the whole was overgrown so thickly with trees and underwood, that I had difficulty in making my way, almost on all-fours, over but a small portion of it.[58]

The place where Bell saw these ruins was about twenty miles from the Kuban River, and quite far from the coast. By itself, Bell's account is nothing more than a clue; but there are other witnesses confirming the Genoese expansion towards the hinterland. In the 1840s, the French engineer Xavier Hommaire de Hell published for the Geological Society of France the account of his travels across Crimea, Caucasus and the steppes between those regions, and the Caspian Sea. While writing about the system of fortresses controlling the Dniester and other routes connecting the highlands of Ukraine with the Black Sea, Hommaire de Hell affirmed that they had been originally built by the Genoese. According to him, Genoese colonists were responsible not only for the fortification in the coastal city of Alkerman, but also for the construction of castles in Bender (Tighina) and in the remote Khotin (Chocim).[59] The French engineer argued that in Khotin the Turks and the Russians had simply renovated the old Genoese structure, and that "the walls . . . bear numerous Genoese inscriptions."[60]

Obviously, more research is needed to illuminate this specific process of expansion into the countryside. However, the information gathered by Bell, Hommaire de Hell, and other nineteenth-century visitors of Ukraine and Circassia seems to explain how the Genoese reached Russia from the Black Sea.[61] The Genoese had previously built castles along the Crimean coast—for example, in Caffa and Soldaia (Sudak).[62] Yet, the existence of a system of fortresses stretching into the mainland would prove that, after the disintegration of the Mongol empire, the Genoese had organized a different kind of network. In fact, we already know that some Genoese decided to establish posts along the routes of the lawless lands beyond the eastern coasts of the Black Sea—more specifically, around the plain of the river Kuban. Perhaps, Ligurian merchants entered the Caucasus region to make sure that its agricultural products would keep reaching the ports of Matrega (Taman), Mapa (Anapa), and Bata (Novorossiysk).[63] Near the mouth of the Kuban, the Genoese founded a colony called Copa (Kopa), which was linking the sea to the Circassian countryside, where they were controlling the production of agri-

Figure 1.1. The Genoese fortress of Soldaia (Sudak), on the Black Sea. ©iStock.com/alexabelov.

cultural goods and (as witnessed by Bell) the land routes towards the port of Maurolaca (Gelendzhik).[64] According to E. S. Zevakin and N. A. Pencko, in Kopa the Genoese were also collecting taxes and administering justice, even though political power had to be shared with Circassian lords.[65] It would therefore seem possible that, as written by Hommaire de Hell, a similar strategy was used by other Ligurians in the north, along the Dniester.

The creation and continuous reshaping of a commercial network at the periphery of the known world, the beginning of an intercontinental slave trade not necessarily as a consequence of warfare, the adaptation to sudden political crises through the use of interchanging business strategies, the growth of a private bureaucratic apparatus based on a consolidated tradition of administrative skills, and the successful establishment of a coastal economy with links to key fluvial routes are all phenomena indicating the emergence of a mature colonial culture. As early as the last centuries of the Middle Ages, and amid countless challenges, Genoese merchants and colonists had woven around the Black Sea a colonial economy. As I aim to show in the last chapter of my book, this process is strikingly similar to the endeavors and achievements of Genoese merchants within the Spanish Americas, a few centuries later.[66]

UNFRIENDLY HARBORS: THE GENOESE IN ENGLAND AND THE OPENING OF THE ATLANTIC

The Atlantic world is a relational concept, so historians searching for the origins of the Atlantic should look for stable, intercontinental (though perhaps discreet, as in the nature of the Genoese) relations built around the Atlantic Ocean. Ligurian merchants were the first group of Italian businessmen to link the Mediterranean and the North Sea exclusively by navigation, establishing a continuous connection and a profitable economic relation through Atlantic waters as early as the 1270s.[67] In particular, the Genoese established commercial colonies in Southampton and London, drawing England into one of the largest trading empires of the time. Later, other Italian merchants (Venetians, Florentines, and Lombards) followed the Ligurian example and tried to penetrate the English market. As explained by Robert S. Lopez, “by 1277–78 Genoese galleys could make the voyage to Flanders and England to a profit, and . . . markets thereafter grew so fast that by the early fourteenth century not only Genoa but also Venice sent regular convoys every year.”[68] The Genoese were coming to England to sell spices, wine, alum, and other products coming from the Mediterranean markets, the Levant, and the Black Sea. On their way back to Italy, they were transporting English wool and cloth. During the thirteenth and the fourteenth centuries,

England was producing the best raw wool in the world, which was then worked in the industrial towns of Italy and the Flanders.

To establish a maritime route from the Mediterranean to London, Southampton, and Boston meant for the Genoese involved to gain an enormous amount of money.[69] But the penetration of the English market was not an easy task. As soon as the first Italian merchants tried to introduce a free-trade mentality, asking to the Parliament to grant them equal commercial rights, English traders and retailers started a long political battle against them. To be sure, the Genoese were not the first alien merchants ever to reach the shores of Britain: during the Middle Ages, Germans, French, and Danes had traded all kinds of goods with England, crossing the Channel and selling products transported on land routes from as far as eastern Europe and the Caspian Sea. But these goods were coming irregularly and were relatively overpriced, as they had been repeatedly taxed on their way to England. In fact, the true novelties of the Genoese arrival in the 1270s were the exclusively maritime transport of the merchandise (from the Mediterranean basin to England, and vice versa) and the stability of the commercial relations that these Italians wanted to build. Local traders and retailers felt particularly threatened by the fact that the Genoese were selling in the English market high quality products at low prices. This was possible because the Genoese, through their vast commercial empire and their knowledge of international markets, were buying spices, wax, silk, alum, finished cloths, and wine in places (relatively) close to the centers of production (or at the sources of supply). Moreover, navigating around the Iberian Peninsula, the Genoese were perhaps the first to avoid the countless duties imposed on the merchants traveling across central Europe and France.

The alien merchants who had previously visited England had not received any legal protection. Therefore, the traders, retailers, and shopkeepers of the main English ports had easily forged legal measures to limit the activities of these foreigners and to minimize their economic intrusion. For example, already in the first half of the twelfth century the burgesses of London protected their monopoly of retail trade in their chart of rights and local laws called *Libertas Londonienis*. According to this text, a foreign merchant was forbidden to sell small quantities of merchandise or to stay in the city for more than forty days.[70] This situation changed with the arrival of Genoese carracks, and precisely because the stable presence of this group of foreigners (assured by their powerful private fleet) and the relatively cheap price of the goods brought by them stimulated the interest of the king and the nobility. For the first time, foreign merchants were going to receive substantial political help in their struggle against the ostracism practiced by town councils and urban retailers. To understand the willingness of the Crown to protect the Italian merchants, we have also to consider that, for the king, a consistent flow of goods from without the country meant that he could increase his customs revenues. In addition, both the Genoese and the Florentines were ready (sometimes compelled) to lend conspicuous sums of money.[71] As a consequence of these conflicting interests, throughout the fourteenth century an abundant and contradictory legislation dealing with alien merchants was produced by Parliament and by some English towns, clearly showing the battle under way between the king and the urban burgesses. When the king was politically strong, legislation protecting alien merchants was passed by Parliament. This happened for example during the reign of Edward III, who was the first king to decisively and consistently challenge the mercantilist structure of the English market. According to Michele Giuseppe Canale, in the 1330s the English monarch had welcomed at court the Genoese Niccolino Fieschi, naming him state counsellor.[72] In addition, with his Acts of 1335 and 1351, Edward III allowed foreign merchants to trade freely, notwithstanding older traditions and local laws. In particular, the statute of 1335 ordered lords, bailiffs, and local authorities to ignore previous trade regulations and to protect foreign merchants from any harassment, seizure of merchandise, and discrimination; all merchants had to be free to buy and sell any goods from and to anybody.[73] The powerful merchants of London reacted with outrage, writing complaints to Parliament and obstructing the king's commercial policy in every possible way. Eventually, they won the battle, and in 1376, taking advantage of a moment of political turbulence, they forced Edward to grant them a charter of privileges that reintroduced all the traditional measures against alien merchants (such as the obligation to be hosted by an English subject and the prohibition to sell by retail).[74]

Admittedly, London was a particularly difficult environment for a foreigner to do business, and there were other English ports with a more friendly local population. More specifically, in Southampton Genoese and Venetians were able to exploit the almost complete lack of long-distance merchants; here, the Italians were glad to leave the retail in the hands of local salesmen, while packing their ships with wool. Hence, the population of Southampton was selling goods coming from the Mediterranean in the hinterlands while the Italians could take advantage of the links between Southampton and wool-farming areas of Southern England. The result was a lively economic alliance between local burgesses and foreign traders, which made Southampton a relatively safe harbor for the Genoese, as emphasized in a study written by Alwyn A. Ruddock in the 1940s. The Italians doing business in Southampton were "allowed to hire many of the town properties, including dwelling houses, lofts, barns, and cellars for storing their merchandize."[75] Some Italians were even being elected "to some of the highest municipal offices in the town."[76] Nevertheless, the condition of an alien merchant remained precarious, and even the Genoese living and trading in Southampton could be harassed, robbed, and at times killed. In fact, documents in the British National Archives prove that the Genoese visiting Southampton could indeed be victims of predatory rivals and local authorities. For example, in a petition to the king dated 1389, some Genoese merchants (led by Barnabus Centurione) lamented that they had been robbed on their way from Spain to London.[77] During the voyage, they had been approached by two English vessels, whose captains offered to accompany the Italians; after two days of joint navigation, the English suddenly boarded the Italian ship and seized the merchandise, claiming that these were enemies' goods and brought the ship to Southampton. Here, the Genoese had tried to obtain justice, bringing the case to the mayor and the bailiffs, but all the local authorities sided with the robbers, and refused to return the ship and the goods, notwithstanding a royal letter with privy seal.[78] In response to this petition, the king granted the appointment of an official to force the authorities in Southampton to deliver up the ship and the merchandise. Another document, this time dated 1403, suggests that the Venetians at times waited for the Genoese carracks to arrive well laden in the North Sea, and then they attempted to assault them.[79]

Despite the examples mentioned, it remains true that for the Genoese Southampton (and the route toward it) was safer than any other English port. So much so, that the Ligurians also seem to have taken advantage of this town as a strategic port of call. In another petition dated 1403, some Genoese merchants appear to have reached Southampton only in order to write to the king, asking for special safe conducts with which to trade in every port and town of the realm.[80] Another petition, written about one year before, discloses the counterstrategy of the Londoners, who intercepted the alien merchants coming from Southampton by land and tried to make them pay customs duties for the second time, while seizing their merchandise and even arresting some of them.[81] It is not surprising then, that in their long struggle to protect the alien merchants visiting England, the monarchs consistently included Southampton on the list of home staples;[82] and later, they granted to the foreigners visiting this port the privilege to avoid the staple of Calais.[83] Yet the friendly Southampton could not always protect the Genoese from their restlessness; the streets of London could be dark enough to engulf a foreigner who had cautiously settled in Southampton but fatefully decided to visit the capital. In 1379, a Genoese traveled from Southampton to London, to propose to the king the transformation of the former into the main English commercial hub and metropolis. The ambitious project would have rewarded the faithful subjects of Southampton, weakened the king's enemies in London, and assured the Genoese supremacy in the English market. However, on a chilly London night the Genoese emissary was assassinated, and the king had to abort the project.[84] This mysterious episode, recalled in the pages of Thomas of Walsingham's *Historia Anglicana*, exemplifies how the Genoese were carrying not only capital and goods, but also an incomparable economic culture, a tendency to adapt to the most hostile conditions, and the capacity to create cosmopolitan hubs for international trade. The inhabitants of Southampton caught a glimpse of all this and tried to establish a mutually beneficial economic alliance; in this context, the Genoese showed once again a remarkable promptness. However, due to the king's weak political position and the violent as well as legislative means employed by the mercantile community in London, the Genoese could not expand their commercial colonies and their family networks across Southern England, so their presence there was, in the long run, inconsequential. In Spain, things would go differently.

UNHAPPY CANDIA, AND THE UNIQUENESS OF GENOA'S MARKET EXPANSION

On a fateful day of September 1363, in the island of Candia (Crete), officials of the Republic of Venice hanged on walls in public squares and doors of government buildings a new decree coming from the metropolis, with which the Senate levied more taxes on the colonies. As the colonists read the edict and as the news ran from house to house, their anger overwhelming their caution, they seized the harbors and attacked their metropolitan compatriots. Days of chaos followed. Inside the warehouses where they were selling their merchandise, or aboard the ships where they were loading cargoes of grapes and other fruit, Venetian merchants were suddenly arrested and dragged by their fellow countrymen into the prisons of Candia's city ports. Numerous revolts across this island had previously culminated in bloodshed, but these were usually ethnic clashes, with the Greek population fighting against colonial rule. This time it was the local Venetian elite that began a rebellion against the centralism of the Venetian empire. The Greeks joined a rebellion that initially was not their own, bringing lawlessness to the countryside and taking advantage of the confusion to massacre many Venetian nobles in their villas.[85] As the Venetian elite gradually restored order and punished the Greek "traitors," the true, specific aim of their revolt was clear: they rose against the republican government and its fiscal system.[86]

Writing at the end of the fifteenth century, the Venetian humanist Marco Antonio Sabellico (1436–1506) recalled a revealing episode of the revolt.[87] While the Venetian Senate was arming a fleet to retake Candia, diplomatic missions kept reaching its shores: the republic would have preferred to avoid a military action against *gentilhuomini Vinitiani*. The rebels, who had initially refused any reconciliation with their motherland, had now witnessed the Greek violence in the interiors and were starting to doubt their ability not only to defend the island from the republican forces but even to simply maintain the Greeks under control. In this situation, asking for a pardon to the Senate seemed to some of the rebels a prudent solution. However, after a long and tense council, "it pleased them [the rebels] to send to Genoa twelve ambassadors, including both some Italians and some Greeks."[88] With this decision, the rebels decided to completely repudiate their Venetian history, status, and blood. While previous commentators had expressed all their shock and rancorous feelings,[89] Sabellico tried to mention this episode with nonchalance, and in an attempt to give an explanation, he introduced it with these words:

> They began to wonder to whom they could give the possession of the island: in order to be sure not to return under the Venetian Dominion. Thus it seemed to them that only to the Genoese they could entrust their fate: both for the power that they had on the sea, and moreover for the ancient envy that they felt toward the Venetian Dominion.[90]

So, the Venetian nobles who started the revolt, once facing a riotous Greek population and the prospect of military defeat, decided to change their own oppressive republic (to which they were linked by family ties, interests, and privileges) with a foreign (and arch-rival). While Sabellico wanted to downplay the episode, the whole event seems especially surprising because the colonial elite in Crete "crafted their individual and family identities to conform to Venetian standards of political and patrician identity."[91] These same Venetian rebels had probably daughters who had married merchants from the metropolis; not infrequently, they had sons who attended the Great Council in Venice and hoped for a governmental post. If these *Vinitiani* wanted to suddenly become part of the Genoese world there had to be some good reason, other than the contingent ones hastily presented by Sabellico.[92] Apparently, once the rebellion became unsustainable, it would have made more sense for the Venetian colonists to accept the pardon from their motherland rather than to call another, equally despotic ruler. What made the idea of a Genoese takeover acceptable to these Cretan *Vinitiani*, however, was that this second, foreign entity was *not* perceived as despotic. In order to be adequately explained, this extraordinary episode needs to be placed in the context of an ideological gap, separating the Genoese colonial and economic mind-set from the Venetian one.[93]

It is necessary to remember that the colonial elite in Crete had rebelled specifically against the fiscal policies of the Venetian government. For all the hard feelings that the Venetian merchants had toward the Genoese, they knew that the Genoese colonies had a different relationship with their metropolis, one that allowed them to organize their local communities around the Mediterranean (and beyond) more freely. Hence, asking for a Genoese intervention did not mean an intention to change an oppressive government with another one; rather, it signified the hope of becoming part of a mercantile and financial system characterized by the lack of a strong metropolitan government. When in 1398 the Genoese consuls of the smaller colonies around the Black Sea received the order to respect a higher authority for matters of foreign policy, this was not the doge or the *Consiglio degli Anziani* in Genoa, but instead the consul of Caffa, the regional hub for Genoese merchants. For Caffa in particular, one could argue that the more this colony grew in economic importance, the more autonomous it became, at least until the 1450s.[94] Furthermore, Genoese officials were never backed by a large public fleet. Even John Dotson, who assigns much significance to the creation of the military magistracy of the *Credenza* in 1282, and while writing about the 1280s and 1290s—which were decades of exceptional communal involvement in naval warfare—has to admit that "while Venetian fleets were built by the state in the famous Arsenal, Genoese fleets were always made up of a combination of communal and private vessels in varying proportions. Often, communal vessels made up the lesser proportion of the fleet."[95] And Michel Balard, in another essay of the same volume, states that "the imbalance between public naval forces and private ones was a constant feature of Genoese history."[96]

Genoa's approach to market expansion seems different from Venice's especially if one looks at the birth of their colonies. Whereas Genoese expansion was usually initiated by private endeavors, and at times (such as in Chios) resulted in peculiar forms of autonomous governance, Venetian empire-building developed as a result of state-run expeditions.[97] At the beginning of the thirteenth century, the Republic of Venice plotted with the French to overthrow the Greek imperial family in Constantinople, and to replace it with Latin rulers.[98] After this coup, the Venetians conquered many islands in the Aegean Sea, including Crete. Sabellico tells the story of this enterprise in his *Historie*, and he is careful to recognize and (as a good Venetian) to glorify the role of the republican government and of the public galleys. In the text, he first explains that the doge granted perpetual possession of the islands to those private citizens who were going to conquer them, move there with their families, and defend them. Yet, the author immediately clarifies on whom most of the burden of the military expedition was:

> But before anything else the public fleet composed by thirty-one galleys was sent to sea. . . . Now almost all the histories, and the authors, which we have read, tell the actions of the private [citizens] before those of the public [fleet]: as if the private [colonists] could have done any operation around the islands before the sea was freed from the pillaging of the corsairs, against whom the public Galleys were forced to fight almost within the very heart of the Adriatic.[99]

Sabellico continues: "to stop the Greek tumults in Candia . . . the Venetians sent a colony to that island. They sent there a certain number of noble knights and a certain number of people as soldiers."[100] The republic "sent a colony": no expression could have sounded more curious to the ears of a Genoese. Venice had not only opened the way and indicated the direction for a colonial expansion. More importantly, the Venetian government authoritatively organized the migration of citizens to specific colonies for political reasons and imposed on them military obligations. An earlier Venetian writer, Giorgio Dolfin (c. 1396–c. 1458) recalls the conquest of Crete by "Renier Dandolo, captain of the *Signoria* and of its *armada da Mar*."[101] Dolfin includes in his chronicle the "pacts and conditions" given by the doge to the colonists sent to Candia; among the conditions that the colonists had to respect, we read that if they discovered any deposit of gold, silver, or any other metal on the island, these were to be considered the property of the metropolitan government.[102] Furthermore, the doge made it clear that "as many times I or my successors shall wish to raise an army, you will do so like the men of Venice without any objection."[103]

There are obviously many consequences of this cultural gap, and they are all recognizable in the political and economic histories of the Genoese and the Venetians. Used to opening new markets and moving to important city ports of foreign countries without virtually any form of support from their government, Genoese entrepreneurs were forced to use economic calculation and to risk private capital in order to open markets. The Genoese merchants were therefore more ready to face political crises and economic transformations. They were also more likely to be welcomed by English, Portuguese, and Spanish monarchs, who did not perceive them as a military or political threat. Of course, the Genoese commercial empire was adaptable, not anarchical: in delicate political contexts, like the Black Sea region, once Genoese merchants and professionals had taken roots, the colonial self-governments developed significantly and sophisticatedly, allowing local consuls to raise enough money for the construction of fortifications like the one still standing today in Soldaia (Sudak), Crimea.[104] But these developments were not dictated by the metropolis as part of a planned imperial expansion. As we shall see, Genoa became more directly involved in the administration of the Crimean outposts only in 1453, when their official possession passed from the commune to a private bank, St. George.

The Venetians, on the other hand, were taking advantage of a politically stable and militarily aggressive state; but they were also dependent on its fate.[105] The Venetians usually followed (or participated in) state-sponsored missions of colonization where the protagonist was the republican fleet, not a group of anonymous entrepreneurs. With the opening of the Atlantic, they were unable to autonomously reinvent their economic role in a changed world. This is perhaps the main reason behind Venice's political transformation into a territorial power.[106] In about fifty years, Treviso, Rovigo, Vicenza, Padova, Verona, Brescia, Bergamo, and Ravenna all fell under the control of the Republic of Venice. "With conquest and lasting occupation of extensive territory it developed a standing army which by the middle of the fifteenth century had become arguably the strongest in Italy."[107] In the meantime, through the growth of the central government, the Venetian oligarchy increased also its internal powers; "from the late fourteenth century, the state was involving itself in an ever-widening range of political, economic, and, especially, social concerns."[108] This whole process was a sort of welfare/rescue for those nobles who had previously taken advantage of the Venetian colonies in the Middle East and in the Levant, and who were now unable to reinvent their economic role in a deeply changed geopolitical situation. They did not lack capital, maritime experience, or commercial tradition; rather, they were lacking an economic culture based on private initiative, diversification of investments, and adaptability. While the Genoese were ready to penetrate the Iberian Peninsula and to reinvest their capital in the Atlantic world, the Venetians fell back on their exclusivist elite to get through the hard times and rule, if not the new ocean, at least their territorial neighbors. Interestingly, this process was seen by some Venetians as a betrayal of the city's maritime and mercantile tradition. Writing in 1501, the merchant Girolamo Priuli condemned the militaristic and expansionist policies carried out by his republic during the fourteenth century with these words:

> The birth and the development of the city of Venice came from the sea and from maritime navigation, and the Venetian riches and treasures came from the sea and maritime travels, yet all this money coming from the sea has been consumed in the mainland . . . from the sea had come wealth and honour and fame, but from the mainland [came] the wars and the spending.[109]

In conclusion, where the Genoese network, lacking a public fleet, was built by private initiatives and through private economic investments, the Venetian empire was relatively centralized and militarized: a creature of the state since the very beginning. Therefore, that the political intrusiveness, the state monopolies and the fiscal pressure of the metropolis were more achingly felt by the Venetian colonists than by the Genoese merchants is not a surprise. In this respect, the Venetians were not exceptional, as their republic was arguably following the pattern of other late medieval powers (such as the kingdom of Aragon).[110] The true exception was Genoa, whose families moved their vessels according to the laws of demand and supply—not following the machinations of a doge or the political agenda of the Senate. Moreover, while much work needs to be done on the fiscal history of Genoa, it seems certain that the amount of taxes paid by Genoese businessmen was low, even "ridiculously low" when compared with the fiscal pressure in other late medieval and early modern Italian states.[111] The Genoese idea of *libertà* was defined and lived in economic terms. As I will show in the next chapters, the Genoese connected and reshaped markets, while overcoming organizational problems and military weakness. In the Black Sea, they eventually centralized their colonial administration by privatizing it, that is, by putting it into the hands of the same merchants and businessmen who were involved in those markets. At home, they kept in check the power of the doge and (when deemed necessary) invited foreign rulers in order to protect their communal constitution and their economic interests.

NOTES

1. Chapter 2 will explain how the Genoese intended and organized their communal republic.
2. Verlinden, *The Beginnings of Modern Colonization.*
3. For the diplomatic documents of this period, see *Trattati e negoziazioni politiche della Repubblica di Genova (958—1797)* (Genova: ASLSP, 1960), in particular n. 433; and A. Ferretto, *Codice diplomatico delle relazioni fra la Liguria, la Toscana e la Lunigiana ai tempi di Dante* (Genova: ASLSP, 1901–1903).
4. In the State Archive of Genoa, a group of manuscripts written in Tunis between the end of 1288 and June 1289 has been preserved throughout the centuries. This collection of documents was published by the University of Genoa in 1986, and it represents an extraordinary window on the everyday life of a colony that has been overlooked by the historiography of the Genoese empire. *Atti Rogati a Tunisi da Pietro Battifoglio (1288–1289)*, ed. Geo Pistarino (Genova: Università di Genova, 1986). To my knowledge, the only cohesive pieces of research about the Genoese in medieval Northwest Africa are H. C. Krueger, "Genoese Trade with North-west Africa in the Twelfth Century," *Speculum* VIII (1933): 377–95; idem, "Early Genoese Trade with Atlantic Marocco," *Medievalia et Humanistica* III (1945): 3–15; and David Abulafia, "L'attività commerciale genovese nell'africa normanna: la città di Tripoli," in *Atti del Congresso Internazionale di Studi sulla Sicilia Normanna* (Palermo: 1973), 395–402. The only historian who has (briefly) treated Battifoglio's file is Felipe Fernández-Armesto, in *Before Columbus*.
5. *Atti Rogati a Tunisi*, deed 68, 99–100. Also, ibid., deed 87, 126.
6. See traces of this clash of interests in ibid., deeds 128 and 129, 179–183.
7. Geo Pistarino, *Atti Rogati a Tunisi*, xxix.
8. See *Maestri e garzoni nella societa Genovese fra XV e XVI secolo*, in L. Gatti, *Un Catalogo dei Mestieri* (Genova: Centro Studi Storia Tecnica, 1980), 46–47.
9. Ibid., deed 19, 29–30.
10. The presence and the economic activities of Genoese noble families in Tunis are documented throughout the Battifoglio's file. For another example, see the notary deed written on June 6, 1289, where we find Tomao Caparagia appointing two members of the Spinola family (Nicolino and Ingueto) as his procurators. Ibid., deed 112, 160–61.
11. Ibid., deed 15, 24.
12. Ibid., deed 54, 78–79.
13. Ibid., deed 45, 66–67.
14. "Possit . . . pecuniam mutuare pro me et meo nomine, usq[ue in] quantitate librarum trescentarum ianuinorum, et quod posit instituere unum procuratorem vel plures, sicut ei melius videbitur, pro me et me[o nomine]." Ibid., deed 45, 67.
15. Verlinden, *The Beginnings of Modern Colonization.*
16. *Atti Rogati a Tunisi*, deed 26, 40–41.
17. "Raynaldo Maffei, civis et mercator Florencie . . . nomine suo et sociorum suorum." Ibid., deed 93, 135.
18. Ibid., deed 83, 120.
19. I shall return to this issue in part II.

20. For an introduction to the relations between Constantinople and the West in this period, see Deno J. Geanakoplos, *Emperor Michael Paleologus and the West, 1258–1282* (Cambridge: Harvard Press, 1959). For a collection of important primary sources, see *Nuova serie di documenti sulle relazioni di Genova coll'Impero Bizantino raccolti dal cav. Angelo Sanguineti e pubblicati con molte aggiunte dal prof. Gerolamo Bertolotto* (Genova: ASLI, 1898), 339–573.

21. Verlinden, *The Beginnings of Modern Colonization*, 32.

22. From the perspective of "cliometrics," or quantitative economic history, it seems clear why scholars have often ignored Chilia. "During the fourteenth and fifteenth centuries, the important Genoese ports in the Orient are four: Caffa, Pera, Chio e Famagosta." Translation from the original: "Nel Trecento e Quattrocento, i grandi porti genovesi d'Oriente sono quattro: Caffa, Pera, Chio e Famagosta." Michel Balard, "Il Sistema Portuale Genovese d'Oltremare (secc. XIII–XV)," in *Il Sistema Portuale della Repubblica di Genova* (Genova: Università degli Studi di Genova, 1988), 338. Balard wrote one of the very first studies of the Genoese activities in the West Black Sea during the thirteenth century, Michael Balard, "Les Gènois dans l'ouest de la Mer Noire au XIV siècle," in *Actes du XIV Congrès International des ètudes byzantines (1971)* (Bucarest: 1975). To my knowledge, the only two works in English mentioning and partly describing the Genoese Chilia are two articles: Constantin C. Giurescu, "The Genoese and the Lower Danube in the XIIIth and XIVth centuries," *Journal of European Economic History* 5 (1976): 587–600; and Dennis Deletant, "Genoese, Tartars and Rumanians at the Mouth of the Danube in the Fourteenth Century," *Slavonic and East European Review* 4 (1984): 511–30.

23. "vendictor vini melis, habitator Chili." *Atti Rogati a Chilia da Antonio di Ponzò (1288–1289)*, ed. by Geo Pistarino (Genova: Università di Genova, 1971), deed 39, 64.

24. "omnes domos suas, et sclavos duos." Ibid.

25. For example, on November 27, 1360, Quirico di Pontremoli sold to Francesco Salvaigo the slave Gata for the sum of five *sommi* of silver. Ibid, deed 1, 3–6.

26. Ibid., deed 9, 16.

27. Ibid, deed 15, 22–23.

28. With the treaty of 1345, the Genoese used Tartar piracy as an excuse to forbid the Venetians to travel directly to Tana without first calling at the Genoese city of Caffa, where all the goods had to be unloaded. The first clause of this treaty stated: "It is forbidden to bring goods of any kind to Tana or to any other place of the Tartar empire by the vessels of either one or the other nation, because of the robberies and the damages suffered by merchants, who have been expelled, imprisoned or killed; rather, the goods must be brought only to Caffa and the other ports under its control toward West." Translation from the original: "Non si dovrà dai bastimenti dell'una o dell'altra nazione portar merci di qualsiasi genere alla Tana, od in altro luogo del tartaro impero, stante i svaligiamenti e danni sofferti dai mercadanti, con espulsione, prigionia e morte loro; ma debbono soltanto portarle a Caffa ed altri porti situati sotto di lei ad occidente." Cited in Michele Giuseppe Canale, *Nuova Istoria della Repubblica di Genova* (Firenze: LeMonnier, 1860), v. 3, 240.

29. *Atti Rogati a Chilia*, deed 61, 103–5.

30. Ibid., deed 85, 151–53.

31. "Acto quod, si dicta sclava se orinaret subtus se, quod dictus Daoch teneatur et debeat et promixit eidem Manoli restituire dictam summam, et eo casu dictus Manoli teneatur et debeat et promisit eidem Daoch restituere dictam sclavam." Ibid., deed 97, 176–77.

32. "I schiavi che [i Genovesi] compreranno e vorranno estrarre dal regno non pagheranno più alcun diritto. Comprandosi però dei schiavi cristiani si farà giuramento di non venderli ai Turchi, né a qualsivoglia persona volesse venderli." Cited in Canale, *Nuova Istoria*, v. 3, 247.

33. To use the Armenian port of Ayas (Lajazzo) and to travel across Armenia was very important for the Genoese commerce with central Asia. Mack Chahin has defined medieval Armeno-Cilicia "as an entrepôt between Europe and Asia." Mack Chahin, *The Kingdom of Armenia* (London: Croom Helm, 1987), 288.

34. About another prototype of the Atlantic slave market, which was the port of Genoa itself, see Domenico Gioffre, *Il Mercato degli Schiavi a Genova nel Secolo XV* (Genova: Bozzi, 1971).

35. The people enslaved by Columbus at this early stage were the same he had described as harmless and good new subjects. The Spanish had yet to come into contact with the Aztec and Inca empires.

36. Among them, the Columbus brothers, Rivaroli, Giannotto Berardi, and Amerigo Vespucci. To understand how, as a consequence of Columbus's decisions, the Florentines Berardi and Vespucci found themselves involved in this first transatlantic slave trade, see Consuelo Varela, "El entorno florentino de Cristòbal Colòn," in *Colloquia sulla presenza italiana in Andalusia nel basso medioevo*, ed. by Alberto Boscolo and Bibiano Torres (Rome: Cappelli, 1984), 125–34.

37. For a meaningful example of Spanish enslaving Moors and Jews in order to obtain rich ransoms, see Miguel Angel Ladero Quesada, "La esclavitud por guerra a fines del siglo XV: el caso de Malaga," *Hispania* 27 (1967): 63–88. To get a sense of how during the *Reconquista* slavery was often a sort of kidnapping for ransom, see Manuela Marin and Rachid El Hour, "Captives, Children and Conversion," *Journal of Economic and Social History of the Orient* 4 (1998): 453–73.

38. Besides Verlinden's book, those interested in the Genoese plantations in the Levant must rely on primary sources; for example, see *Quatre titres des propriétés des Génois à Acre et à Tyr*, ed. by Cornelio Desimoni, Archives de l'Orient latin, 2 (1884). Only sporadically the Genoese system of agricultural exploitation is mentioned in works treating the Latin kingdoms; see for instance Jonathan Riley-Smith, *The Feudal Nobility and the Kingdom of Jerusalem* (London: Macmillan, 1973), 53.

39. About the readiness with which the Italians enslaved Native Americans and (in contrast) the doubts of Queen Isabel, see Helen Nader, "Desperate Men, Questionable Acts: the Moral Dilemma of Italian Merchants in the Spanish Slave Trade," *The Sixteenth Century Journal* 33 (2002): 401–22.

40. See *Atti Rogati a Chilia*, xxxi–xxxiii.

41. The colonies on the Northern and Eastern shores, ruled by the Genoese government in Caffa, were sovereign (granted a variable degree of cooperation with local lords or Tartar authorities); instead, the colonies on the Western shores of the Black Sea, especially Galata and Pera (neighborhoods of Constantinople), were a sort of *imperium in imperio*. The lack of studies dealing with the Genoese in the Black Sea is striking. Besides the already mentioned works by Michel Balard, the rare (and dated) exception is Georges I. Bratianu, *Recherches sur le commerce génois dans la mer Noire au XIIIe siècle* (Paris: Geuthner, 1929); for an account that focuses more on the slave trade, see idem, *La mer noire; des origines à la conquête ottomane* (Munich: Societas academica Dacoromana, 1969). Louis Mitler has proved the stubborn resistance of Genoese commerce in Galata in his article "The Genoese in Galata: 1453–1682," *International Journal of Middle East Studies*, 10 (1979): 71–91. For a more recent but merely introductory reading, see Charles King, *The Black Sea* (Oxford: Oxford University Press, 2004), 82–104.

42. *Atti Rogati a Chilia*, deeds 50 and 51, 84–86.

43. Ibid., deed 50, 84.

44. On the Treaty of Nymphaeum, see John Dotson, "Venice, Genoa and Control of the Seas in the Thirteenth and Fourteenth Centuries," in *War at Sea in the Middle Ages and the Renaissance*, ed. John B. Hattendorf and Richard W. Hunger (Woodbidge, Suffolk: Boydell Press, 2003), 121–122. For one of the most important investigations of medieval trade in the Levant, see Eliyahu Ashtor, *Levant Trade in the Later Middle Ages* (Princeton, NJ: Princeton University Press, 1983).

45. *Atti Rogati a Chilia*, deed 31, 50–51.

46. Ibid., deed 32, 52–53.

47. Pera was the colonial neighborhood of the Genoese within the city of Constantinople.

48. Ibid., deed 40, 67–67.

49. Ianino was going to travel with the Guisulfis brothers, who "have to feed both him and his servant." "teneatur nutrire ipsum Ianinum et eius famulum." Ibid., deed 41, 69.

50. Ibid., deed 41, 68–70.

51. Ibid., deed 62, 105–7.

52. "In nomine Domini, amen. Carlo Iane de Mexembre grechus condam Papa Leonis confessus fuit et in veritate recognovit Anthonio de Finario, filio Manuelis, presenti et solempniter stipulanti, se ab ipso Anthonio habuisse et recepisse in Chili tantam quantitatem sui argenti boni et mercantilis." Ibid., deed 63, 107–8.

53. "infra dies novem proxime venturos postquam dictum lignum fuerit aplicatum [ad umum] ibi." Ibid.

54. This happened of course also in Chilia, where Genoese shipowners could borrow money from Genoese businessmen such as Mogolo di Camilia. See the restless money-lending activities of Mogolo in the month of May 1361, in ibid., deeds 64, 65, 68, 69, and 70, 109–13, and 118–24.

55. Ibid., deeds 66 and 67, 113–18.

56. Before these events in the 1340s Chilia and the northern shores of the Black Sea were less vital to the Genoese network than appears to be the case at the time of Ponzo writing his deeds in 1361. The Tartar sieges of Caffa as well as their piracy mentioned in the treaty of 1345 with Venice must be understood in the light of these changes.

57. Giurescu, "The Genoese and the Lower Danube," 589–90.

58. James Stanislaus Bell, *Journal of a Residence in Circassia During the Years 1837, 1838, 1839* (London: Moxon, 1840), v. 1, 243.

59. Khotin is about 400 miles from the Black Sea.

60. Xavier Hommaire de Hell, *Travels in the steppes of the Caspian Sea, the Crimea, the Caucasus, &c.* (London: Chapman and Hall, 1847), 425. Originally published as *Les steppes de la mer Caspienne, la Crimee et la Russie meridionale* (Paris: Bertrand, 1843–45).

61. About the traces of economic relations between the Genoese colonies in the Black Sea and Russia, see Cornelio Desimoni, *Nuovi Studi sull'Atlante Luxoro* (Genova: ASLSP, 1868), 181.

62. Balard, *La Romanie génoise.*

63. Another reason to penetrate in the highlands may have been to attempt a recovery of those routes linking the Caspian Sea to the European markets.

64. E. S. Zevakin and N. A. Pencko, "Ricerche sulla Storia delle Colonie Genovesi nel Caucaso Occidentale nei Secoli XIII–XV," in *Miscellanea di Studi Storici* (Genova: Bozzi, 1969), 26–27.

65. Ibid.

66. Even Felipe Fernández-Armesto, who believes that the Genoese never played a significant role in the Atlantic, has incidentally but appropriately admitted that "[t]he same surnames crop up repeatedly all over the Genoese world, from the Black Sea in the thirteenth century to the Caribbean in the sixteenth." Fernández-Armesto, *Before Columbus*, 106.

67. Renée Doehaerd, *Les relations commerciales entre gênes, la Belgique et l'outremont d'aprè̀s les archives notariales génois es aux XIII et XIV siecles* (Bruxelles and Rome: Academia Belgica, 1941).

68. Robert S. Lopez, "Majorcans and Genoese on the North Sea Route in the Thirteenth Century," *Revue Belge de Philologie et d'Histoire* 29 (1951): 1166.

69. About the importance of Boston, in Lincolnshire, see William G. Hoskins, *Provincial England* (London: Macmillan, 1963), 12.

70. *Libertas Londonienis*, London, British Library, MS Additional 14252, fos. 104v–105v. Also published in *Die Gesetze der Angelsachsen*, ed. by Felix Liebermann (Halle, 1903), v. 1, 674–75.

71. In the case of the Florentines, money-lending was their main business in England. Only the Alberti family was trading on its own ships; until 1429, the other Florentines did not possess a fleet able to trade with England, so they rented the vessels. And when in the 1430s Florentine voyages became more regular, it was too late: the Genoese had taken over almost all the trade of goods, taking advantage of a period in which the Florentines had been expelled from the English market due to their war against the pope (War of the Eight Saints, 1375–1378). For a study of the most successful Florentine traders in England, see G. A. Holmes, "Florentine Merchants in England, 1346–1436," *The Economic History Review* 13 (1960): 193–208.

72. Canale, *Nuova Istoria*, 291. The Fieschi were a noble and powerful family in Genoa; and for them to be able to influence the king of England in a way that favored Genoese businessmen operating there must have been a precious political card to use in the republic's internal struggles. On the other hand, the presence of Niccolino at court was surely seen by the Londoners as another proof of the alliance between the king and alien merchants.

73. *The Statutes of the Realm* (London: George Eyre and Andrew Strahan, 1810), v. 1, 270.

74. *Historical Charters and Constitutional Documents of the City of London*, ed. by Walter de Gray Birch (London: Whiting, 1887), 67.

75. Alwyn A. Ruddock, "Alien Merchants in Southampton in the Later Middle Ages," in *The English Historical Review*, 61 (1946), 4.

76. Ibid., 6.

77. The National Archives, Kew, Special Collections (Petitions), SC 8/216/10773.

78. The fact that the Genoese already possessed an official document from the monarch ordering the restitution of seized goods seems to indicate that this was not the first petition written by the Genoese merchants to the king.

79. The National Archives, Kew, Special Collections (Petitions), SC 8/232/11560.

80. The National Archives, Kew, Special Collections (Petitions), SC 8/230/11465.

81. The National Archives, Kew, Special Collections (Petitions), SC 8/22/1098.

82. With staple I here intend a fixed place where a specific good was to be traded and taxes concerning it were to be collected.

83. *Statutes of the Realm*, 2 Ric. II, stat. i, c. 3; 2 Hen. V, stat. ii, c. 6; 2 Hen. VI, c. 4; 8 Hen. VI, c. 17; 14 Hen. VI, c. 2.

84. Thomas of Walsingham, *Historia Anglicana* (Wiesbaden: Kraus, 1965), 407–9.

85. For an account of the revolt, see Sally McKee, "The Revolt of St. Tito," *Mediterranean Historical Review* 9 (1994): 173–204. For a history of Venetian Crete and a study on the complex social rivalries within the island, see idem, *Uncommon Dominion: Venetian Crete and the Myth of Ethnic Purity* (Philadelphia, 2002).

86. The economic reasons behind this revolt are acknowledged also in Silvano Borsari, *Il dominio veneziano a Creta nel XIII secolo* (Napoli: Fiorentino, 1963), 55; and Mario Gallina, *Una società coloniale del Trecento: Creta fra Venezia e Bisanzio* (Venezia: Deputazione editrice, 1989), 11.

87. On Sabellico and the propagandistic tone of his writings, see Eric W. Cochrane, *Historians and historiography in the Italian Renaissance* (Chicago: The University of Chicago Press, 1981), 83–86.

88. "Piacque adunque loro mandare a Genova dodici Imbasciatori parte Italiani, et parte Greci." Antonio Sabellico, *Historie Vinitiane* (Venice, 1544), 113.

89. Antonio Morosini (ca. 1365–1433) had defined the Venetian elite involved in the revolt as "the most unjust of traitors . . . guilty and evil"; in the original text "iniquisimi traditori . . . rie e malvaxii." Antonio Morosini, *Morosini Codex* (Ghezzo and Melville-Jones: Padua, 1999).

90. Translation from the original: "incominciarono a rivolgere nell'animo loro a chi potessero dare il possesso dell'Isola: percioche non si assecuravano di tornare sotto il Dominio Vinitiano. Onde sola a Genovesi parve loro di poter commetter la salute loro: si per la potenza, ch'essi havevano in mare, et si anchora per l'antica invidia, ch'essi portavano al Dominio Vinitiano." Sabellico, *Historie Vinitiane*, 113. The Genoese welcomed the embassy, but they did not help the rebels, probably because, at that moment, there was no Ligurian family willing to arm the vessels needed to break the Venetian siege around Crete.

91. Monique O'Connell, "The Venetian Patriciate in the Mediterranean: Legal Identity and Lineage in Fifteenth-Century Venetian Crete," *Renaissance Quarterly* 57 (2004): 466–67.

92. And it is not enough to merely point out the Greek component of the rebellion and of the embassy sent to Liguria: that also the Greeks of Candia were willing to accept Genoa as a new ruler does not solve the mystery; instead, it complicates the matter. The Venetians of the metropolis thought that their rebel compatriots were "moved by envy" (Sabellico writes that those who thought to ask Genoa for help were *da invidia mossi*); but envy of what?

93. John J. Norwich, *A History of Venice* (Harmondsworth: Penguin, 1983), 236–37; and Michael E. Mallet and J. R. Hale, *The Military Organization of a Renaissance State: Venice, c. 1400 to 1617* (New York: Cambridge University Press, 1984), 12. Norwich goes as far as to

liken the Cretan rebellion against Venice to that of the American colonists against Britain four centuries later.

94. According to Theodore Bent, "so important did Caffa become that the Genoese found it necessary in 1398 to grant its inhabitants more share in the government." Theodore Bent, *Genoa: How the Republic Rose and Fell* (London: Kegan Paul, 1881), 114. As we shall see in chapter 3, the Genoese in the metropolis were conscious of the autonomy of their colonies, and in several late medieval celebrative poems they gave merit for their commercial network to the anonymous Ligurian merchants living in distant trading posts, rather than to Genoa's communal government.

95. Dotson, "Venice, Genoa and Control of the Seas," 123.

96. Michel Balard, "Genoese Naval Forces in the Mediterranean during the Fifteenth and Sixteenth Centuries," in *War at Sea*, ed. John B. Hattendorf and Richard W. Unger (Suffolk: Boydell Press, 2003), 137.

97. On the history of the *maona*, the association of Genoese private investors administering the island of Chios, see the important collection of documents published in "Documenti della Maona di Chio (secc. XIV–XVI)," in *Atti della Società Ligure di Storia Patria, nuova serie*, ed. Antonella Rovere, volume XIX, 2 (Genoa: SLSP, 1979). On the history of this Genoese colony, see Philip P. Argenti, *The Occupation of Chios by the Genoese and their Administration of the Island, 1346–1566* (Cambridge: Cambridge University Press, 1958); and Geo Pistarino, "Chio dei Genovesi," *Studi medievali* 10 (1969): 3–68.

98. The fundamental reading on these events as well as on the principal political processes characterizing medieval Venice is Thomas F. Madden, *Enrico Dandolo and the Rise of Venice* (Baltimore: John Hopkins University Press, 2007). Marco Pozza has presented key documents on the crusade led by the Venetian doge. Marco Pozza, *I patti con l'impero latino di Costantinopoli, 1205–1231* (Rome: Viella, 2004). See also William Miller, *The Latins in the Levant, a History of Frankish Greece* (New York: Dutton, 1908); and *The Latin Conquest of Constantinople*, ed. Donald E. Queller (New York: Wiley, 1973).

99. Translation from the original: "Ma Avanti tutte le cose l'armata publica di trent'una Galea fu ridotta in mare. . . . Ora quasi tutte le historie, e auttori, che letto habbiamo, mettono i fatti de privati avanti a publici: quasi che potesse essere avenuto, che alcuna operatione intorno le Isole habbia potuto esser fatta col'havere de privati: avanti che'l mare fosse da latrocinii de corsari impedito: con li quali quasi ne confini del seno Adriatico le Galee publiche fossero astrette a combattere." Sabellico, *Historie*, 63. It is striking to reflect on the fact that the Republic of Venice had thirty-one galleys at its disposal for a single expedition (and while involved in other military confrontations), as early as the beginning of the thirteenth century.

100. "Per raffrenare i tumulti Greci in Candace . . . in essa Isola i Vinitiani colonia mandarono. Dicesi anchora, che vi mandarono de nobili certo numero di cavaleria, et della Plebe pedoni." Ibid. On the expeditions of colonists organized by the Venetian government, see Gherardo Ortalli, "Venezia e Creta. Fortune e contraccolpi di una conquista," in *Venezia e Creta*, ed. idem (Venezia: Istituto veneto di scienze, lettere ed arti, 1998), 9–32: see in particular 24–25. Ortalli points out that these "operations guided from the capital" lasted for forty years (25).

101. Giorgio Dolfin, *Cronicha dela nobil cità de Venetia et dela sua provintia et distretto* (Venice: Cicogna, 2007), 228.

102. Ibid., 229.

103. "Et quante volte nui voremo far exercito et li nostri successori, vui faré come fa li homini de Venexia senza alcuna contradition." Ibid., 231.

104. For an example of colonial self-government, see the Statutes of Caffa. Amedeo Vigna, "Codice diplomatico delle colonie tauro-liguri durante la signoria dell'Ufficio di S. Giorgio," in *Atti della Società Ligure di Storia Patria*, volume VII, 2 (Genova: Tipografia del R.I. de'Sordomuti, 1879), 634–66.

105. In the words of one of the greatest scholar of this city republic, in Venice "the state, where trade was concerned, left nothing to chance; and by 1400 it was taking over more and more of Venetian economic life. The days of private enterprise on the grand scale were almost gone. All the merchant galleys were built in the Arsenal and state-owned; the Republic kept the monopoly of many of the most profitable routes and cargoes. . . . As always, increased public

ownership, led to increased taxation." John J. Norwich, *A History of Venice* (Harmondsworth: Penguin, 1983), 272.

106. An important work on these themes is Michael E. Mallet, "La conquista della Terraferma," in *Storia di Venezia* (Rome: Istituto della Enciclopedia italiana, 1996), ed. Alberto Tenenti and Ugo Tucci, vol. IV, 181–244. Several studies have looked at more specific issues related to Venice's territorial expansion: besides the already mentioned work by Mallet and Hale, *The Military Organization*, see for instance David S. Chambers, *The Imperial Age of Venice, 1380–1580* (London: Thames and Hudson, 1970); Michael Knapton, "Venezia e Treviso nel Trecento. Proposte per una ricerca sul primo dominio veneziano a Treviso," in *Tomaso da Modena e il suo tempo* (Treviso: 1981), 41–78; and Stefano Barbacetto, *"La più gelosa delle pubbliche regalie"* (Venezia: Istituto veneto di scienze, lettere ed arti, 2008). That Venice's transformation in a large territorial state was also a consequence of the Venetian elite's inability to address the progressive loss of the Levantine markets was already clearly stated in the 1960s: Carlo Vanzetti, *Due secoli di storia dell'agricoltura veronese* (Verona: Giuliari, 1965), 3.

107. Michael Knapton, "Venice and the Terraferma," in *The Italian Renaissance State*, ed. Andrea Gamberini and Isabella Lazzarini, (Cambridge: Cambridge University Press, 2012), 147.

108. Stanley Chojnacki, "Political Adulthood in Fifteenth-Century Venice," *American Historical Review* 91 (1986); 795.

109. "Il principio et sublevatione dela citade veneta he proceducta dal mare et navigatione maritime, e le richeze et texori venetti sonno devenuti dal mare et viagij maritimi, et tutti questi danari venuti dal mare sonno statti consumati in la terraferma . . . dal mare heranno pervenute le richeze et li honori et la dignitade, et dala terraferma le guere et le spexe." This passage is from Girolamo Priuli, *Diarii*; quoted in Innocenzo Cervelli, *Machiavelli e la crisi dello stato veneziano* (Napoli: Guida, 1974), 183.

110. On the link between Aragon's militarism and its commercial decline, see J. H. Elliott, *Imperial Spain, 1469–1716* (Harmondsworth: Pelican, 1970), 36.

111. Giovanni Assereto, *Le metamorfosi della Repubblica* (Savona: Ferraris, 1999), 84. Assereto uses the word "irrisoria" in particular to describe Genoa's fiscal revenues in the sixteenth century.

Chapter Two

The Business Network of Giovanni da Pontremoli and Genoa's Anti-Tyrannical Institutions

As described in chapter 1, the Genoese late medieval colonial system was characterized by private entrepreneurship, geographical vastness, and adaptability. In particular, adaptability was favored by the relative absence of a centrally planned and state-run military and political expansion. This facilitated movements of capital toward more profitable markets and determined the fluidity of the Genoese intercontinental network. In order to understand the model of business organization developed by Genoese merchants (their colonial "techniques," as Charles Verlinden would call them),[1] the first half of this chapter deals with the strategies adopted and the networks built by a fifteenth-century businessman. The second half of the chapter will then contextualize this case study by presenting the constitutional history of Genoa and some unique institutions of the metropolis.

UNITY AND ECONOMIC ENTANGLEMENT

Tom Scott has observed that, "unlike Venice, Genoa never sought to construct a colonial *territorial* empire."[2] Indeed, as we have seen in the previous chapter, the colonies composing the Ligurian network were usually established without state-run military expeditions or a centrally planned political strategy. This fact raises an important question: how were the Genoese hubs kept together? Such a problem needs to be fully addressed, in part because of the extremely diverse nature of some of the Genoese colonies presented so far. Where Chilia and her sister colonies of the Black Sea all had consuls, statutes, and even international treaties recognizing them, the Genoese colonies in England were simply communities of merchants living in a foreign country, autonomously organized and enjoying a sort of unofficial friendship with the monarch. To treat the issue of unity means unavoidably to return to the problem of distance, which was especially felt by the Genoese because of the geographic (though not territorial) expansion of their network. In order to grasp the functioning of this multiform and mutant body—the Genoese intercontinental system of commercial colonies—it is useful to analyze a rare source, which allows us to look at the economic culture and the private network of a Ligurian merchant. In doing so, I will move the perspective from the periphery to the metropolis.

The archive of the Bank of St. George preserved the copies of 166 letters written by the Genoese merchant Giovanni da Pontremoli.[3] Pontremoli was a town in the region called Lunigiana (at the periphery of the Republic of Genoa), which during the late Middle Ages often fell prey to other political entities (especially Milan).[4] People from this area had traditionally been attracted by the port of Genoa, where they migrated already during the thirteenth and fourteenth centuries. Giovanni lived in Genoa during the fifteenth century, and his activities represent the typical application of the Genoese economic culture that is the subject of this book. The reason why Giovanni's letters survived has to do with his multiform businesses; he was not only a merchant, but also a tax collector for the Bank of St. George.[5] In the year 1439, Giovanni bought the office of tax collector for the duties on grain. After his death, some of his private letters were copied in the file of the *Cabella granorum* (the account book for the duties on grain).

It is possible that Giovanni initially needed a stable income to start his import-export business. Thus, his work for the Bank of St. George may be seen as a way to fill the financial gap separating him from the merchant community in Genoa. Giovanni needed to save some money, a first capital to subsequently invest in trading activities. The letters in the file, showing a well-established business touching the shores of three continents, were written between 1453 and 1459, about fifteen years after his purchase of the office of tax collector. This is not to say that in 1439 Giovanni was not already involved in the commerce of wool and labored cloths; yet, the economic position of Giovanni had probably improved during the period of time between 1439 and 1453. And whatever the means chosen by Giovanni to accumulate capital, by 1453 we find in him a successful merchant, with a network of representatives and friends spread across the known world. He was, however, a different kind of merchant than the adventurous explorer of new markets, the seaman and colonist typical of the previous centuries. He was not meeting other merchants in exotic North African warehouses: rather, he was planning his investments from his house in Genoa. The dangers he met were financial, not physical, as he was able to manage his numerous businesses without moving from the Ligurian capital. This shows us that the sophisticated nature of the Genoese economy stimulated a remarkable diversification of activities also within the mercantile groups. In an age of shattering military defeats and political earthquakes, the continuous Genoese presence on the stage of international commerce was a miracle of adaptability, through accumulation of capital, industriousness, and freedom to move from collapsing markets to rising ones.

The first two letters in the file, dated July 6, 1453, were written after the news of the fall of Constantinople had reached Genoa. Shocked by the dramatic events in the Levant, Giovanni did not hide his emotions and his reflections. In the missives that were sent to Tommaso de Fornari and Bartolomeo de Persio, his representatives in Chios, Giovanni writes: "my soul is so shattered that I would wish to be dead rather than hearing news such as this one, and now I see clearly that because of our sins we are eventually and undoubtedly forsaken by God."[6] The loss of Pera, the Genoese colony within Constantinople, was clearly only the beginning of the end for the Genoese possessions in the Black Sea region and in the Aegean. Giovanni seems to see the sins of his people as the main reason of such catastrophic event. But after expressing his sadness, he quickly turned his attention to his brother-in-law, Stefano de Pinu, who worked as his *procuratore* in Pera. Giovanni feared that Stefano could have been killed, together with the other Christian inhabitants of Byzantium, "whose majority they say has been massacred."[7] He thus asked both de Fornari and de Persio to conclude his businesses in Chios, to investigate the fate of de Pinu, and to try to collect the money that de Pinu was managing (3,500 lire).[8]

The next letter in the file, dated October 30, 1453, was written by Giovanni to his brother-in-law, Stefano de Pinu, for whose life he had feared.[9] We understand that Stefano had somehow been able to escape from Pera, finding refuge in the island of Chios. Reading the next letters to his representatives in Chios, we learn how Giovanni was involved in the trade of cloths, cotton, and pepper. After the fall of Constantinople, Caffa became the main Genoese hub in the region. Situated at the center of the Black Sea, and controlling the commercial routes to eastern Europe and western Asia, Caffa had always been a pivotal colony in the Genoese network. Now, its importance grew even more, and Giovanni quickly focused his attention there. In a letter written in December 1453 to another of his representatives based in Chios, Nicola de Tacio, Giovanni agrees with the idea of purchasing goods in the market of Caffa, and in particular he asks for spices and jewels.[10] The legal institution of *procuratio*, which as I have previously shown was already used by the Genoese in the thirteenth century, became by the fifteenth century their main instrument of business organization.

However, the *procuratio* by itself was not enough to unite a vast and loosely organized system of colonies. If a merchant like Giovanni da Pontremoli had concentrated his investments exclusively on one of the many Genoese markets, such as the Levant, we could not talk about a properly Genoese colonial network, because the various markets would not be integrated. But Giovanni did not have representatives only in the Levant. Genoese economic culture saw profit precisely as the combination of these three activities: long-distance trade, connection of remote markets, and diversification of investments. A merchant would acquire more wealth if he was present (or represented) in both the points of supply and the markets where the demand (and, as a consequence, the price) was higher.[11] This was not a sort of theoretical speculation, but a living culture, an attitude and knowledge, guiding the Genoese in their everyday life and in their economic endeavors. On May 10, 1454, Giovanni wrote a message to his representative Iacopo da Monleone, who was then embarking on a vessel heading for Tunisia. With this sort of short memorandum, Giovanni intended to inform his employee about the cargo loaded and what he had to do once in Tunis.[12] Giovanni was sending to Tunis two big bales of cloths, among which some precious "vermilion cloths of London" (*drapi vermegii de Londres*). Iacopo had to sell them either in Bona or in Tunis, only at a high price, as specified by Giovanni, who added: "if you cannot sell them for money, rather than bringing them back, I would like you to try to barter them for goods that you think we could better sell here [in Genoa], such as wax, leather, and other things, as you will best discern."[13] In this document, London and Tunis are drawn into an intercontinental market built around Genoa not by state-sponsored military adventures, but by the presence (if not physical, at least legal) of a great number of Genoese merchants like Giovanni. The ideal place to sell a certain item at a high price could also be the cheapest center of production of another one, which could be sold at a profitable price in Genoa or in yet another market. Thus, the geographic (but not territorial) extension of the Genoese commercial empire was at the same time a feature and a consequence of the Genoese mercantile, entrepreneurial, and colonial culture.

While the institution of *procuratio* was surely the most important instrument of business administration for Giovanni, he also wrote letters to a number of notables, sailors, relatives, and other merchants, apparently in order to inform them about the tasks of his representatives. In reality, this was a system of informal control, an attempt to solve the problems of distance and dishonesty. For example, in the case mentioned above of the Genoese and English cloths sent to Tunisia to be sold under the supervision of Iacopo da Monleone, after writing the letter to him Giovanni immediately wrote two other letters, one to Costantino de Marinis and the other to Martino Giustianiano. Giovanni informed these two men living in Tunis about the cargo he had entrusted to Iacopo da Monleone and asked them to assist him.[14] Even more interestingly, on the same ship on which Iacopo was traveling, another man, Bartolomeo Mirone, who worked aboard as *subscri-*

ba, was given a small quantity of cloth by Giovanni to sell in Tunis. At first glance, this may seem a strange decision to make. Why would somebody, having already a representative going to Tunis to sell merchandise, assign the same task with a smaller quantity of the same goods to another man? The reason is that Giovanni did not want to concentrate too much power in the hands of a single individual. Behind the courteous words written in the letters, there was a precise scheme of control from distance. Assigning a small, apparently insignificant job to the *subscriba* Bartolomeo Mirone allowed Giovanni to make him work together with Iacopo once in Tunis.[15] Simply put, the two representatives were controlling each other, and Giovanni could also learn at what price the cloth was sold by each of them in the same period and in the same market. Moreover, thanks to this strategy, Giovanni had an excuse to write a letter to the *scriba* Bartolomeo de Calvi, who was Mirone's boss on the ship, wishing him a good journey, and asking him with diplomatic words to control Mirone: "therefore, my brother, I pray you that it will not be too demanding for you to offer them all the help, advice and support that you can."[16]

A thorough reading of the Pontemoli file proves that this intricate exchange of missives surrounded almost every business transaction concluded by Giovanni. Having three or four representatives in the same place was also part of Giovanni's strategy, especially in the distant Caffa and in the lucrative hub of Chios. On this island, Giovanni's procurators (among whom, after the fall of Constantinople, there was also his brother-in-law Stefano de Pinu) were being consistently informed about their respective tasks, so that they could keep an eye on each other (or even compete with each other, thus obtaining for Giovanni the best profit). Having continuous communications with many procurators and friends was a strategy that Giovanni did not use only to control his employees in distant harbors. This is exemplified by the case of Agostino da Bargagli, a man Giovanni had sent to Milan to sell rhubarb, and who wrote him that he had not been able to accomplish his task. Thanks to one of his numberless contacts (Iacopo de Amendola), Giovanni knew that it was actually possible to sell rhubarb at a profitable price in Milan. With this piece of information, Giovanni replied to his unsuccessful procurator to openly reproach him.[17] We do not possess the answer written by Agostino da Bargagli, but the quarrel went on for a while, since in a letter dated about two years later, Giovanni once again complained to Agostino about his incapability to sell rhubarb in Milan, and told him that another Genoese procurator had successfully sold it in nearby towns.[18] The fact that Giovanni continued to hire Agostino as procurator suggests that he was not a bad employee, or at least that Giovanni was not really disappointed by his work in Milan. This seems to indicate that the net of informers at Giovanni's disposal was at times used simply to put pressure on his representatives and make them feel as if constantly under scrutiny—in spite of the distance separating them from their boss.

Notwithstanding the tangled system of control and division of tasks ideated by Genoese merchants like Giovanni da Pontremoli, some representatives could still take advantage of distance and periods without communications to steal part of the profit. Giovanni never had the proofs of these acts of dishonesty, but he was an experienced and astute merchant, consistently informed about the prices of his merchandise in each of the Genoese colonies. Thus, he could sense when a representative was committing fraud, and at times, his letters have a note of frustration, or even accusation, as he complains about long periods of silence or reticence in transferring the money gained from a cargo. For instance, in a letter to de Fornari in Chios, Giovanni complained about the representative's long period of silence, and expressed surprise and disappointment at the low price at which he had sold the last cargo of cloths.[19] In another letter, this time to Nicola de Tacio, he complains about other representatives and alludes to the good conduct that every merchant should have (the *more mercatorum*). Then, in a significant line, Giovanni adds: "one coin honestly earned can benefit more than a thousand coins dishonestly taken."[20]

DIVERSIFIED TRADE

In the Genoese system, unity resulted from private networks, but also from the diversification of investments and the integration of markets, which were freely pursued by countless merchants. This is evident when we consider that Giovanni da Pontremoli sent letters not only to Pera, Chios, Caffa, and Tunis, but also to other places in North Africa (such as Costantina and Bona), Sicily, Corsica, Florence, Milan, Switzerland, and Spain. In particular, the markets in Barbary, after the loss of Pera, quickly became the most important economic theater for Giovanni. I have already presented the complicated exchange of letters regarding a shipment of cloths sold in Tunisia, but many other missives, indeed the majority of those copied in the file, were directed to North Africa. This movement from the collapsing Levant to Barbary did not, admittedly, represent an absolute novelty: the economic relationship between Genoa and North Africa had ancient origins and had been one of the reasons for the rivalry with Barcelona throughout the Middle Ages. Nonetheless, the fall of Constantinople undoubtedly hastened the movement East-West already noted by Charles Verlinden.[21] The Genoese (unlike the Venetians) readily adapted to the political changes of the fifteenth century moving their investments towards Africa, Spain, and the Atlantic, whose Northern waters they had first visited with Mediterranean vessels as early as the 1270s.[22]

However, one could still harbor doubts about the movement East-West and explain the impressive number of missives sent by Giovanni to the ports of Barbary simply as the continuation of preexisting business relations, especially considering that we do not possess any letters written before the fall of Constantinople, thus it is impossible to compare Giovanni's economic presence in North Africa before and after 1453. So, where are the proofs of a quick movement of capital from the Levant to the Occident? A first clue is in the movement of the representative Nicola de Tacio, whose residence had been the island of Chios and whose travels between there and the markets of the Black Sea I have already mentioned. On June 25, 1455, Giovanni ordered to de Tacio to immediately leave the Levant and to come back to Genoa.[23] Then, Nicola is mentioned in a long letter written between August and October 1455 to the representative Gaspare de Nigro and his brother Oliviero de Nigro, who were working for Giovanni in Costantina and Tunis. In the very last postscript of this letter, dated October 10, Giovanni recommends Nicola so that he would quickly receive every support he may need for his new job.[24] And one year later we have proof that Nicola de Tacio had indeed settled down in Tunisia, where he was in charge of selling cargoes coming from Genoa. On October 27, 1456, Nicola was in Genoa, ready to leave on a ship heading for Tunisia; on this vessel, Giovanni had loaded a variety of goods: barrels (*caratelli*) and bags of pastry (*tarta*), cloths, and jewels.[25] In the memorandum written in this occasion, Giovanni grants to Nicola extensive powers, suggesting him to sell everything he can and barter the rest for any kind of good that he will judge profitable to bring back to Genoa. Hence, Giovanni decided to move Nicola de Tacio, who was among his most trustworthy and experienced representatives, from the Levant to Tunisia.[26] Evidently, Giovanni was quickly transferring to the North African route his cargoes of Genoese and English cloths previously sold in the Eastern markets. This seems a clear indication of the prompt movement of capital from East to West, but there is more proof.

In the years after 1453, Giovanni da Pontremoli frantically searched for new Genoese representatives living in North Africa and having years of experience in working in the North African market. This attempt to find new outlets for his merchandise emerges from many passages in Giovanni's missives. In numerous letters written in 1456 to three merchants living in Bona (Bartolomeo Cosio, Ottaviano Imperiale, and Pietro de Coronato), Giovanni expressed his joy about the beginning of these professional collaborations.[27] That he urgently needed outlets for his merchandise is confirmed by the fact that he did not hire these men, but rather he proposed to them the sharing of every profit. But the African ports were not important only to sell. Because the grain coming from the Black Sea started to diminish, the Genoese took advantage of the large geographic extension of their commercial empire. Therefore, having lost his business in the hub of Pera, Giovanni da Pontremoli used his most skilled man, Nicola de Tacio, and his new Genoese contacts in North Africa in order to purchase grain, cereals, and other food supplies.[28] When, in the years following 1453, Giovanni quickly increased his investments in North Africa and established new business collaborations with people working in the Berber markets, he was simply applying the Genoese economic culture to the changed macroeconomic situation. He was, to be sure, building upon solid foundations, since, as I have shown in chapter 1, the Genoese had already diversified their interests and multiplied their markets in the previous centuries. The Genoese were already in Tunisia and they had been the first navigators to open the Atlantic; what they needed now, was to quickly hasten a process, the movement East-West, that they had started.

While Tunisia became undoubtedly the most important hub for Giovanni da Pontremoli, there were many other markets where he could (and did) invest from Genoa. Two of these were Sicily and Spain. From the letters written to representatives working in Sicily, it seems that the importance of this island had to do with the trade of grain. For example, in a letter dated August 1, 1457, Giovanni orders his procurator in Palermo to purchase wheat, to be later sold in Genoa at a higher price.[29] That same summer he was busy searching for other markets where wheat could be found at a low price, as proved by a letter to Lorenzo da Rapallo, his contact in Corsica.[30] Sicily seems to have been the preferable point of supply because there Giovanni could sell leather and wax at a high price, thus more profitably juxtaposing export with import.[31] But the Genoese economic presence was never a one-way flow; therefore, Giovanni was also able to sell other products such as cloths in Corsica.[32] Concerning Spain, Giovanni da Pontremoli wrote an interesting letter on July 2, 1459, in which he gave instructions to his representative Giuliano Tarigo. Tellingly enough, Giuliano was leaving Genoa without a specific destination: Giovanni asked him to sell a piece of velvet anywhere he could.[33] If Giuliano was not able to sell the velvet, he had to barter it for wax, wool, leather, or grain. Thus, Giovanni was not among those Genoese who had already penetrated the Iberian market during the previous centuries; nonetheless, precisely his unfamiliarity with the Spanish market makes his letter more revealing, as it confirms both the movement East-West and the fluidity of the Genoese commercial system. By 1459, due to the loss of Constantinople and the disastrous political situation in the Levant, it seems that the Genoese were diversifying their investments within the western Mediterranean. Giovanni successfully reduced his exposition to the eastern political earthquakes by gradually increasing his presence in Barbary. There, he found Genoese associates and attempted to expand his network as quickly as possible. In Spain, the situation was more complicated, due to the longstanding rivalry between Genoa and Barcelona. However, by the first quarter of the sixteenth century, the Genoese had replaced Barbary with Spain as their main market in the western Mediterranean. As we shall see in the second part of this book, it was precisely in the new Spanish kingdom(s) that the Genoese would eventually find an ally that shared their economic interests, offered a compatible (and even complementary) idea of governance, and found itself engaged in a breathtaking (and profitable) effort of empire building across the ocean.

THE ROLE OF CAPITAL

Neither the extension of the Genoese colonial world nor the far-reaching economic relations and endeavors of Genoese citizens like Giovanni da Pontremoli would have been possible without the previous accumulation of private savings. Admittedly, the diversification of trade and the colonial skills developed in different markets throughout three centuries were decisive components of the Genoese economic success, in the face of dramatic geopolitical developments. Yet, one cannot diversify one's investments if one does not reinvest part of the profits in a new market. The availability of capital is an indispensable prerequisite for economic development; and the willingness to immediately reinvestment part of the profits is absolutely necessary to obtain long-term prosperity. Giovanni da Pontremoli was able to start (or expand) his business only after accumulating a certain amount of money. That a considerable part of his profits were saved and reinvested in the family business (thus triggering innovation and cushioning international crises) tells us something about the Genoese economic culture. Commercial colonies and the exploration of new markets came only after—and as a consequence of—private saving. The role played by the Italians in the commercial revolution and economic growth of Europe had much to do with their understanding of this first, fundamental step in the chain of large-scale production and long-distance economic relations. When a merchant accumulates capital, he is acquiring the means to optimize production, improve techniques of manufacturing, build (or rent) the fleet necessary to penetrate a remote market, and hire a net of representatives giving him the advantage of knowing the prices in different regions (thus purchasing and reselling a certain good in the most profitable hubs). Following this economic principle, since the later Middle Ages the Genoese saved money not only to solve the retention of value problem, but also to reinvest it in their multiform economic activities—hence contributing to what Robert S. Lopez called the commercial revolution.[34]

Reinvestment, in this case, could mean a very broad range of private expenditures that aimed not only at improving productivity or fastening transportation, but also at collecting precious information. To understand this, one may simply think of the many representatives kept by Giovanni da

Pontremoli on his business's payroll. As we have seen in the pages above, these men were admittedly in charge of overseeing the transportation and the retailing of cargoes bought and sold by Giovanni. But they were also constantly required to inform Giovanni, through a regular correspondence, about the presence of certain goods in certain markets and the relative fluctuation of prices. Thus, it is not surprising that Genoa became one of the cosmopolitan capitals of the Mediterranean world, since there foreign businessmen could not only sell and buy almost every kind of merchandise, but also gather information and invest their capital. Saminiato de' Ricci, a wealthy Florentine banker, lived in Genoa for many years precisely because of these reasons. His name is associated with a *manuale di mercatura* written in Genoa.[35] This document suggests both that Genoa held attraction for foreign investors and that the Genoese had developed a thorough and efficient system of financial communication and market prices evaluation. By 1396, the year when de' Ricci wrote (or commissioned) his document, Genoa had become one of the best places where a businessman could prepare a *manuale* which contained detailed information about currency exchanges, duties, and prices of all the major ports of the Mediterranean world and of the North Sea.

Presenting a peculiar document—the file of private letters written by a fifteenth-century Genoese merchant—the first part of this chapter has given some pragmatic examples of what it meant to be a Ligurian businessman. My findings also suggest that the Genoese moved their investments and activities from the East to the West without following a communal policy, but rather taking advantage of their previous presence in markets such as northern Africa and Sicily. Unavoidably, the themes treated above raise particular questions. Did this economic culture developed during the Middle Ages contribute to shape the early modern Genoese understanding of *libertà*? Were there in Genoa a civic culture and a constitutional arrangement that somehow favored saving and reinvestment of capital? How did the Genoese perceive and describe themselves? It is legitimate to wonder what men like Giovanni da Pontremoli wanted at home. What institutions did they device in order to better accumulate and reinvest capital while preventing the communal government from jeopardizing their commercial interests? What kind of regime were they ready to support, and how did this affect future Hispanic-Genoese relations? Indeed, the Genoese showed a tendency to limit the disruptive effects of both factional strife and unchecked government spending, in order to preserve their dynamic, business-oriented, and pragmatic idea of *libertà*. They achieved this, at least in part, thanks to the creation of the Bank of St. George, a unique association of creditors which soon acquired political, fiscal, and diplomatic powers. The second half of this chapter illustrates the main stages of this process, thus contextualizing Pontremoli's story.

INSTITUTIONAL CHANGE AND "MODESTISSIMA AUTORITÀ"

The multiform economic activities of the Genoese, as exemplified by Giovanni da Pontremoli's business, suggest that cumulative behaviors and reinvestment of capital brought long-term economic progress. That this cumulative behavior was common among the Genoese is also the conclusion of Giovanna Petti Balbi, who has described the typical Genoese as "spending a great part of his life accumulating wealth," and as an individual driven by "mercantile mentality, proto-capitalist ideology, and the habit of doing his/her own business."[36] However, late medieval and early modern Genoese businessmen were also aware of "negative pressures": the internal and external predatory powers threatening their entrepreneurship and jeopardizing a stable prosperity in the cosmopolitan network they had built.[37] Interestingly, the Genoese usually interpreted external threats as a consequence of the divisions within the free city. This fear of political divisions and the anti-tyrannical institutions devised by the Genoese to protect their private wealth were both underpinned by an intellectual discourse, a civic cosmology, and a peculiar idea of liberty that is rarely spelled out in the sources, but that is nevertheless possible to bring to light. Genoa's republican tradition has to be rediscovered not only to study the historical roots of the Genoese presence in the Atlantic world—that is the main objective of this book—but also to widen the historiographical debate concerning Renaissance republicanism.

The archives of Genoa preserve manuscripts that help us to shed some light on the institutional framework adopted by the Genoese since the beginning of the fourteenth century to amortize the public debt[38] and to limit the political power of the *cappellazzi*.[39] Because of the scarcity of Genoese sources directly dealing with political philosophy and republican ideals, these documents have to be considered if we wish to understand what kind of regime a Genoese businessman like Giovanni da Pontremoli was willing to support. Therefore, I here briefly present and contextualize the laws of 1303, 1340, 1363, and 1413, as well as some of the powers taken over by the Bank of St. George in the colonies. The intention is to delineate the culture behind this form of self-government, studying the strategies used by the Genoese to render safe capital accumulation and to prevent the establishment of a local *signoria*.[40] That late medieval and Renaissance Genoese had been successful in limiting the power of their highest political office was something already clear to the most astute of their contemporaries, as it transpires from these words, written by Niccolò Machiavelli in the 1520s:

> In the city of Genoa, when it lives in *libertà*, a chief is elected, who is called Doge; he is not an absolute ruler, nor can he autonomously take decisions, but rather as a leader he proposes what has to be later deliberated by their [the Genoese people's] magistrates and *Consigli*.[41]

The stream of reforms defining (and thus limiting) the power of the executive branch had begun more than two centuries before—even before the creation of the dogeship. In the next pages, Genoa's early budgets are analyzed because they constituted the first instrument used by the Genoese fluid elite to influence the structure of the body politic and to limit the *podesta*'s (and the doge's) powers.

A Genoese document dated 1303, comprising a number of reformative laws, is among the first manuscripts planning the yearly expenditures of an Italian city-state.[42] On April 1, 1303, the Genoese *podesta*, with the *Consiglio degli Anziani* and the *consilium maius* (an assembly comprised of hundreds of citizens), approved a reorganization of the offices administering the public finances; but more importantly, they also approved a budget and amortized the debt.[43] This budget was intended to plan (and limit) all the expenses of the central government; other money was going to be spent for special necessities and for the administration of the debt.[44] The public debt, which had been created already during the past centuries through voluntary loans made by Genoese citizens to their government, had to be periodically amortized and regrouped. But how exactly did these loans work? Canon Law condemned any form of interest on a loan as usury; therefore, the Genoese lent money to their government without an interest rate, but receiving instead the revenue coming from an indirect tax (*gabella*).[45] Since it was impossible to precisely calculate the amount of money that the tax was going to provide, Canon Law was not broken.[46] The manuscript of 1303 signals a significant innovation in this system, with the creation of a secondary market for the public debt; this was achieved through the regrouping of old *compere* (large private loans to the commune), which were then divided into bonds, called *luoghi*. According to the laws of 1303, the *luoghi* were to be considered as *bona mobilia*, which could be sold and bought, while the revenue coming from them (or better, from the *gabelle* linked to them) was to be counted in special registers called *cartolari*. The secondary market of *luoghi* represented a form of safe investment for the Genoese people, who could take advantage of their republic's debt to accumulate savings. Saving constituted the first capital—money to be later invested in the real economy, triggering commercial expansion, sophistication of colonial techniques, and economic growth. In sum, what we can learn from the manuscript of 1303, studying it from the perspective of the Genoese economic culture, is that the Genoese, as early as 1303, began to systematize and regularly approve budgets for fiscal years. Moreover, the Genoese had transformed the public debt into a profitable bond market, where they could invest money in times of crisis on the international scenario (which means, every time their colonies were under threat or in a phase of transition), or simply when they were searching for a long-term, domestic, and safe investment.[47] Finally, it is interesting to note that in the file of documents dated 1303 there is no trace of any significant fund allocated to the defense of the colonies.[48]

The revolt of 1339 signalled the beginning of the dogeship for life, a form of government that would last until the reforms of 1528. The events surrounding this change of regime have been often interpreted as a popular revolt, similar to others happening in Italy during the first half of the fourteenth century. This interpretation was possibly also inspired by Giuseppe Verdi's opera entitled *Simon Boccanegra* (1857), in which a tangled plot develops along the themes of romantic love and social conflict, without mentioning public debt or financial distress; it was then elaborated in the academic world by Le Mesurier.[49] More recently, Andrea Zorzi has argued that the revolt of 1339 was "the successful establishment of a 'popular' government."[50] Admittedly, the rebellion had (at least initially) an anti-aristocratic tone. A crowd gathered before the palace of the *capitani* decided that electing a non-aristocratic *abbate* was not enough to check the nobles' power, so it overthrew the oligarchic government and nominated a popular general, Simone Boccanegra, as doge. Simone, a sort of epic figure in the Genoese memory, was doge twice, from 1339 to 1344, and from 1356 to 1363.[51]

Yet, according to Mario Buongiorno, both the revolt of 1339 and the tragic end of Boccanegra's second dogeship had to do with the struggle against the factional use of public revenues. While it is true that in 1344 Boccanegra went to exile because of an aristocratic reaction (a fact that apparently strengthens the traditional explanation of the 1339 revolt as a conflict between *nobili* and *popolari*), on the other hand it is important to remember that in 1363 Boccanegra was poisoned probably because of his greed, which had caused an increase in public spending. This would suggest the peculiarly economic meaning of *libertà* for the Genoese, who could not tolerate a predatory government, either in the hands of a *nobile* or not. Besides pointing out the skyrocketing trajectory of the doge's salary under Boccanegra's watch, Buongiorno brings to the reader's attention the fact that in the thirty-four years after the murder of the popular general and the noble (yet not the *nobili*) families' return to power, the public expenditures slowly stabilized, becoming almost absolutely static.[52] Thus, the true aim of the 1339 popular revolt had not been merely the establishment of a popular or democratic government; and the priority in the following decades remained to avoid the creation of a seigneurial dynasty. Buongiorno's argument is not necessarily incompatible with Zorzi's (and Le Mesurier's) thesis of a clash between two different groups; but calling them "noble and popular" risks to be a meaningless abstraction. Political factions in Genoa did exist, but they were not the result of opposing, monolithic social classes. Gabriele Adorno, the man who became doge after Boccanegra's death, came from a merchant family and was a *popolare*; yet, he exiled all Boccanegra's family, and was himself eventually overthrown as soon as his government was deemed to have become too fiscally demanding.[53]

Unfortunately, the laws and the budgets approved between 1303 and 1339 have been destroyed during the 1339 revolt. However, we know that during the period of time missing from the archives, the Genoese had continued their tradition of annual budgets, improving them with the introduction of a double entry. The earliest public budget that has survived (after the laws of 1303) is a document dated 1340, and it presents some modern innovations, being the first public accountancy to use methods borrowed from the merchant community, such as the double entry *introitus et exitus* (revenues and spending).[54] However, while the state accounting in Genoa was undoubtedly systematic, its study is not simple. Not all the documents have survived, and those still preserved in the State Archive are scattered in many different registers. This fact shows the overlapping functions of particular offices and the lack of a centralized authority regarding special spending.[55]

The Genoese fiscal system was in constant evolution. The changes occurred between the pioneering laws of 1303 and the budgets of the 1340s (such as a new heading for the doge's salary and higher stipends for the castellans) had to do with the new political constitution of the republic, the appearance of a doge for life, and the resulting personal connections between the doge and the men appointed as castellans in the *Riviere*.[56] Nonetheless, a conscious reformative tendency was present throughout the fourteenth and the fifteenth centuries, also during periods of political stability. For instance, several copies of a 1413 manuscript, whose nature is similar to the reformative laws of 1303, have survived in the Genoese archives.[57] Dated November 19, 1413, these laws follow the structure of an ordinary budget for the coming year. Nonetheless, some innovations set this document apart from the other budgets. The laws of 1413 were written under the dogeship of Giorgio Adorno, who was a strong leader and a skilled politician. He was able to raise the stipend for his office and to obtain more money for his political initiatives. At the beginning of the list of expenditures, just after the introductory paragraph, the preserved manuscripts report: "To provide for the magnificent lord the doge and his family, eight thousands six hundreds and twenty-five lire, or: lb. 8,625."[58] At the end of the manuscript, we find written: "Also as provision for what the magnificent lord doge will see, two thousand lire, or: lb. 2,000."[59] Yet, notwithstanding the notable political leverage of this doge, Adorno's laws also contained the first cap for the special spending, another indication of the Genoese elite's determination to stabilize expenditure. The special expenditures—money not provided for in the budget—had been until then the highest outflows for the government, even though they were debated in the *Consiglio degli Anziani* and in the offices dealing with specific issues.[60] With the inclusion of the special spending in the ordinary budget, the Genoese were at the same time admitting that certain special expenditures had become regular and also were trying to reduce the excuses to spend even more. The new heading did not contain any deadline or specific description, but it aimed at covering all unforeseen necessities, as it simply read: "For any extraordinary expense that may occur, three thousand lire: lb. 3,000."[61]

Another document of great interest for the study of the Genoese institutions is the *Regulae Communis Ianuae* written in 1363. Contrary to the annual budgets, the *regulae* were exceptional laws, produced to reaffirm the constitutional organization of the Genoese government after periods of crisis. Unfortunately, almost all the fourteenth- and fifteenth-century *regulae* have been lost or destroyed; but the text of the *regulae* of 1363 has been almost entirely preserved.[62] Penned right after Boccanegra's poisoning, the intent of this document is clear since its preamble:

> Having chosen this dogeship as form of government, in order to prevent the doge from degenerating into tyranny through the abuse of the other high officials selected for the utility of the *res publica,* it was necessary both to limit the danger of his [the doge's] authority through an adequate act of moderation and to restrict his power in inviolable terms through laws formulated according to the tradition.[63]

Temperare and *limitare* ("to limit" and "to restrict") are the key words. Twenty-four years earlier the Genoese had changed their political regime, establishing the dogeship for life. With this constitutional law, they were not repudiating that decision; rather, they had learned that a charismatic man could use the highest office to transform the republic *in tirannidem*. Hence, the Genoese people needed to intervene, defining the roles of every public office, and "limiting" the doge's authority. This was neither a rejection of the Genoese juridical system (*more legum*) nor an aristocratic coup, but instead an "act of moderation" absolutely in line with the tradition of communal self-government.

> Having confirmed [all the assembled citizens] that, while Simon Boccanegra was suffering from very grave illness, the citizens of Genoa and the inhabitants of the villages and the suburbs had realized the serious dangers, discord and scandals where they had been put . . . they understood that if they were going to be governed and commanded by him [Boccanegra] in the future, they would have been brought to destruction and final extermination, unless the Genoese commune and people unanimously selected a new commander and governor for the future.[64]

The Genoese people writing this document lay the blame for the political crisis on Boccanegra, their former hero, confirming that the labels of *nobili* and *popolari* did not indicate immutable groups or unreserved support. Furthermore, this passage adds a republican, almost collegial tone to the civic effort, underlining the participation in the process of the Genoese living without the metropolis (those in the "villages and suburbs," which means in the other Ligurian towns and in the rural areas of the *Riviere*).

After the long preamble, the *regulae* of 1363 consists of 172 articles, which represent a detailed account of the republic's medieval offices, but also a constitutional project that was yet to be realized in practice. The first article—*De civitate Ianuae per ducem de populo perpetuo gubernanda*—designated the doge as the head of the state, but as one keeps reading the other articles important limits (explicit and implicit, direct and indirect) to his authority quickly emerge. To be precise, even the first article, contradicting its title, immediately clarified that the republic was to be governed by the doge "and by twelve councilors."[65] Yet it was the third article—*In quibus consistit baylia domini ducis et consilii*—that implicitly established what is arguably the most significant anti-tyrannical rule: "if the doge is absent, then at least nine of the councilors have to be present, and then at least eight of those nine councilors have to agree."[66] In other words, the councilors could in certain cases take a decision without the doge, while on the other hand the *regulae* did not allow him to govern without the council. But this was not enough. The Genoese feared that a particularly charismatic doge could somehow attempt to obtain a stable partisan majority in the council. Thus, another truly fundamental principle of the *regulae* adopted in 1363 (beside the contraposition between doge and council) was the reaffirmation of the traditional division of offices among the Genoese social and political groups. The doge could not place men of his faction in these key positions. In addition, these offices (among which the fiscal and the judiciary ones) were to remain independent from the central authority, constituting the true bulwark against the rise of a *signoria*. Possibly the most significant example of this principle is the article number 31—*De prohibita intromissione iusticie domino duci et consilio*. The administration of justice was to respect the traditional courts and legal systems previously established in Genoa and in the other towns and villages of Liguria; moreover, "about the cases, both those under way and those in the future, both civil and criminal, [we order that] the doge and the council have neither the powers, nor any jurisdiction to know, define or direct them."[67] To prevent the doge and the council from jeopardizing the rule of law and centralizing the administration of the republic, the Genoese had first introduced annual budgetary laws and now were assigning a new role to the medieval offices divided among cross-factional—and thus innocuous—social groups. Groups such as *nobili* and *popolari*, or merchants and artisans were not the true origin of civic conflict, but rather the remains of a medieval hierarchy that in Genoa had never been immobile. And as more wealth was created, accumulated and reinvested, the Genoese society became more economically fluid. The main fear was the rise of a centralized authority able to plunder the huge capital accumulated by the Genoese, and not by chance article 96 of the 1363 constitution—entitled *Quod officia Mercancie et Gazarie sint et remaneant*—stated that the decisions concerning trade and colonial affairs were not among the doge's (or the council's) prerogatives. In particular: "we decide and order that the offices of Trade and *Gazaria* are and have to be and have to remain what they have usually been, and that they have their own jurisdiction and powers and administration."[68] The "act of moderation" embodied by the *regulae* of 1363 was completed by the powers given to the *sindacatori*. According to the article entitled *De quatuor syndicatoribus eligendis*, the magistrates called *sindacatori* represented the whole *civitas*, were in charge of overseeing the correct application of the constitutional order, and could judge the conduct of the doge, the councilors, and the officials. In other Italian city-states, the *sindacatori* usually judged a citizen at the end of his mandate; however, because the doge stayed in office for life, in this article the Genoese specifically explained that the *sindacatori* could investigate the doge's respect for the other institutions of the commune at any time.[69]

The creation in 1407 of the *Casa delle compere e dei banchi di San Giorgio* should be interpreted more as the continuation (and audacious sophistication) of this well-established tendency to limit the power of *podesta*, councilors, and doges than as an exceptional and unprecedented event. Because the Genoese did not want political factions to use the government as a predatory apparatus and public spending as an instrument of patronage, they had consistently tried to keep taxation and expenditures under control.[70] But while before 1407 the Genoese mercantile elite prevented the establishment of a *signoria* by attempting to protect and restate the traditional communal *diritto*, with the Bank of St. George the businessmen who had lent money to the commune progressively replaced the republican offices. Initially born to once again amortize the public debt, the Bank of St. George would gradually become an executive body, through which creditors and investors wisely managed the finances of the republic, took political decisions, and even administered the Levantine colonies. All this was done to the detriment of the dogeship and the *cappellazzi*, but also of those traditional offices that had failed to promptly protect the Genoese interests in distant lands, or that could not guarantee the sound administration of the fiscal revenues in the *Riviere* (thus endangering the private savings invested in the debt market). It was as if the republican institutions were slowly emptied of their effective powers, in order to more effectively achieve a diverse set of objectives—protection of private capital from predatory political factions; rule of law and self-government in Genoa; authoritative diplomatic representation in the colonies. The eight *Protettori* and the members of the Assembly of the Bank of St. George were a fluid and diverse elite, quite the opposite of the exclusivist Venetian patricians. The bondholders of St. George were businessmen who had both experience in accounting and administration, and consistent contacts throughout the Mediterranean world. The *Protettori* represented all the Genoese who had invested in the public debt's market, and they had to efficiently and pragmatically manage an increasingly complex structure, eventually dealing not only with finance, bonds, and loans, but also with public offices, collection of taxes, and foreign policy. Because of their delicate and powerful duties, the *Protettori* were elected by lot and rotation, and they were replaced once a year. A document dated 1453 gives evidence of the shrinking of government prerogatives and the expansion of St. George's administrative activities.

In 1453, when the news of the fall of Constantinople reached Genoa, the situation appeared tragic not only for what was lost (Genoese lives, the possession of Pera, and all the Genoese properties there), but also for what was suddenly in extreme danger—Caffa and all the colonies around the Black Sea. Neither the doge, Pietro Campofregoso, nor the republican institutions could do anything to defend the sea route to Caffa or to help the Genoese merchants, doctors, notables, artisans, and sailors scattered between Greece and the Caucasus. In this situation of emergency, facing one of the most dramatic crises in the history of the republic, the Genoese refused to entrust more financial resources or more power to the doge. The idea of raising an emergency tax or to allow the government to borrow more money never crossed the Genoese people's minds.[71] Instead, the Genoese decided to take matters into their own hands. With Pietro Campofregoso playing the role of spectator, in November 1453, the Genoese (self-)government (through a "consegio grande") sent a letter to the *Protettori* of St. George, asking to this institution to take over the possession of all the Black Sea colonies that had survived the Ottoman fury:

> understanding the necessity as urgent and the desire of the citizens to do this with promptness, believing that in this way the money necessary for this provision could be found, we wished to have the opinion of the citizens by a vote, from which we also had universally confirmed that it is good to cede the possessions of Caffa and of that vast sea to the administration of the office of St. George, from which the resources and the remedies for the preservation of those colonies shall come . . . to discharge our duties we have deliberated to submit this matter before you: so that you can decide first of all whether you believe it is appropriate for the office of St. George to accept the government of those possessions or not.[72]

The Genoese evidently thought that the "preservation of those colonies" (*salvatione di quelle cosse*) was more important than keeping up appearances. Thus, from 1453, those same Genoese merchants and businessmen enriched by the Levantine trades would guarantee the money necessary for the defense of the colonies and would be in charge of delicate diplomatic relations.[73] Giovanni da Pontremoli was in Genoa during the dramatic days in which the decision was taken; and his name, *Johannes de Pontremulo*, is indeed listed in the archival document among the 275 bondholders who were called by the *Protettori* of St. George to vote on whether the *Banco* had to accept the administration of the colonies offered by the commune.[74] A few days later, in a private letter to his brother-in-law, Giovanni wrote: "I consider this as good news, the colonies of Caffa have been given to the venerable Office of St. George, which I believe will govern them in a different and better way than what was done until now, and so may please the Almighty."[75] These sincere words seem to reflect the Genoese climate of opinion described by Machiavelli:

> those [Genoese] citizens have removed their love from the Commune as a tyrannized institution, and they have given it to St. George as a well and moderately administered organization; from here come the frequent and deep mutations of government, and that they [the Genoese] obey now one citizen, now a foreigner, because only the Commune changes government, but St. George does not. So much so that, when the Fregoso and the Adorno fight for power, because what is disputed is only the government of the Commune, most of the citizens step aside and leave it to the victor; similarly the office of St. George does nothing, except, once the winner has taken the government, [he is] made to swear to respect its [St. George's] independent laws. These laws have never been broken so far, because [St. George] having weapons and wealth and its own government, it is impossible to break them without the risk of a dangerous rebellion. This is a truly rare case, one that has never been seen by philosophers in their numerous speculations and studies about Republics, to see within the same circle, among the same citizens, *libertà* and tyranny, civic life and corruption, justice and wickedness; because this is the only order that that city filled with ancient and venerable laws is able to maintain. And if St. George was to govern the whole city, which in the future will surely happen, then this would be a Republic more memorable than the Venetian one.[76]

The Genoese left street fights and honorary titles to the *cappellazzi*, while the businessmen, the merchants and the professionals made sure that the public debt was well administered and their colonies in the Black Sea were saved from catastrophe.[77]

The limits to centralized authority posed by the stream of reforms emerging from this brief study of Genoese archival sources illustrate the importance of institutional change in the history of Genoa. As put by Douglass C. North, "institutions have been devised by human beings to create order and reduce uncertainty in exchange."[78] Genoa was the center of an intercontinental commercial system; by the end of the thirteenth century, it had broken the barriers to economic growth that are typical of agrarian societies. This means that with colonies in strategic points of supply and a long history of private market expansion, Genoese merchants had the exceptional opportunity to profit from long-distance trade, diversify their professional activities, and improve their economic conditions. In this context, it is not surprising that

Genoese businessmen coming from different social backgrounds and working in different fields felt the need to protect private capital from predatory political factions. Merchants traveling around the known world, bankers furnishing capital for economic expansion, professionals who had invested in the public debt's market, recent immigrants coming from rural areas, and artisans laboring raw materials imported from the colonies all agreed on one, fundamental issue: they did not want their money to be diverted to the pockets of doges or military leaders. That some nobles could share interests, values, and (basic, anti-tyrannical) political aims with merchants, notaries, representatives, and shop owners appears unlikely only if we think of social classes as watertight compartments; but in the Genoese world, "for most individuals above the lower levels of personal mediocrity, simultaneity of careers was a social, economic, political, and cultural fact."[79] Thus, for example, a Genoese noble was often also a shipowner and a businessman. This "simultaneity of careers" is important in order to understand the economic culture behind the institutional change and republican conservatism documented in this chapter without necessarily or exclusively using the concept of social mobility.[80] Also the documents related to Giovanni da Pontremoli well exemplify the fluidity of the Genoese society and the cross-class contacts favored by a thriving economic system. There is evidence that Giovanni's relatively modest but undeniably flourishing business put him in contact with powerful noble families, with which at times he entered into partnership—and with which he shared entrepreneurial values and economic interests.[81]

All this is not to say that as early as 1303 the Genoese had in mind a coherent project of constitutional governance. In fact, as we saw, the Genoese were pragmatic enough to admit in the preamble of a fundamental piece of legislation that they had misjudged Simon Boccanegra's inclinations. Nonetheless, in the documents that have survived, it is possible to detect a gradual definition of those delicate, "moderating" roles assigned to communal institutions (institutions such as offices, but also codes, budgetary laws capping spending, and constitutions meticulously regulating the political process). In the case of Genoa, the strict relationship between economic development and sophistication of institutional structures seems to furnish a convincing conceptual framework. "A capital market entails security of property rights over time and will simply not evolve where political rulers can arbitrarily seize assets or radically alter their value."[82] In the fifteenth century, the Genoese continued their process of institutional change quite creatively, as they transformed the republic's fiscal problems in an opportunity to partly replace the communal government with an innovative financial institution—a chartered bank that was administrated by the same entrepreneurs who had accumulated savings, investing them in public bonds (*compere* and *luoghi*). As a result of the budgetary reforms, the *regulae*, and the increasingly political role played by the Bank of St. George, "doges could not control the finances of the commune, and the financial restrictions placed on them did much to inhibit their ambitions to behave like lords of Genoa."[83] And the words written by the Genoese Andrea Spinola (1562—1631) well summarize the centuries-long effort by the Ligurians to limit the political prerogatives of the factional leaders who became doges:

> This word of Doge, or *duce*, whichever we prefer to say, is a civil name that indicates not who dominates, but rather the one who goes ahead escorting, and guiding. This is why the heads of some free republics are called Doges. To these heads the laws give appearances and honours, but only *the most modest authority.*[84]

CONCLUSION

The study of Giovanni da Pontremoli's intercontinental business shows the Genoese entrepreneurial mindset in action and constitutes a clear example of market expansion, private economic calculation, and adaptability over time. This story has been here put into context, by juxtaposing to it an investigation of the constitutional history and political culture of the metropolis. Both the communal and the private institutions presented in this chapter indicate a consistent (and largely successful) desire—shared by different generations and social groups of the Genoese citizenry—to protect the rule of law, to limit the power of the doge, to create financial self-government, and to safeguard economic prosperity.[85] As a consequence of centuries of colonial and commercial expansion in areas not directly controlled by their state, the Genoese appreciated the profitability of private networks and elaborated a constitutional order with strong anti-tyrannical provisions. As we shall see in the next chapter, in this vision there was no space for a large public fleet (nor for regular state-led military adventures), while the periodic, nominal submission to representatives of foreign governments was not considered necessarily at odds with the enjoyment of freedom.

NOTES

1. See, for instance, Charles Verlinden, "Italian Influence," 199, 209, 211.
2. Tom Scott, *The City-State in Europe, 1000–1600* (Oxford: Oxford University Press, 2012), 76. I shall return to the key concept of territorial state (which was consistently rejected by the Genoese) in chapter 5.
3. A.S.G. Archivio del Banco di San Giorgio, *Cabella granorum*, sala 37/26. The letters have been published in *Lettere di Giovanni da Pontremoli, mercante Genovese: 1453–1459*, ed. Domenico Gioffre (Genova: Università di Genova, 1982).
4. For a local history of Pontremoli, see Giovanni Sforza, *Storia di Pontremoli dalle origini al 1500* (Firenze: Franceschini, 1904). For a more recent history of the region, but from

the perspective of its literary presence in Dante's *Divina Commedia*, see the article by Livio Galanti, "La Lunigiana nella Divina Commedia," in *Corriere Apuano* (22 March 1980).

5. The Bank of St. George and its role in the institutional history of Genoa are treated in chapter 3.

6. "Tantum habeo animum altaratum quod fere ante voluissem mortuus fuisse quam audire nova similia et clare video quod propter peccata nostra sumus ad extremum et, sine dubio, derelinquit nos Dominus." *Lettere di Giovanni*, letter 1, 3.

7. "dicunt in maiori parte trucidaverunt." Ibid.

8. Ibid., letter 2, 5–6.

9. Ibid., letter 3, 6–9.

10. Ibid., letter 7, 16–17.

11. "In one respect, medieval trade differed totally from modern trade. Today most goods are sold before they are shipped. . . . Medieval trade, however, with few exceptions involved venturing. An assortment of goods was shipped to a distant place in the expectation that it would be sold at a remunerative price and that the merchant would be able to make his returns in other commodities demanded at home." Raymond de Roover, "The Organization of Trade," in *The Cambridge Economic History of Europe*, ed. M. M. Postan, E. E. Rich, and E. Miller (Cambridge: Cambridge University Press, 1963), 44.

12. "Memoria vobis Iacopo de Monleone parte mea Iohannis de Pontremullo." Ibid., letter 9, 19. The rest of the letter is written in Genoese dialect, with some words in Latin.

13. Translation from the original, in Genoese dialect: "quando no li poessi vende a la monea, avanti che tornarli cocie, laudo e conforto che voi overe e cerchae de baratarli in roba de la qua a voi paere possasene cocie megio trarne li soi dine, como soe ceyra, core e in altre cosse, como meggio a voi parra." Ibid., 20.

14. Ibid., letters 12 and 13, 23–25. In particular, note the sentence "ideo deprecor vos non sit vobis grave eidem Iacobo porrigere omne conscilium et auxilium quod ei porrigere potestis," on 24.

15. Ibid., letter 10, 21–22.

16. "Ideo, frater, si oportet, deprecor vos non sit vobis grave toto posse vestro sibe porrigere omne auxilium, conscilium et favorem quod vobis possibile sit." Ibid., letter 11, 23.

17. "ex quo satis admiratus fui, attento quid per duas vestras nobis scripsistis et potissime quia in reditu de hic Iacobus de Amigdola michi dixerat potuisse ipsum vendere ad lb. VIII libra una, sed, attenta commissione nostra, non ellexit illud facere." Ibid., letter 62, 79.

18. Ibid., letter 138, 190–91.

19. Ibid., letter 6, 14–16.

20. "Plus iuvat unus denarius bene acquisitus quam mille male acquisiti." Ibid., letter 120, 165.

21. "It is clear that there was a general movement from east to west, from the time of the Crusades until the seventeenth and the eighteenth centuries. This movement was a complicated process of reciprocal influences among European colonies in the Levant and the European metropolises on the one hand, and the colonies of the Atlantic archipelagoes, the African continent, and the American continents on the other." Verlinden, *The Beginnings of Modern Colonization*, 32.

22. About the establishment of regular economic relations between the Mediterranean and the North Sea, and about the Genoese colonies in Southern England, see chapter 1.

23. "quam cito potestis, huc accedatis quia ad partes illas non laudo moram amplius faciatis." *Lettere di Giovanni*, letter 38, 53.

24. "Presentem vobis mitto per Iacobum de Monleone cui ad vos cicius capitando quam Nicolaus de Tacio qui ad vos cito erit detis totum quod in nostro est quia bene tempus est, semper si dictus Nicolaus ad vos veniet ipsum vobis recomando et omnia nostra eidem detis cicius quam alio et de toto advisetis." Ibid., letter 41, 58. The letter begins on 55.

25. Ibid., letter 86, 103–4.

26. De Tacio's decision to immediately exploit Caffa's market after the fall of Pera, and before receiving Giovanni's orders (see again letter 7), shows a courageous spirit and intelligent thinking. Concerning his trustworthiness, consider the words with which Giovanni talks about Nicola in letters sent to other people: he does not ask to control him, but rather he

introduces him as a faithful employee and a friend (see for example letter 3 to his brother-in-law, where toward the end Giovanni mentions Nicola as a "bona persona").

27. See letter 95, 118; letter 96, 119; and letter 122, 167. About Pietro de Coronato, see in the letter 102 (sent to Giovanni Battista Mirono) this passage on 132: "bonam spem habeo in Petro de Coronato, quia audio et vidi est bona persona."

28. See, for instance, letter 94 to Nicola de Tacio, in particular on 114.

29. Ibid., letter 115, 156–59.

30. Ibid., letter 112, 151–54.

31. About this, see, for example, letter 113, on 154–55, where Giovanni demands to his representatives Iacopo and Tommaso da Cassana the profits of an old cargo of wax, and he also asks them to send him information about the variations in the price of this good.

32. Ibid., letter 108, 142–46. In particular see 145.

33. "in Ispania, vel ubi melius videbitur." Ibid., letter 164, 247.

34. Robert S. Lopez, *The Commercial Revolution of the Middle Ages, 950–1350* (Cambridge; New York: Cambridge University Press, 1998).

35. *Il manuale di mercatura di Saminiato de' Ricci*, ed. Antonia Borlandi (Genova: Di Stefano, 1963).

36. "il genovese, teso per gran parte della vita all'accumulo . . . la mentalità mercantile, l'ideologia precapitalistica, l'abitudine ad ordinare le proprie cose." Giovanna Petti Balbi, *Governare la città. Pratiche sociali e linguaggi politici a Genova in età medievale* (Firenze: Firenze University Press, 2007), 31.

37. As Alan Macfarlane has argued in his book *The Riddle of the Modern World*, political powers throughout history have hampered the process of capital accumulation. According to the British anthropologist and historian, these negative forces were either internal or external to the society that was developing. The internal "predatory tendencies" lay in the structures of power that were typical of agrarian societies, and in those social groups ready to increase their control over an opulent community in order to extort more resources; the external "predatory tendencies" were instead represented by economically backward but militarily powerful neighbors. Alan Macfarlane, *The Riddle of the Modern World: of Liberty, Wealth and Equality* (London: Macmillan, 2002). In particular, see 270–71.

38. At least since the nineteenth century, some historians have been interested in the development of Genoese budgetary laws. See Giuseppe Banchero, *Genova e le due Riviere* (Genova: Pellas, 1846), in particular 350–53; Heinrich Sieveking, *Studio sulle finanze genovesi nel medioevo e in particolare sulla Casa di San Giorgio* (Genova: ASLSP, 1905–1906); and Angelo Boscassi, "Le spese della Repubblica di Genova nel 1349," *Gazzetta di Genova* 2 (1915). Sieveking's book remains the most thorough study, indispensable even today. For a recent, but more general introduction to the Genoese financial system see Giuseppe Felloni, *Genova e la Storia della finanza: una serie di primati?* (Genova: Tormena, 2005).

39. The term *cappellazzi* (literally, big hats) indicates the two families usually fighting for the dogeship in fifteenth-century Genoa (the Adorno and the Campofregoso). See Riccardo Musso, "Lo stato cappellazzo. Genova tra Adorno e Fregoso (1436–1464)," *Studi di storia medievale e diplomatica* 17 (1998): 223–88.

40. Given the history of political turbulence in Genoa, the fact that this city did not see the rise of a family dynasty (*signoria*) has puzzled historians. See for example Ernesto Sestan, "Le origini delle signorie cittadine: un problema storico esaurito?" in *Italia Medievale* (Napoli: Edizioni Scientifiche Italiane, 1968), 193–223. Arturo Pacini has suggested that the continuous civic conflict for the dogeship was partly counterbalanced by the fact that public offices were evenly divided among *nobili* and *popolari*, merchants and artisans. Arturo Pacini, "Ideali repubblicani, lotta politica e gestione del potere a Genova," in *Politica e cultura nelle repubbliche italiane dal Medioevo all'Età moderna*, ed. Simonetta Adorni Braccesi e Mario Ascheri (Roma: Istituto Storico Italiano per l'Età Moderna e Contemporanea, 2001), 189–236 (see, in particular, 199–201).

41. Translation from the original: "Nella città di Genova, quando la vive nella sua libertà, si crea per liberi suffragi un capo, il quale chiamano Doge; non perchè e'sia assoluto principe, nè perchè egli solo deliberi, ma come capo proponga quello che dai magistrati e Consigli loro si debba deliberare." Niccolò Machiavelli, *Istorie Fiorentine* (Firenze: Barbera, 1883), 177. Ma-

chiavelli did not perfectly describe the functioning of the Genoese political system, but he absolutely grasped the limits placed on the doge's authority in Genoa.

42. Archivio di Stato di Genova, *Membranacei di San Giorgio*, ms. IV (*Regule Comperarum Capituli*), cc. CLXXXVII r.–CLXXXXVIII v.

43. The total expenditure mentioned in the text is L. 26.244, distributed as follows: L. 4.915 for the central government (included the salary for the *podesta*); L. 5.290 for the defense of the city and the police; L. 16.039 for the defense and the local offices (such as the castellans) in the *Riviere*. The territories around Genoa, traditional possessions of the republic, were called *riviere*, a word meaning coasts.

44. The Genoese nobility was never able (at least before the 1570s) to impose an exclusivist system following the model of the Venetian *Serrata*. Geo Pistarino, "La spesa ordinaria della Repubblica di Genova nella crisi del 1461–1462," in *Miscellanea di Storia Ligure in memoria di Giorgio Falco* (Genova: Università di Genova, 1966), 239–63. Moreover, the Genoese people could control the spending (and taxation) not only through the *nobili* and *popolari* sitting at the *Consiglio*, but also because merchants, artisans, and notaries had shares of those offices and bureaucratic positions, which had a say in the deliberations concerning the fiscal policy of the state. On this important point, see Rodolfo Savelli, "'Capitula,' 'Regulae,' e pratiche del diritto a Genova tra XIV e XV secolo," in *Statuti città territori in Italia e Germania tra Medioevo ed Età moderna*, ed. G. Chittolini e D. Willoweit (Bologna: Il Mulino, 1991), 447–502.

45. Usury was condemned by the Church already during the patristic period. Arthur Vermeersch, "Usury," in *The Catholic Encyclopaedia* (New York: Robert Appleton, 1912), v. 15, 235. See also the letter written by Leo the Great to the bishops of Campania, Picene and Tuscany, dated October 443. In this missive, called *Ut nobis gratulationem*, the Pope condemned usury not only among the clergy, but also among the laity.

46. Genoese businessmen were used to turning into administrators and officials. Already during the Middle Ages "Genoese capitalists often took over the administration of public revenues also in foreign states." Translation from the Italian edition: "capitalisti Genovesi spesso assunsero anche all'estero l'amministrazione delle rendite dello stato." Sieveking, *Studio sulle finanze genovesi*, 109, note 4.

47. At least since the fifteenth century, Genoese investing in *luoghi* were not only businessmen like Giovanni da Pontremoli. For example, public debt's bonds were used as donations to religious communities, or to pay for the construction of chapels. See the scraps of parchments in Archivio di Stato di Genova, *Ordini Religiosi*, n. 672 (1423–1543).

48. This is not to say that the central government did not spend money at all on the colonies; but maritime expansion and defense were left primarily to private captains, and the doge was not supposed (nor furnished with the economic means) to control the commercial and political life of the Genoese overseas communities. See Mario Buongiorno, *Il bilancio di uno stato medievale: Genova, 1340–1529* (Genova: Università di Genova, 1973), 42.

49. E. A. Le Mesurier, *Genoa. Her History as Written in her Buildings* (Genoa: Donath, 1889), 91–95.

50. Zorzi, "The Popolo," 155.

51. See Petti Balbi, *Simon Boccanegra*.

52. Buongiorno, *Il bilancio di uno stato medievale*, 51, 73, 77.

53. Luigi Maria Levati, *Dogi perpetui di Genova (1339–1528)* (Genova: Certosa, Marchese & Campora, 1928), 39–47.

54. Archivio di Stato di Genova, Antico Comune, II–MCCCXXXX (*Massaria*).

55. Nowadays, most of these documents can be found in the section called *Antico Comune*, where some budgets have been preserved in the file of the *Massaria Communis Ianue*, while others in the collection of the *Magistrorum Rationalium*; to achieve a precise understanding of the expenses mentioned in these manuscripts, at times it is useful to consult also other files, such as the *Castrorum Communis Ianuae*, Archivio di Stato di Genova, *Antico Comune*.

56. One of the (few) legal powers of the Genoese doge was to appoint the local officials and castellans in the *Riviere*. Yet, also in this case the doge could hardly appoint his men, as he had to consider the privileges of local families.

57. Archivio di Stato di Genova, *Leges Genuenses*, ms 133, cc. 96 r.–100 v.

58. "Pro provisione magnifici domini ducis et familie sue libras octomillia sexcentas viginti quinque, sive: lb. 8.625." Ibid.

59. "Item pro provisionatis, secundum quod videbitur magnifico domino duci, libras duomillia; lb. 2.000." Ibid.

60. For a recent study of one of the greatest debates concerning public spending in Genoa, the one focused on the opportunity to arm a public fleet of galleys, see Kirk, *Genoa and the Sea*.

61. "Pro diversis expensibus extraordinariis dietim occurrentibus, libras tria millia: lb. 3.000." Ibid.

62. The *regulae* of 1363 have been published in 1901. *Regulae Communis Ianuae anno MCCCLXIII, tempore ducatus domini Gabrielis Adurni conditae*, in *Historiae Patriae Monumenta*, v. XVIII (Torino: Bocca, 1901), c. 243–388. This edition is important because it tried to combine the original manuscripts, nowadays lost or scattered. However, this work does not have a translation, as it simply presents the original Latin text; moreover, it is by now a very rare volume, and given the importance of this constitution a new edition, with a historical introduction and a complete translation, would be much needed.

63. Translation from the original: "Quo Ducali regimine preellecto, ne per abusum prelatis utilitati Republice commodis principantis (*sic*), ydem Dux in tirannidem declinaret, necessarium fuit et opere precium potestatem ipsius congruo moderamine temperare Ducaleque arbitrium regulis inviolabiter limitare, editis more legum." *Regulae Communis*, c. 243.

64. "attendentes parlamentum predictum quod, domino Symone Buchanigra multa et periculosa infirmitate gravato, cives Ianue et homines civitatis burgorum et suburbiorum videntes se in magnis periculis, discordiis et scandalis constitutos . . . et si in futurum per ipsum regeretur seu gubernaretur ad finalem destructionem et exterminium deduceretur, nisi de alio prorsus duce et rectore concorditer per comune Ianue et populum Ianue provideretur." Ibid., c. 246.

65. Ibid., c. 257.

66. "Si vero fuerint in absentia domini ducis, tunc debeant esse presentes ad minus novem ex ipsis consiliariis, et tunc debeant ex ipsis novem vocibus esse concordes octo ad minus." Ibid., c. 262.

67. "Et de ipsis causis, motis et movendis, tam in civilibus quam in criminalibus, dominus dux et consilium nullam potestatem habeant, seu aliquam iurisdicionem ipsas cognoscendi et diffinendi, seu etiam tractandi." Ibid., c. 284.

68. "Statuimus et ordinamus quod officia Mercancie et Gazarie sint et esse debeant et totaliter remanere prout hactenus solita sunt, et habeant illam iurisdicionem potestatem et bayliam." Ibid., c. 343. The *Officium Gazariae* had been created in 1303 (when Caffa was rebuilt) to deal with the administration of the colonies in the Black Sea; tellingly enough, the consul in Caffa was under the authority of this office, and not under the control of the *podesta* or, later, the doge.

69. Ibid., c. 325–331.

70. The Genoese gradually eliminated all direct taxes, at the same time favoring the transfer of fiscal powers to the Bank of St. George. Buongiorno, *Il bilancio di uno stato medievale*, 25–30.

71. To be more precise, the government did ask the Bank of St. George for a loan, but simply in order to send a diplomatic mission and many gifts to the Ottoman Sultan. The hope was to spare the fortified Genoese citadel in Constantinople from being sacked; but before a decision was taken, the terrible news of the capture and destruction of Galata reached Genoa.

72. Translation from the original: "intendendo la necessitae esser grande e lo dexyderio de li citaín esser che cossí se facia cum ogni celeritae pensando per quella via se podesse trovare forma a quelli dinae chi fosseno necessarij a tale provisione: ne parse haverne per via de scruptinio lo parei de li citeín: da liquae tandem universalmente trovamo esser questa sententia che ben fosse arembare le cosse de capha e de quello mare mao a logoverno de lo officio de sanzorzo: da loqual nascesse la forma e li rimedij per salvatione di quelle cosse. . . . per nostro descharego avemo deliberao de proponere questa materia davanti da voi: acioche poi possae in primis deliberare se ve pare ben che lo officio de sanzorzo a nome delle compere acceptae lo governo de quelle cosse o non." Archivio di Stato di Genova, *Manoscritti di San Giorgio*, IV

(*Diversor. Negotior.*), 1453–1480, 60 v. Also published in Amedeo Vigna (ed.), "Codice diplomatico delle colonie tauro-liguri durante la signoria dell'Ufficio di S. Giorgio," in *Atti della Società Ligure di Storia Patria*, volume VI (Genova: Tipografia del R.I. de'Sordo-muti, 1868), 24–25.

73. See the deliberation of the eight *Protettori*, assembled together with 275 citizens who had invested their savings in the *compere* and *luoghi* managed by St. George. Ibid., 25–32.

74. The name of Giovanni is listed in the document on 31.

75. "bonum terminum capere possent habendo apodiatas partes illas Caffe venerando Officio Sancti Georgii, qui teneo alio modo ut utiliori illas gubernabit quam ab inde in antea factum fuit et sic placeat Altissimo." *Lettere di Giovanni*, letter 5, 12.

76. "quelli cittadini hanno levato l'amore dal Comune come cosa tiranneggiata, e postolo a San Giorgio come parte bene ed ugualmente amministrata; onde ne nasce le facili e spesse mutazioni dello stato, e che ora ad uno loro cittadino, ora ad uno forestiero ubbidiscono, perchè non San Giorgio ma il Comune varia governo. Talchè quando intra i Fregosi e gli Adorni si è combattuto del principato, perchè si combatte lo stato del Comune, la maggior parte de' cittadini si tira da parte, e lascia quello in preda al vincitore; nè fa altro l'uffizio di San Giorgio, se non quando uno ha preso lo stato, che far giurargli l'osservanza delle leggi sue; le quali insino a questi tempi non sono state alterate, perchè avendo armi e danari e governo, non si può senza pericolo di una certa pericolosa ribellione alterarle. Esempio veramente raro, e da' filosofi in tante loro immaginate e vedute Repubbliche mai non trovato, vedere dentro ad un medesimo cerchio, intra i medesimi cittadini, la libertà e la tirannide, la vita civile e la corrotta, la giustizia e la licenza; perchè quello ordine solo mantiene quella città piena di costumi antichi e venerabili. E s'egli avvenisse, che col tempo in ogni modo avverrà, che San Giorgio tutta quella città occupasse, sarebbe quella una Repubblica più che la Veneziana memorabile." Machiavelli, *Istorie Fiorentine*, 317.

77. Robert Sabatino Lopez, one of the most important historians dealing with the Genoese medieval colonies, wrote: "We do not wish here to treat the details of Saint George's administration [of the Levantine colonies]: but we can say for sure that even though it did not have impetuses and it did not perform miracles, it was nonetheless careful and honest. Much attention was given to the supply [of the colonies], to the renovation of the fortifications, to the reorganization of the local budgets. Most of the officials named by the *Protettori* were more diligent, more capable, more honest than those in the last period of the republican rule." "Non vogliamo entrare nei particolari della gestione di San Giorgio: ma possiamo dire senz'altro che se non ebbe slanci e non fece miracoli fu però oculata e onesta. Molte cure furono dedicate all'approvigionamento, al restauro delle fortificazioni, al risanamento dei bilanci locali. In maggioranza i funzionari nominati dai Protettori furono più diligenti, più abili, più probi di quelli degli ultimi tempi del dominio diretto genovese." Lopez, *Storia delle colonie genovesi*, 421. Documents showing how the Bank of St. George governed the Levantine colonies in the 1460s can be found in Amedeo Vigna (ed.), "Codice diplomatico delle colonie tauro-liguri durante la signoria dell'Ufficio di S. Giorgio," in *Atti della Società Ligure di Storia Patria*, volume VII, 1 (Genova: Tipografia del R.I. de'Sordo-muti, 1871).

78. Douglass C. North, "Institutions," *The Journal of Economic Perspectives* 5 (1991): 97.

79. Robert L. Reynolds, "In Search of a Business Class in Thirteenth-century Genoa," *The Journal of Economic History* 5 (1945): 10.

80. On the social mobility in the Italian communes, see in particular Robert Sabatino Lopez, *Naissance de l'Europe* (Paris: Colin, 1962), 277–79, and 284–312.

81. For example, letters written in 1457 and 1458 prove the partnership of Giovanni with the noble Eliano Spinola. See *Lettere di Giovanni*, letter 120, in particular on 165; and letter 152, in particular on 223. Giovanni also participated in both the forms of Genoese self-government: medieval communal offices (he was a tax collector, once again thanks to his business's profits, with which he had been able to purchase such office); and Banco di San Giorgio (where he took part in the historic decision on the Levantine colonies).

82. Douglass C. North, "Institutions," 101.

83. Shaw, "Concepts of *Libertà* in Renaissance Genoa," 180. According to Shaw, only during the fifteenth century the Genoese understood that they had to limit the power of noble factions, and only with the famous reforms of 1528 they were successful in doing so ("by the

later fifteenth century, these factions [Adorno and Campofregoso] seem to have been losing their grip, as more and more Genoese grew tired of them," ibid., 188). However, the process of political reform was under way at least since the beginning of the fourteenth century.

84. "Questa parola di Doge, o duce, che dir vogliamo, è nome civile, significando, non chi signoreggi, ma chi come scorta vada inanzi, e che guidi. Di qui è che i capi di alcune republiche libere si chiamano Dogi. A capi tali sogliono le leggi dar apparenza e prospettiva, ma *modestissima autorità*." Emphasis added. Biblioteca Universitaria di Genova, *Ricordi*, ms. B.VIII.26, 75.

85. In fact, such conclusion constitutes a challenge to the teleological narrative often employed to describe the (supposedly unavoidable) rise of the modern, territorial state.

Chapter Three

Self-Government and Self-Perception

Foreign Protectors, Cosmopolitanism, and the Genoese Identity

After the fall of Constantinople, the Genoese could have decided to create a public fleet and to grant more powers to the communal government in order to defend their Crimean colonies. Instead, they decided to transfer the government of the colonies to the private businessmen of St. George. This move is noteworthy, because it shows the Genoese's distrust of their doge as well as their belief in the power of private arms—even when facing extraordinary challenges. Although Genoa's decision may appear bizarre, its results were impressive. Under the guide of the Bank of St. George, the Ligurian fortresses and city-ports in the Black Sea were able to survive for another twenty-two years. This was possible also because, in these exceptional circumstances and being surrounded by enemy forces, the Genoese colonists were ready to accept a certain level of administrative coordination and political centralization.[1] Yet, they accepted this precisely because they knew that the orders they received were not coming from a doge for life, but rather, in a sense, from themselves, since the *Protettori* were basically an alternating group of businessmen. This is why St. George's rule was perceived as reasonable, benevolent, and efficient. More importantly, this is why the Genoese refused to admit that the fall of Caffa was, eventually, unavoidable, and instead placed the blame of that disaster befalling their colonies in 1475 on the *discordia*, the division within the city. All these themes deserve attention, because they tell us something about Genoese perceptions of politics and freedom, and, as we shall see, they are linked to the political history of the metropolis.

DISCORDIA AND ITS CONSEQUENCES

In 1453, when Constantine Palaeologus, the last Byzantine emperor, fell while fighting the Ottomans at the feet of Constantinople's crumbling walls,[2] the Black Sea region ceased to be what it had been for centuries—a chain of hubs shakily controlled by Christian rulers and merchants, the door to Asian steppes, and the place where Tartars, Greeks, Genoese, and Venetians alternatively fought and did business with each other. But the fall of Constantinople was hardly unexpected. The rise of the Turks had been under way for decades, while the Italians were powerless spectators, some of them wishfully hoping to maintain their privileges under the Sultan's rule. By the 1430s, the Ottomans—who had conquered Adrianople as early as 1365, making it their capital—controlled all the territories around Constantinople. The Greek emperor had asked for help several times to the distracted and divided European kingdoms; but by the 1440s, every hope was lost. The Spanish traveler Pero Tafur, visiting the Black Sea in the 1430s and composing the memoirs of his voyage in the 1450s, wrote: "the Greeks are now completely destroyed, as already at that time Constantinople was the only fortified place they had. . . . The Turks well took revenge for Troy! Even before I arrived, and before Constantinople had been taken, the Greeks were as subject as they are now."[3] After 1453, it was clear that the whole Black Sea would have soon become part of the Ottoman possessions. And the situation of the Genoese hubs along the coasts of the Black Sea became even more desperate with the fall of Trebizond, in 1461.[4] Thus, when Caffa eventually fell in 1475, the true surprise was not the definitive end of the Genoese presence in the Black Sea, but rather the fact that Caffa had resisted for so many years after the fall of Constantinople. Every observer should have seen the sack of Caffa as the inevitable outcome of an unsustainable geopolitical situation. Yet, somebody in Genoa read the loss of Caffa in a very different way, giving a curious interpretation of this tragic event.

This interpretation can be found in a bound volume consisting of nine different manuscripts, preserved at the Archivio di Stato of Genoa. We do not know who collected them, even though it is possible that the volume was either prepared or purchased by a member of the Pallavicini family in the sixteenth century.[5] The third manuscript in the bound book is listed in the index as *Discorso delle Discordie seguite in Caffa con Tartari*, but leafing through the volume until the actual text, one discovers that whoever wrote this reflection on the last period of the Genoese Caffa decided to entitle it *1474—Discorso della Discordia fra Genovesi*. The true title of the document draws the reader's attention not to the external threats (Tartars, Turks), but rather to the internal strife affecting the city. Tellingly enough, the anonymous author begins his account with these words:

> In Caffa there was discord among the Genoese. The Great Turk asked them to return some young slaves who had escaped from Trebizond, and he demanded to have them back especially because the Tartar captain of the Country, called Eminec, had made himself his tributary, promising to help him in every enterprise. And even though the Genoese knew about this, the representative [of the Great Turk] left without having the fugitive slaves back, so they tried to apologize in every possible way. And in this moment, hate and division were born among the Genoese, because some of them favored Eminec while others were against him and in order to remove him from the country invited the Emperor of the Tartars to Caffa, asking him to bring Eminec with him and with the intention to poison him. But when everything was ready to poison him the other Genoese, those who favored him, warned him, so he did not want to drink or eat anything. And even though it was still possible for the Genoese to kill him since he still was in their house, the discord among them was so serious that they could not agree on what to do, wondering about the consequences.[6]

The key concept in these lines is evidently the *discordia*, the internal divisiveness preventing the Genoese in Caffa from acting effectively. The desperate geopolitical situation is not described, as the author immediately focused on the factional strife within Caffa; the document does not mention the fall of Trebizond, and the political relation between the Genoese and the Tartars is not explained.

In 1474, the Genoese were administering Caffa thanks to the benevolence of the Tartar Khan, who was glad to use the Italian ships to connect his territories with a large commercial network.[7] The territories around Caffa were all controlled by the Tartars, who brought to the Genoese market a great quantity of slaves (whom were often sold by the Genoese to the Egyptians).[8] But with the falls of Constantinople and Trebizond, the Genoese of Caffa found themselves living in a narrow strip of land, a handful of cosmopolitan fortresses on the coast.[9] The Crimean Khanate became a vassal state of the Sultan, and it is not unlikely that some Tartar leaders began to see the Genoese as the last remains of a lost world, a riotous and weak group of greedy Latin intermediaries. With the Ligurians gone, and the Turk ships visiting the Crimean coast, they could have continued to sell slaves and agricultural goods, possibly even obtaining a higher profit. It is therefore revealing that the Genoese author of this manuscript chose not to address this deteriorating political and military situation in the Black Sea region. In fact, the title of the manuscript and the first two pages of the text clearly reject the idea that the loss of Caffa was inevitable and due to external forces. This shows the conviction that the fall of Caffa was not due to its military weakness or to the inefficiency of St. George's governance; rather, the author believed that only an unfortunate disagreement within the Genoese community and the ambitions of some local Genoese prevented the city from maintaining its independence and prosperity for many other decades. As the document proceeds, the theme does not change, and the *discordia* among different Genoese factions continues to be the true subject of the story. According to the anonymous writer, after the failed assassination attempt, the Genoese and the Tartar emperor officially deposed Eminec, naming as new captain of the country (which meant, a new Tartar chief controlling the Crimean territories behind the coastal line) a man called Saetor, son of a former captain.[10] Yet, Eminec was a wily political actor; according to the manuscript, he escaped from Caffa together with Chaydar, brother of the Tartar emperor, promising to make him the new khan and beginning to plunder (*facendo gran danno*) the countryside around Caffa. At this point in the text, the author wrote:

> Thus the Emperor came again to Caffa, and he decided to remove both his brother and Eminec his Captain. And he [the Tartar Emperor] would have obtained this if the Genoese who shared the government had found an agreement . . . in their discord. As a consequence the Turk Armada reached Caffa, on the last day of March.[11]

The Genoese apparently blamed the arrival of the Turks on their own *discordia*.[12] And the author then briefly describes the great joy expressed by the Turks when they were informed of the ongoing civil war tormenting Caffa and the countryside.[13]

The siege laid by the Turks caused suffering and deaths in Caffa, so

> four ambassadors of the Land [Caffa] were elected and they went to the General of the Armada, called Amat Bassa. These ambassadors were: ser Giuliano dal Fusto, ser Battista d'Allegro, ser Sisto Servicio, and ser Gregorio Rosso, and after the negotiation with Bassa they were promised their freedom along with their factions and their possessions, and seven other families. They [our ambassadors] declared [to the other people of Caffa] that they had reached an agreement [with the Turks] so that all the people and the properties would have been safe, and immediately the insignia of the Turk were put on the doors and the walls.[14]

Hence the Ottomans entered the city, and the ambassadors' lie was soon discovered. The four betrayers had their lives spared, and the Turks respected the agreement, allowing them to flee, together with their clans and their money; also another twenty-eight families (seven chosen by each ambassador) were spared, but had to remain in Caffa, and pay tribute.[15] The manuscript consoles the reader by adding that thanks to the secret agreement between the four ambassadors and Amat Bassa, "almost four thousand people" were pardoned, "all according to the desire of the aforementioned ambassadors." Not surprisingly, "the ambassadors did not want to stay in the City with the others, and were sent by ship, together with their wives, families and possessions, to Constantinople, where many of them died from plague."[16] "But those who remained slaves in Caffa"—that means, those who were neither part of the ambassadors' clans nor among the thousands saved through the ploy of the seven additional families chosen by each ambassador—"were captured and put in jail as soon as the Turks entered the city, and their properties were sacked . . . their screams, as well as the screams of the women hitting their own cheeks, rose up to the sky, with unbelievable cries, which would have moved both the living and the dead to pity."[17]

What is the historical vision emerging from this account? And who was its intended audience? The first question can be answered considering the importance given to the concept of *discordia*. From the beginning of the manuscript (indeed, from its title), the Genoese are depicted as the arbiters of their own destiny. The Ottomans appear "as a consequence" of internal divisions, so the external predatory power is never the true subject of the account. Instead, the political instability (*questo disparere*), due to the attempt by different Genoese factions to use the Tartars in order to obtain political power in the city, is the theoretical framework within which the crisis is conceptualized and interpreted. The question concerning the audience can be partly answered thanks to a second text, written by the same anonymous writer(s). It is a quite rare philosophical reflection on the *res publica* that immediately follows the text on the fall of Caffa. The two texts are linked, the second of them not being listed in the index of the miscellanea as an independent manuscript; moreover, the ink and the calligraphy are exactly the same (while they change in the other manuscripts composing the bound volume). This second text is entitled *Qui cuncta discordiis civilibus fessa nomine Principis sub Imperium accepit*, a Latin sentence that may be a quote from Cornelius Tacitus's *Annals*.[18] The rest of the document is in Genoese dialect. The manuscript does not mention the previous story, and it immediately begins with a general reflection on an ideal *res publica* and the consequences of *guerre e discordie civili*.

> The most propitious opportunity, and also the most timely, that could happen to one, who desires to take over his own *patria*, which has already been living for several years in *libertà*, [is] when in this *patria* for some time there have been and maintained civil wars and discords.[19]

The manuscript continues with a description of the decisive moment, when a citizen plotting to become prince can act more successfully. "When, for whatever reason, the City will be divided in factions and parties, then that will be the best time for him [the prince] to reveal his intentions."[20] According to the author, once the citizens are tired of internal strife and political disorders, they are more willing to entrust the government to a dictator.

> and thus as the ships that are hit by storms and scared by the dangers of the Sea welcome the possibility to take refuge in those ports that in normal conditions

> they would have avoided and hated due to their being controlled by enemies and foreigners, and like some birds, among those which are more afraid of the hunters, when they are chased by the hawk, or by other birds of prey, go, hoping to save themselves, even into the arms of the hunter, so in the same way those cities that in a tranquil and peaceful state would have hated the name of Prince more than anything else, when for some time suffering from domestic, civil weapons and with no hope of a nearby friend, easily go to take refuge under the authority of one who steps forward, almost as [if they were] inside the safest harbor.[21]

The document ends explaining how the future prince usually behaves during the delicate period of civil strife; he pretends to be a moderate man (*sempre d'animo composto*), who is uninterested in power and is not part of any faction.

Notwithstanding the apparently different topics treated by the two texts, the reflection on the end of *libertà* has something in common with the account of Caffa's fall. Given the medieval history of Genoa it is not bizarre that the anonymous author decided to focus on the internal divisions crippling a *res publica.* In the first manuscript, he recounted a tragic event in Genoese history through the use of key concepts that were familiar to the Ligurian audience—discord, division, factional strife, betrayal of the city. Caffa's fall, according to this interpretation, was not the consequence of the changed geopolitical and military situation in the Black Sea region; instead, it was a personal controversy between the local Tartar commander, Eminec, and one of the factions of Genoese merchants within Caffa to spark a regional crisis eventually ended by the Turk intervention. The space given in the account to the betrayal of the four Genoese ambassadors is also revealing: throughout the story, the focus remains on the *discordia* and on the plots done by powerful political characters. The second text draws an additional lesson from what happened in Caffa. When suffering from *guerre e discordie civili*, a republic risks seeing the rise of a despotic prince. Once again, the danger does not come from without the city, but from within. The foes are not Muslim conquerors or Renaissance dukedoms, but one ambitious, authoritarian citizen. Finally, of particular interest is the importance given in the second text to the time that is necessary for the people to get tired of divisions and to accept the end of *libertà.* This means that whoever wants to become a tyrant needs to be patient; but, more importantly, this also means that there is the opportunity for the city to save its freedoms and to act in the period of time between the beginning of civil war and the rise of a prince. What the anonymous writer does not explain is *how* the republican institutions should act. Given the history of Genoa, it is possible that the answer to this problem was considered obvious. In order to protect their freedom and to avoid the rise of a prince, the Genoese often turned to a foreign ruler. Interestingly enough, in the passage quoted above, the author, while enumerating the conditions that are necessary for the internal threat—the would-be tyrant—to successfully take over the city, stated that there has to be "*no hope of a nearby friend*." At this point, we shall consider more documents and look at some telling episodes in the political history of the metropolis.

FOREIGN PROTECTORS AND GENOA'S FREEDOM

In 1395, Liguria was afflicted by civil conflicts between different factions; in Genoa, the doge Antoniotto Adorno was not able to reestablish order, and the population was afraid to lose its liberties.[22] Facing a crisis that could jeopardize the communal institutions and provoke a civil war, the Genoese still refused to grant more military and political powers to their doge. Instead, during a general council on November 10, they decided to give to Antoniotto Adorno a diplomatic mandate in order to negotiate with the king of France. At the beginning of this assembly, the notary Antonio di Credenza clearly explained the meaning that such a decision could have. The Genoese, he said, were gathered to decide whether "it is good for us to take a *signore*, who can reintegrate this city and be our chief, and protect the *libertà* of this city, so that the city will not be destroyed by the discords among the Genoese."[23] Otherwise, the Genoese could have chosen either to join a league of states that would have helped them to restore internal order, or to establish "a new form of government . . . preserving our liberty without the help of any *signore*."[24] The Genoese chose the first solution, allowing the doge to negotiate with a foreign ruler. The loss of sovereignty (here intended as formal political independence) was therefore not in contrast with the Genoese concept of *libertà*; rather, the king of France was seen as a powerful ally by those who wanted to avoid a civil war and the establishment of a sectarian, local dynasty. The Genoese feared more the tyranny of a compatriot than the rule of a foreign *signore*. To be sure, the Ligurians were not willing to tolerate a predatory ruler, no matter how far he lived from Genoa; similarly, they did not want to rewrite their constitution. They were giving up their nominal independence precisely in order to maintain their communal offices, their tradition of limited public expenditure, and their economic environment. "Essentially, all they wanted was for the prince to send a governor, who would have the powers and the salary of the doge, and who would govern together with the *Anziani*."[25] As well documented by Christine Shaw, the foreign powers called by the Genoese were rarely abiding by the meticulous agreements signed with the city-state. A foreign ruler saw in Genoa an opportunity to sell the goods of his territories through one of the most important Mediterranean hubs; secondly, he was probably attracted by the private wealth of the Genoese merchants. The fact that, notwithstanding the tensions and the revolts characterizing Genoa's relations with the foreign rulers chosen from time to time to protect its freedom, the Genoese people continued throughout two centuries to give up their sovereignty in order to stop civil wars that could have ended with the rise of a native Ligurian tyrant seems surprising. Evidently, the Genoese knew the strength of their private arms and thought that a foreign yoke was easier to shake off than the regime of a compatriot. But, more significantly, the Genoese also continued to believe that while "a nearby friend" was in charge of their state, *libertà* could survive. The kind of freedom lived by the Genoese and shaped by their history of institutional change did not exclude a temporary loss of political independence. Hence, Genoa's freedom did not have much in common with the sovereignty-*libertas* celebrated by the Florentines.

In 1464, the Genoese felt that their *libertà* was endangered and curtailed precisely by what they considered the most dangerous kind of threat: a local doge trying to establish a *signoria*. The Genoese humanist Agostino Giustiniani (1470–1536) described with these words the situation in Genoa:

> And in the year 1464, in the month of February, the city being under the Dogeship of Paolo Fregoso, the Duke of Milan took possession of Savona . . . in Genoa during the previous two years there had been great discords among the Fregoso family; and the city had changed *Rettori*, which means Magistrates, several times, so that eventually it was taken by Archbishop Fregoso, as we have said above; and because he found himself so powerful over the Genoese people, together with Obietto di Flisco, and the other conspirators, they shamelessly transformed the public *libertà* into tyranny: many were taking revenge for past insults and assaulted those whom they hated; the Magistrates were not respected, and virtue was nowhere to be found: every seditious and arrogant man was honoured and praised; crimes and wickedness were not punished, the innocence of honest men was not safe in the midst of such confusion; and everything was done according to the vicious desires of Paolo and Obietto, and divine as well as human things were in a state of chaos, so that all the good men were complaining about this situation and were crying for the common miseries.[26]

Thus, in Giustiniani's account, "tyranny" and "confusion" are identified as the enemies of *libertà*. The Genoese freedoms die when the rule of law is absent ("the Magistrates were not respected") and when the political power is concentrated in the hands of a few leaders ("everything was done according to the vicious desires of Paolo and Obietto"). These lines give us, though indirectly, a rare definition of *libertà* coming from the mouth of a Renaissance Genoese. *Libertà*, in Giustiniani's view, means two things: first, an ordered political process—one that respects the functioning of those institutions (both political and private) that limit centralized power; and second, the rule of law—that is the pivotal condition for economic prosperity and the respect of property rights. The attention paid by Giustiniani to the economic consequences of a predatory government is confirmed by the lines that follow in the account:

> This was the terrible time when St. George's *luoghi* [bonds] were not worth more than three lire, and many good men from both the factions had left the city, searching for places that they judged safe, and many nobles had gone to Savona, and they pleaded with the Duke Francesco to free the city from the tyrannical yoke of the Fregoso.[27]

The Genoese chose once again to resort to the help of a foreign ruler in order to reestablish internal order, avoid the disintegration of their institutions, and solve a financial crisis. This time, the man chosen for the delicate role of discreet protector was none other than the personification of the Renaissance prince, the astute professional *condottiero* and the self-made duke of Milan, Francesco Sforza.[28] On May 24, 1464, the *Protettori* of St. George sent a letter to the Levantine colonies, communicating that the city of Genoa was now under the *dominio* of the Duke of Milan. The tone of the missive is revealing:

> for divine providence, to which we shall always be grateful, and by the will of the citizens, the government of this city has been transferred to the most illustrious and most powerful *signore* duke of Milan, who has not only confirmed but also increased all our privileges; he has shown great attention to the good of these *compere* [St. George]. Similarly, he has shown a singular love for all that concerns the good and the pacification of this city and the benefit of the citizens, so much so that the city and the citizens seem to have reborn; and *they already begun to build ships, to trade and to invest.* So that, God willing, we will let the world know that the Genoese have reestablished their affairs.[29]

Economic considerations are clearly at the center of this letter addressing the state of the polity and a change of regime in Genoa.

According to Giustiniani, Sforza was not only backed by the king of France and welcomed by the Bank of St. George. There was also a majority of Genoese citizens—*una gran parte dei cittadini*—actively involved in the coup of 1464 and directly inviting the duke of Milan to take over Genoa—*pregavano il Duca Francesco che volesse attendere a liberare la città di Genova.* While it is impossible to determine the percentage of Genoese that supported the duke, we do know that this number was significant enough to allow him to take the republic without fighting and to force Paolo Fregoso to escape. But whatever the size of this anti-seigneurial group might have been, its ideas and its rhetoric are what matters here. These ideas and rhetoric can be found in a fascinating manuscript written in February 1464, and containing a political poem with which the Milanese party within Liguria begged the duke to intervene.[30] In the first stanzas, the anonymous author(s) presented Genoa as a gracious widow (*Genova viduella*; *la vidueta cossì gratiosa*), who is waiting for her new husband to come. The first husband is identified as Filippo Visconti, the duke of Milan who had ruled Genoa just a few decades before; while the new husband is the recipient of the poem, Francesco Sforza. The Genoese writing this document wished to describe the previous experience under the Milanese authority as a period of peace and prosperity:

> Oh how happily under that *signore* [Filippo Maria Visconti]
> I lived a good time with strength
> And then with sadness
> For twenty-eight years I was widowed![31]

This rhetoric was instrumental in presenting Sforza as the external arbiter, the just ruler, who could stop the endless civil strife and bring Genoa back to the "strength" of its past days. But who exactly had to be blamed for the current situation? The text is outspoken:

> Fregoso, Adorno, Montaldi and the Guarco family
> Have done with me what they desired;
> But I still hope in God
> That from their hands I will be liberated.[32]

The anti-*cappellazzi*, anti-seigneurial tone of the poem is clear. The Genoese preferred to formally lose their independence rather than keep it under these circumstances. Yet, for the aim of this chapter, the most important lines of the manuscript concern neither the hated Fregoso nor the beloved duke of Milan. In a passage that opens a window on the way in which the Genoese perceived their own identity, the author(s) lamented the loss of Pera and invited Francesco to consider the riches accumulated by Genoa with sweat and blood (*sudore et sangue*). This wealth (and how it was created) is what defined Genoa. In the text, the widowed city goes on and says to Francesco:

> Think, if you would like,
> About my half-stolen dowry;
> And check whether any woman
> Is richer than me in all Christendom.[33]

The central theme is wealth and, of course, its origin: the commercial empire.

> What other bride in the whole world as many ships
> Can give you as I will,
> If you with my desire
> Agree, as it seems?[34]

The creation of wealth and the maritime power are what made Genoa unique to the eyes of the Genoese writer(s). Because the wealth and the colonial network had been jeopardized by predatory enemies both within and without the Ligurian community, the Genoese were willing to give their dogeship to a foreigner and to join the Milanese *dominio*, hoping to restore peace, order, and prosperity.

> I can neither count nor write to you
> How many fortresses and maritime colonies
> I have lost, poor me,
> Only because I am infirm for so long.
> When I think of it, it seems frightening
> The many ships with great riches,
> Which by many bands
> Have been stolen from me on the sea.
> . . . I was rich but now I am like a garden,
> Where everybody comes and picks the salad.[35]

The most important concepts used by the author(s) to describe (and define) Genoa are economic prosperity and commercial enterprise; in the whole manuscript, no other theme or keyword is given as much space as "wealth" and "riches." Renaissance Genoese understood freedom as the freedom to go into business, to save and to (re)invest capital; such freedom could exist only in a society where institutions—intended as constitutional laws, local codes, offices, magistrates, private banks, and parallel juridical systems—guaranteed property rights and weakened the doge, therefore preventing the creation of a centralized, predatory *signoria* guided by one of the urban factions. The Genoese were pragmatic enough to realize that at times the communal constitution failed to accomplish its delicate mission. The concentration of authority in the hands of divisive leaders and the disrespect for the communal laws could prevent the traditional distribution of power and endanger the creation, the accumulation, and the property of "riches." To solve these periodical crises, the dogeship, which was the symbol of Genoa's independence but just one part of the complex and entangled body called *res publica*, could and indeed had to be amputated. In theory, this meant maintaining the constitutional structure of the medieval commune and replacing the Genoese doge with a foreign governor. Until the previous century, also Florence and other Italian cities had at times found refuge under the formal leadership of a foreign ruler.[36] Yet, in Genoa this medieval tradition continued throughout the fifteenth century and, as we shall see, was still a viable solution in the sixteenth.

SELF-PERCEPTION AND COSMOPOLITANISM

The sources presented so far have shown that the Genoese maintained a traditional form of republicanism—strengthened by the development of a peculiar non-governmental institution like St. George. They did not intend *libertà* as political sovereignty vis-à-vis other polities, and they feared internal *discordia* more than an ordered and financially profitable submission to a foreign ruler. Now, we shall briefly consider two manuscripts whose authors' intention was primarily (if not solely) the description and the celebration of Genoa and its citizens. The Genoese were primarily preoccupied with making money, so they did not write masterpieces of political thought; neither did they indulge in numerous philosophical debates on the best government.[37] So, it is hard to exaggerate the importance of these documents, because they constitute rare intellectual reflections on the late medieval and early modern Genoese identity and reveal how deeply the economic activities of the Genoese shaped their self-perception, defined their common political goals, and strengthened their cosmopolitan spirit.

The first of these documents is a manuscript preserved at the Biblioteca Vaticana, and written at the beginning of the fifteenth century.[38] The anonymous writer addressed his poem to the personification of Genoa:

> Genoa, who they say was founded by Giano,
> Ancient city, powerful at war, famous for her trophies,
> . . . Now you head for the ocean and Gades,
> Where kindly Thetis welcomes the tired horses of the sun;
> Now you like to visit the oriental peoples from whom you bring
> At home riches, jewels and many goods
> That you, so wealthy, send across the western world.[39]

The humanist environment surrounding the composition of the text is clear, with the author lauding the mythological origins of Genoa, and after a few lines introducing other pagan figures (the nymph Thetis, mother of Achilles, and Apollo's horses) to describe the distant lands and seas visited by the Genoese people. Yet, the characteristics of Genoa appear different from those of the other Renaissance city-states; neither the artistic achievements nor the territorial expansion were the pride of this republic, but rather its ceaseless maritime explorations, its thriving commerce and its riches. After comparing the Genoese youth with that of the Roman Empire, the writer exalted the houses, the buildings and the marbles of the Ligurian metropolis. But the most audacious and wonderful of all the urban landmarks was the port:

> We cannot forget the harbor, famous for its lighthouses,
> Full of different kinds of vessels, and of many navigators,
> Which was not built by curved cliffs or by the sea shaping an arch,
> But rather by a massive pier built with vast deed
> And immense expense.[40]

The description of the harbor continues for a few lines, and then the manuscript ends mentioning the "dire *discordia*" affecting the citizens.[41]

In the closing lines of the poem, the broader, non-temporary picture of Genoa emerging from the manuscript follows the themes of trade, wealth, and industriousness. Interestingly enough, the author did not single out any Genoese *condottiero,* doge, or famous merchant; the protagonist of the poem is the average Genoese, or better the whole Genoese people, able to transport riches on its vessels and to build portentous masterpieces such as the spacious, deep, safe harbor. What the author wanted to celebrate was not a basilica, a painting or a statue; he was interested in the architecture of the city only insofar as it reflected the wealth accumulated there by its astute and "handsome" citizen-businessmen (*Nec vero populous ulla formosior urbe est*). More space is dedicated to the port precisely because it represents a pragmatic, commercial infrastructure: the heart of the city's economic life.

The second manuscript that we shall consider is not a poem, but a *laudatio*, written by an anonymous Genoese to celebrate his city, at the request of other cultured compatriots. This oration, composed in the 1430s, was initially meant to be read in public, in front of "an assembly of erudite men."[42] The writer began the text with a lengthy introduction where he humbly stated how inadequate his skills were for the task. Next, he explained that his intention was to describe "the position and the beauty of the city; its riches; and its nobility."[43] The way in which these three themes are treated in the text reveals how the Genoese perceived themselves and judged their achievements. The first part of the *laudatio*, which had to be dedicated to "the position and the beauty of the city," gives indeed little space to the geographic characteristics of the Ligurian region and to the beauty of Genoa's buildings. The Genoese industriousness and the city's port quickly emerge as the true subjects of this part of the oration.

> Why should we not call divine work this wonderful port, built by the hands and sweat of our ancestors? In fact, it was built by an art that was more divine than human, among deep currents and frequent blasts of wind. . . . Why should I talk about the arcades built over it? Why [should I talk] about that beautiful tower linked to it [the port], which shows at night the entrance of the harbor to the ships so that they, shaken by the storm, do not hit the rocks or the nearby beaches? This building is so amazing that it is hard to judge what is higher between its cost and its marvel.[44]

Evidently, to the eyes of a Genoese the most praiseworthy beauty was a useful beauty. The port is once again at the center of a description of Genoa, because it represents the power on sea, the heart of an intercontinental trade, and the place through which exotic riches and foreign travelers enter the city. Its very existence was a proof of Genoa's genius and wealth. And so the writer continued for many lines to praise this wonderful port, which surpassed the harbors of Rhodes and Naples, and had made the city as famous as Athens.[45] Before concluding this first part of the *laudatio*, the author considered the underground tunnel collecting the drain water of the city, the aqueduct bringing clean water to the metropolis, and the villas built by the Genoese on the steep crest of Liguria's mountains.[46] Neither the beauty of Liguria's landscape nor the beauty of artistic achievements found space in the writer's mind and work: what deserved praise were the symbols of an advanced and efficient urbanization, the fruits of the Genoese businessmen's capital and industriousness.

The second part of the *laudatio*, which according to the author's initial intentions had to describe Genoa's "riches," begins with the praise of the Genoese "illustrious citizens," an expression that is not followed by a list of famous names, but rather by a description of the economic activities through which the Genoese had accumulated their exceptional wealth. This means that the Genoese did not celebrate their wealth per se, but rather the commercial enterprises and the colonial network that were the true origin of their capital. While a Renaissance Florentine would have probably named painters and writers among his "illustrious" fellow citizens, the author of this text avoided mentioning the name of any individual Genoese; instead, he focused his attention on the number of Genoese who had invested their money and their lives in trade and business.

> It is impossible to go to a country so hidden or to a region so far away that you would not find many Genoese *merchants* there. In fact, what island, within or without this world, what land on the sea is lacking a Genoese? Go among the oriental or the occidental peoples, those who inhabit the north and those in the south, and you will see that all corners are filled of and swarming with men from our city, like the richest fountain. And if all those powerful and famous colonies, such as Bonifacio, Pera, Caffa and Chio were all to be assembled together, which walls could ever contain so many citizens? . . . although many colonists have left [Genoa], although such a great number of citizens are in business around the world, and although some terrible *discordia* has dispersed a great number of them, there is no nearby city that surpasses it [Genoa] for number of citizens.[47]

The Genoese living in the colonies and those "dispersed" around the world were thus still part of the Genoese community and actually deserved to have much space dedicated to them in this *laudatio*. This is not a mistake or a long digression in the text; the anonymous author revealed here the most precious among all of Genoa's "riches." Having so many merchants in so many city-ports, from Corsica to the Black Sea, from the northern seas to the southern lands was indeed what made Genoa both unique and wealthy. These documents obviously challenge the idea that civic space and social body were understood in the same way across central and northern Italy. In particular, the recent thesis proposed by Fabrizio Ricciardelli, who stresses the importance of the "town square"[48] and then goes as far as to say that in the Italian city-states "the circle of walls marks the boundary between order and chaos, between organised space and savage nature, between good and bad,"[49] does not work in the case of Genoa. The Genoese were not particularly fond of any "town square" simply because they were not interested in political participation nearly as much as in economic prosperity. This is why they celebrated their port, which was their door to the world. The model citizen for a Genoese was not a man who had been born and raised in Liguria, and whose horizon was limited by the city walls; on the contrary, the author of this manuscript placed at the center of a *laudatio* of Genoa those Genoese who spent a great part of their lives far from the Ligurian (and Italian) shores. And the Genoese merchants in distant lands continued to organize their communities according to pragmatic and profitable principles of inclusion, so that sellers and buyers could freely enter the markets opened by the Genoese. Interestingly enough, the cultural entanglement and the cosmopolitan environment resulting from this mind-set were not a cause of embarrassment for our writer, but rather proofs of the peaceful, civilizing, and stable economic expansion achieved by the Genoese:

> It is a witness to the vastness of its [Genoa's] dominion the city of Pera, well-known among the famous and very bellicose peoples of Thrace, which was bettered by the industriousness and work of our ancestors . . . It is preeminent witness and best example of it that densely populated city on the Scythian shore, which is called Caffa, where, because there is a multitude not only of Latin but also of Greeks, Armenians, Jews and other peoples of every race, it is surely difficult to judge which one among its many riches should be the first to be praised: perhaps the diversity of languages and dialects, or the variety of cults and religions, or the unheard-of multitude of citizens, or the beauty and the fame of the city.[50]

The last section of the manuscript is dedicated to the "nobility" of the Genoese people, and once again the economic culture of his fellow citizens is at the center of the author's reflection.

> Now consider with me, I beg you, oh citizens, what is the nobility or magnificence of the Genoese . . . I believe to be the highest their intelligence in acting and in treating the things of this world, the expertise in trading and sailing, the art of fighting and the strength especially in maritime wars.[51]

"Treating the things of this world," "trading and sailing." This is how the Genoese perceived themselves—as economic actors and shrewd businessmen. There is no mention of indispensable, uniquely Genoese political institutions; there is no rhetorical laud dedicated to the history of the republic.[52] The colonies are celebrated as places of encounter, entrepreneurship, and commercial success. This was the culture underpinning the reforms and the institutional change documented in the previous chapter. If the Genoese had a civic philosophy, its objective was to foster the conditions that allowed them to "be Genoese": anti-tyrannical laws and security of property rights. Not by chance, as the author continued to praise the Genoese "nobility," the theme of private wealth resurfaced repeatedly in the *laudatio*.

> In fact, the reputation of our people is so widespread that those who go to trade in foreign lands do so being transported by Genoese ships, and doing so they travel so safely, away from winds and storms, that it is as if they were sailing inside a harbor. By these abilities and this activity, we accumulated so many riches that the fortunes of some of our citizens equal those of kings.[53]

And while the pride of many Renaissance city-states was their rule over weaker neighbors and the territorial dominion expanded through the military exploits of *signori* and *condottieri*, the Genoese were deliberately refraining from building a large territorial entity: "What should I say then about the modesty of the [Genoese] citizens? It is well-known that in every aspect of life the Genoese nation has been moderate and more careful than the other Italian peoples, as it respects the foreign territories and dominion."[54]

The unmistakably Genoese spirit of these words appears distinctly if we contextualize them in the historical landscape of fifteenth-century Italy. A comparison with the Republic of Venice may be once again opportune. Since the 1380s, the Venetians increasingly focused their energies on a series of terrestrial military initiatives in Northern Italy, which transformed their republic into a large mainland entity, while providing the patricians with hundreds of new military posts and public offices.[55] Recent research by Sandra Toffolo has juxtaposed Venice's territorial expansion with the works of contemporary Venetian writers, who variously described, conceptualized, and justified the new mainland state. For instance, Jacopo d'Albizzotto Guidi (b. 1377), in his work *El sommo della condizione di Vinegia*, described in these unapologetic terms the conquest of Padua:

> Of the city of Padua and of the Padovano
> they [the Venetians] have acquired the land
> with their strength and with swords in their hands.
> And if my mind is not mistaken here,
> there are more strong castles, with more territory,
> which they have won by the force of war.[56]

Toffolo suggests that, even when Venetian authors like Guidi later downplayed the role of violence and stressed the benefits of Venice's expansionism, they did it not so much because of a genuine uneasiness felt towards state-led military endeavors as because of the eerie aura that Venice had started to acquire in the eyes of other Italians. In fact,

> in the early phases of expansionism Venetians really did not see a problem in bluntly referring to violent acquisitions of territory. Only later in the century, when foreign hostility towards Venice was growing, did it become clear that it was probably safer to stress the peacefulness and beneficial influence of current Venetian rule, rather than its violent beginnings.[57]

Indeed, it would have been difficult for fifteenth-century Venetians to repudiate their long tradition of state militarism in the Mediterranean and in Italy. As put by Mallett and Hale, "if the need for a permanent military commitment emerged very slowly on the Italian mainland, such a commitment was apparent much earlier in the empire overseas."[58]

CONCLUSION

In order to better understand the Genoese definition of *libertà* and Genoa's intellectualization of its history and identity, this chapter has analyzed manuscripts that show how the Genoese conceptualized (and reacted to) periods of crisis. One of the most important findings is that Genoa's idea of *libertà* did not necessarily entail formal political independence. I then presented some rare celebratory documents that open a window on the way in which the Genoese perceived themselves and celebrated their city. The entrepreneurial, business-oriented, and mercantile mindset of the Genoese is confirmed by the economic themes that they used to define their identity. In particular, the Genoese portrayed themselves evoking economic images and praised their commercial colonies as much as (or even more than) their metropolis. What made a Genoese "a Genoese" was not his blood, his ancestors or his residence, but rather his business activities, his "simultaneity of careers," his relation with the sea, and, more in general, his talent for accumulating wealth. Arguably, this economic culture was one of the reasons behind Genoa's peculiar form of self-government and republicanism. The fact that a Genoese's objectives were accomplished usually away from home, often in foreign territories, and always in city-ports connecting numerous markets, rendered the Genoese less sensitive to the theme of independence/sovereignty and more fond of security in the exchange of goods and capital. In this context, the meaning of *libertà* coincided with prosperity and economic freedom. The resilience of this intellectual and political framework eventually differentiated Genoa's republicanism from that of other late medieval and Renaissance states—including the other famous maritime republic, Venice—and is pivotal in order to explain the origins of the Hispanic-Genoese alliance.

NOTES

1. On the organization given by St. George to the colonies, including the regular replacement of consuls and castellans in Caffa, Soldaia (Sudak) and Cembalo (Balaklava), see the documents collected in Vigna (ed.), "Codice diplomatico," v. VI.

2. A few decades later, the epic scene was told with these melancholic words by the Venetian Marco Sabellico: "Having shown the Imperial insignias, so that being recognised he would not have been taken as prisoner, with the naked sword he impetuously entered the Turk multitude. And courageously fighting, the Prince worth of eternal glory died at the hand of the enemies. And dying, he added his body to the ruin of the other Greek Emperors." "Onde disposte l'insigne d'Imperatore, accioche essendo conosciuto non fosse fatto prigione, con la spada nuda entro impetuosamente nella moltitudine de Turchi. Et fortemente combattendo il Principe degno di eterna memoria per man de nimici mori. Et morendo aggiunse il suo corpo con la ruina de gli altri Imperadori Greci." Sabellico, *Historie Vinitiane*, 238.

3. "los griegos están del todo desfechos, fasta aquí non avía otra cosa enfiesta si non Constantínopla. . . . ¡Bien an fecho la vengança de Troya los turcos! que áun ante que yo viniese e Constantinopla fuese tomada, tan subiectos estavan como agora." Pero Tafur, *Andanças é viajes de Pero Tafur por diversas partes del mundo avidos: 1435–1439* (Madrid: Miguel Ginesta, 1874), 167–68.

4. For a history of the Empire of Trebizond and of its relations with the Italian merchants, see Sergej Pavlovic Karpov, *L'Impero di Trebisonda, Venezia, Genova e Roma: 1204–1461* (Roma: Il Veltro, 1986). In English, the best monograph on Trebizond remains William Miller, *Trebizond: The Last Greek Empire* (Amsterdam: Hakkert, 1968), which was originally published in 1926 (New York: Macmillan).

5. Archivio di Stato di Genova, *Manoscritti*, n. 707. I found this volume among the untitled manuscripts, where it is listed as *miscellanea Pallavicini*.

6. "Li Genovesi erano fra loro in discordia in Caffa—Il Gran turco li mando a domandare alcuni garzoni schiavi ch'erano fugiti di Trabisonda e tanto più credeva haverli, quanto ch'il Capitano de Campagna delli Tartari chiamato Eminec s'era fatto suo tributano con promissa d'esserli favorevole in ogni impresa, il quale trattato e convegno havuto notitia li Genovesi, et essendosi partito il mandato dal Turco senza risolutione delli garzoni ricercati, procurarono d'escusarsi con ogni loro potere. Et in questo mentre nacque fra loro odio, e divisione, perche parte di essi Genovesi favorivano Eminec, e parte erano suoi contrari e per scacciarlo de Campagna fecero venire a Caffa l'Imperatore de Tartari, facendoli condur seco il d'Eminec con intintione d'avenenarlo. Et essendosi apparecchiati per darcilo gli altri Genovesi ch'erano in suo favor l'avisorno, e lui non volsi magnare ne bevere cosa alcuna. E sibene era in potir de Genovesi, li quali lo potivano far morire essendo in casa loro con tutto ciò la discordia ch'era fra loro fu di tanta importanza che fra loro non si potiron accordare, dubitando d'alcun male che li potesse intervenire." Ibid., ms. 3, 1–2.

7. "As long as the Tartars maintain the economic and political organization of the first period, with nomadic camps rather than towns, with cloths and fabrics used instead of coins for bartering, they have no reason to impede the commercial activity of the Crimean ports, which function as their windows on the world." "Finchè i Tartari conservano l'organizzazione economica e politica dei primi tempi, con accampamenti mobili in luogo di città, con impiego di stoffe o di telerie in luogo di moneta per gli scambi, non hanno alcun motivo di ostacolare l'attività commerciale dei porti della Crimea, che sono come le loro finestre sul mondo." Lopez, *Storia delle colonie genovesi*, 297.

8. "The city [Caffa] is large, as large as Seville, or larger, with about twice as many inhabitants, Christians and Catholics as well as Greeks, and all the nations of the world. They say that the Emperor of Tartary would have conquered and destroyed it many times, but the lords and common people of the surrounding territories would not consent to it, because they use the place for their evil doings and thefts, and their great wickedness, such as father selling son, and brother selling brother. . . . In this city they sell more slaves, both male and female, than anywhere else in the world, and the Sultan of Babylonia has his agents here." "La çibdat es grande, tan maña ó mayor que Sevilla, é de gente çerca de dos tanto, ansí de xpianos católicos como de griegos é todas la naçiones del mundo. Dizen quel Emperador tártaro la avríe alguna

vez tomada ó desfecha, salvo que los señores é las gentes comunes de las tierras veçinas non gelo consienten, porque en ella é con ella obran de sus maldades é de sus furtos, é grandes travesuras que fazen, ansí como vender padre á fijo ó hermano á hermano. . . . Aquí se venden mas esclavos é esclavas que en todo lo otro que queda del mundo, é aquí tiene el soldan de Babylonia sus factores." Tafur, *Andanças é viajes*, 161–62.

9. Some interesting letters written by Florentine merchants who described the economic situation in Pera and Caffa during the 1390s have been published in *Atti della Società Ligure di Storia Patria, nuova serie*, volume XI, 2 (Genoa: SLSP, 1971), 345–59.

10. Ibid., ms. 3, 2–3.

11. "Onde di novo l'Imperatore torno a Caffa, e procuro di deponere suo fratello, e Eminec suo Capitano. Il che havia ottinuto se li Genovesi che governavano fra loro si fussero accordati . . . in questo disparere fu si che giunse l'Armata del Turco a Cafa, a l'ultimo di Marzo." Ibid., ms. 3, 3.

12. The conjunction used in the document is "fusi che," a Genoese expression that could be literally translated "so it happened that." In my translation, I decided to use the words "as a consequence." At any rate, the connection drawn by the writer between the internal strife in Caffa and the arrival of the Turks is certain.

13. Ibid., ms. 3, 5. This fact obviously undermines the previous argument that the Turk armada came "as a consequence" of the Genoese factional divisions; yet the aim of this chapter is not to meticulously establish what happened or to furnish a political history of fifteenth-century Caffa. Instead, this manuscript is being analyzed here because it indirectly helps us to understand the intellectual framework of its author(s). At any rate, another contemporary manuscript, a letter written by a Tuscan merchant resident in Caffa and taken as prisoner by the Turks, confirms the outline of events recounted in the Genoese document and concurs in blaming the fate of Caffa on internal factionalism. This missive was published in Amedeo Vigna, "Codice diplomatico delle colonie tauro-liguri durante la signoria dell'Ufficio di S. Giorgio," in Atti della Società Ligure di Storia Patria, volume VII, 2 (Genova: Tipografia del R.I. de'Sordo-muti, 1879), 239–46.

14. "furono eletti quattro ambasciatori della Terra, li quali andorno dal Generale dell'Armata nominato Amat Bassa furono gli Ambasciatori: ser Giuliano dal Fusto, ser Battista d'Allegro, ser Sisto Servicio, e ser Gregorio Rosso, e dopo il negotiato col Bassa hebbino gratia d'esser liberi, con tutti della lor corti, e facolta con altre sette famiglie. Il nostro diedero da intendere che s'erano accordati con che fussero salve le persone, e la robba, e subito furono poste alle porte l'Insegne del Turco et alle muraglie." Ibid., ms. 3, 6–7.

15. The story of the ambassadors' betrayal is confirmed in a letter written by the Tuscan merchant. Vigna, "Codice diplomatico," 239–46.

16. "Gli Ambasciatori non volsero restar ne la Citta con alquanti altri, e furono mandati con un naviglio con le mogli e figlioli e facolta a Costantinopoli ove giunti morirno molti di peste." Ibid., ms. 3, 8.

17. "Ma quelle pover famiglie che restorno schiave a Cafa, nel intrar li Turchi dentro furono presi, e posti alla Catina, e poste a sacco le loro facolta . . . le gridi di essi, e delle donne che si battivano le guance andavano al cielo con pianti incredibili da far compassione a morti, non che a vivi." Ibid.

18. Tacitus's sentence is: "Pompei Crassique potentia cito in Caesarem, Lepidi atque Antonii arma in Augustum cessere, qui cuncta discordiis civilibus fessa nomine principis sub imperium accepit." Cornelius Tacitus, *Annals*, book 1, chapter 1.

19. "La più bella occasione, e la più opportuna, che possa avvenire ad uno, il quale dissegna di impadronirsi con nome di Principe della sua istissa patria di già vissuta molti anni in libertà, e quando nella istissa patria per qualche corso di tempo si sono conservate e mantenute Guerre e discordie civili." Archivio di Stato di Genova, *Manoscritti*, n. 707, ms. 3, 11.

20. "quando per qualsivoglia occasione sara divisa la Citta in fattioni e parti all'hora sara tempo molto opportuno nel quale egli si cavi la mascara." Ibid., ms. 3, 12.

21. "come le navi agitate dalle procelle e sgomentati dai perigoli del Mare, hanno per gran merce il potersi ricoverare in quei porti, i quali non essendo astretti dalla necessita havribbono rifiutati e schifati come di huomini nimici e diffidenti, e si come alcuni Ucelli anco di quelli ch'hanno piu paura dell'Uccellatori, ad ogni modo quando sono cacciati, o dal sparviere, o dal

falchetto, o da altri uccelli rapaci hanno per gran ventura l'andarsi a salvare in fino dentro al seno istisso del cacciatore cosi quelle istisse Citta le quali in stato tranquilli, e pacifico niente havevano piu odioso che il nome di Principe quando poi si trovano per lungo tempo travagliate da armi domestiche, e civili senza speranza di vicino amico, facilissima cosa é che quasi in un porto in seno sicurissimo vadino volentieri a riporsi sotto l'imperio di chi discretamente si fa loro in contro."

22. For a history of the political situation in Genoa during these years, see Giovanna Petti Balbi, "Tra dogato e principato: il Tre e Quattrocento," in *Storia di Genova: Mediterraneo Europa Atlantico*, ed. Dino Puncuch (Genova: SLSP, 2003), 233–324.

23. "che per noy sea ben arrembarse de segnor, lo qua possa reintegrar questa citae et tegnerne in cadello, et mantegnei la libertao de questa citae, a zo che ella no vegna in ruynna per li discordii li quay sum inter li Zenoeyxi." *Les origines de la domination française à Gênes, 1392–1402*, ed. Eugène Jarry (Paris: Picard, 1896), appendix, document x.

24. "dar forma de governo . . . e mantegney la nostra libertae senza aminiculo de alcum segnor." Ibid.

25. Shaw, "Concepts of *Libertà* in Renaissance Genoa," 181–82.

26. "E l'anno di mille quattrocento sessanta quattro, del mese di febbraro sendo la città sotto il Ducato di Paolo Fregoso, il Duca di Milano mandò a pigliare la possessione di Savona . . . e in Genova i due anni passati furono gran discordie fra i Fregosi insieme; e la città aveva cambiato molte volte Rettori ossia Magistrati insino a tanto che pervenne in mano dell'Arcivescovo Fregoso, come abbiamo detto di sopra; il quale poichè si vide costituito in questa potenza sopra il popolo genovese insieme con Obietto di Flisco, e con gli altri fautori, messa da canto ogni vergogna, convertirono la pubblica libertà in tirannia: molti si vendicavano delle ricevute ingiurie dei tempi passati, e molestavano quelli che avevano in odio; i Magistrati della città non erano onorati, e alla virtù non si trovava luogo: ogni sedizioso e ogni temerario era onorato e apprezzato; i malefici e le scelerità non erano punite, l'innocenza degli uomini da bene non era secura tra tanti ribaldi; e tutto si faceva alla sfrenata volontà di Paolo e di Obietto, e ogni cosa divina come umana era in confusione, tal che tutti gli uomini da bene si dolevano di questo tempo, e piangevano le comuni miserie." Agostino Giustiniani, *Annali della Repubblica di Genova* (Genova: Canepa, 1854), v. II, 439–40.

27. "Questo è quel calamitoso tempo nel quale i luoghi di S. Giorgio non valevano oltre venti tre lire, e una gran parte dei cittadini uomini da bene dell'una e dell'altra fazione s'erano partiti dalla città, e ridotti in qualche luoghi che stimavano securi, e molti nobili erano andati a Savona, e pregavano il Duca Francesco che volesse attendere a liberare la città di Genova dal tirannico giuoco dei Fregosi." Ibid., 440.

28. On Francesco Sforza and his policies, an important source is Giovanni Simonetta, *Le memorabili e magnanime imprese di Francesco Sforza* (Rubbettino, 2009). Among the literature treating the Sforza dynasty, see Georges Peyronnet, *Il Ducato di Milano sotto Francesco Sforza, 1450–1466* (Firenze: Olschki, 1958); and the conference publication Gli Sforza a Milano e in Lombardia e i loro rapporti con gli Stati italiani ed europei (1450–1535) (Milan: Cisalpino-Goliardica, 1982).

29. Emphasis added. "per diuina prouidentia a la quale semper hauemo gratia, il dominio de questa inclita cita de voluntade de li citadini est transferto in lo illustrissimo et potentissimo signore duca di Milano, il quale ha tuti li nostri priuilegij non solum confirmato sed etiam augmentato. A quello tenda al bene de queste compere ha dimostrato grande affectione. Similiter in tuto quello concerne il bene de questa citate pacifico et utilitate de li citadini ha dimostrato singulare amore, adeo che pare la citate et li citadini prhendere grande recreatione, et tale che già se adrissan a fabricare de naue et fare quello est de multi trafichi et auiamenti. si che annuente deo se m andera per lo mundo li genueisi hauere reintegrato le cosse sue." The letter is preserved at the Archivio di Stato di Genova, among the *Missive Off. Caffe*, 1464–1475, folio 11 v. It was also published in Vigna (ed.), "Codice diplomatico," v. VII, 1, 298–99.

30. Archivio di Stato di Milano, *Potenze Estere (Missive)*, 1464–1465, ms. 67, c. 34–r. 36.

31. "Hai quanto lieta soto tale Signore/Vissi bon tempo con gran uigoria,/Et poi con melenconia/Vintioto anni facta viduella!" Ibid.

32. "Fregosi, adorni, montaldi e casa guardia/Di mia persona chan soto il suo desio/Ma spero pur in dio/Che da loro mane sarò liberata." Ibid.

33. "Pensa un pocho, sei ti piace hormai,/Alla mia dote meza rampinata;/Et guarda se donna nata/Più richa di me saria fra chripstiani." Ibid.

34. "Qual sposa dii mondo tante bone nave/Dare ti po quante farò io,/Se tu al mio desio/Pur condesendi, como mostri in vista?" Ibid.

35. "Contare ni scrivere io ti poria,/Quante castelle et terre di marina/Ho perso, haime meschina,/Sol perchè inferma sono cotanto tempo.—Quando ci penso, mi pare uno spavento/Le tante nave con richeze grande,/Quale da molte bande/Robate mi son state per lo mare. . . . De richa che io era sono facta un orto,/Doue ciascun uene per insalata." Ibid.

36. Ricciardelli, *The Myth of Republicanism*, 27.

37. As rightly observed by Riccardo Ferrante, "it has to be underlined how in Genoa little is written about politics, or—for example—about law. Between the Middle Ages and the Modern era the political literature is in fact limited to a small number of authors, few of whom possess broad theoretical perspectives." "va innanzi tutto sottolineato come a Genova si scriva molto poco di politica, come—ad esempio—si scrive molto poco di diritto. Tra Medioevo ed età moderna la letteratura politica si limita infatti a un numero ristretto di autori, pochi dei quali con prospettive teoriche di ampio respiro." Ferrante, "Legge e Repubblica," 238.

38. Biblioteca Vaticana, *Reginensi latini*, ms 1393, cc. 115 v.–116 v. This document has been published in *Contribuzioni alla storia di Genova specialmente nella poesia* (Genova: ASLSP, 1888), 657–60.

39. "Ianva, quam perhibent Iano condente locatam,/Urbs antiqua, potens armis, preclara tropheis, . . . Nunc Oceanus Gadesque petuntur,/Defessos ubi Solis equos Thetis hospita condit;/Nunc libet Eoas gentes invisere, gazam/Inde domum multas gemmas mercesque referre,/Occiduum, locuples, que totum mittes in orbem." Ibid., 657–58.

40. "Non portum transire decet farisque celebrem/Navigio omni, crebro et vectore refertum,/Quem non curvati scopuli aut sinuatus in arcum/Tam pontus statuit moles quam actà profundo/Et sumptu immense." Ibid., 658.

41. Ibid., 659.

42. Biblioteca Civica Berio di Genova, ms. 1.3.14, cc. 1v-12r.

43. "Dicam primum de situ et ornatu urbis, secundo de opibus, postremo de nobilitate." Ibid.; the word "nobility" (*nobiltà*), here has to be intended as fame, reputation.

44. "Quid nobilis ille portus, maiorum nostrum manu atque opera factus, nonne divinum opus merito appellabimus? Est enim inter altissima freta et crebris ventorum flatibus facile tumentia, divino verius quam humano artificio, iactus. . . . Quid referam porticus superstructas? Quid turrim illam ornatissimam coniunctam ad ostendendum portus ingressum navibus noctu, ne tempestate compulse in saxa incidant aut in vicinia littora? Est sane eius generis ec moles, ut iudicatu difficile sit utrum maioris sit admirationis an sumptus." Ibid. For a history of Genoa's port, see Francesco Podestà, *Il porto di Genova: dalle origini fino alla caduta della repubblica Genovese* (Genova: Spiotti, 1913). See also Natale Malnate, *Della storia del porto di Genova dalle origini all'anno 1892* (Genova: Istituto sordo-muti, 1892).

45. Biblioteca Civica Berio di Genova, ms. 1.3.14, cc. 1v-12r.

46. Ibid. On the history of Genoa's aqueduct, see Francesco Podestà, *L'acquedotto di Genova: 1071–1879* (Genova: Istituto sordo-muti, 1879).

47. Emphasis added. "Licet necuique ullas tam abditas terras comeare, licet ullas tam longiquas abire regions, quin quoque te contuleris, ibi plurimos Genuenses negociantes reperias. Que nam insula vel intra vel extra orbem terrarum iacet, que maritima regio est Genuensi homine vacua? Pete orientales, pete occidentals populous, pete ad austrum, pete ad Arcton habitantes, omnes profecto angulos nostris hominibus redundare et, quasi uberrimum fontem, scatere perspicies. Quid si congregentur atque iterum unum in corpus redigantur potentes ille ac preclare colonie, Bonifacium, inquam, Pera, Caffa et Chios, que tunc latitudo menium capereid civium poterit? . . . quamvis tot colonie hinc deducte fuerint, tam ingens preterea civium numerusper terrarum orbe passim negocietur, tam multos et fatalis quedam dissensio disiecerit, a nulla tantum finitiarum urbium, prestantissimorum civium numero, vincitur." Biblioteca Civica Berio di Genova, ms. 1.3.14, cc. 1v-12r.

48. Ricciardelli, *The Myth of Republicanism*, 75.

49. Ricciardelli, *The Myth of Republicanism*, 108.

50. "Est testis etiam lati dominii Pera urbs, celebres inter illustrissimos et bellacissimos Tracie populos, maiorum nostrorum manibus atque opera adaucta . . . Testis est locuplex et exemplum omnium maximum urbs illa popolasissima in ora Scythica, quam Caffa appellamus, in quam, cum non ex Latinis modo, verum et ex Grecis, Armeniis, Iudeis et omnis pene generis gentibus conventum sit, difficile sane est iudicare quid potissimum, ex omnibus eius ornamentis, sibi laude ante omnia vindicet: an linguarum idiomatisque diversitas, an cultum regionumque varietas, an civium inaudita frequentia aut oppidi pulchritudo atque auctoritas." Ibid.

51. "Nunc que civium prestantia et splendor sit animadvertite, queso, mecum accuratius . . . Iudicio est summa in agendis tractandisque rebus humanis prudentia, navigandi negociandique scientia, bellandi ars ac fortitudo maritimis presertim bellis insignis." Ibid.

52. The Tuscan Enea Silvio Piccolomini (later Pope Pius II), who visited Genoa in 1432, wrote: "Not much interested in scientific inquiry, they [the Genoese] study grammar only as much as it is strictly necessary and do not love the other studies; but when they smell opportunity of commerce, they immediately come forward." "Scientie parum cupidi, grammaticam ad necessitatem student, cetera studiorum genera parvi faciunt; quando quidem de emptione seu venditione respirant, procantur omnes." Enea Silvio Piccolomini, "Description of Genoa," published in *Der Briefwechsel des Eneas Silvius Piccolomini*, ed. Rudolf Wolkan, *Fontes rerum austriacarum* (1909) LXI, letter 6.

53. "Ea sane opinio de gente nostra ubique diffusa est ut qui mercandi gratia alienas transadeunt, Genuensium navigio invecti, non secus quam si portu navigarent, ventorum ac pelagi securi, per alta deferantur. Hisce artibus, hac industria,ad eum divitiarum cumulum ventum est ut iam quorundam, civium fortune civilem modum superent ac regulorum opes exequent." Biblioteca Civica Berio di Genova, ms. 1.3.14, cc. 1v–12r.

54. "Quid autem loquar de huius civitatis modestia? Est sane id vulgatissimum ut per omnes vite partes Genuensem populum esse ante omnes Italicas nationes moderatum ac polliticum, ab alieno agro imperioque absinentissimum." Ibid.

55. See chapter 1.

56. Jacopo d'Albizzotto Guidi, quoted in Sandra Toffolo, *Depicting the City, Depicting the State. Fifteenth-Century Representations of Venice and the Venetian Terraferma* (PhD diss., European University Institute, 2013), 186.

57. Toffolo, *Depicting the City, Depicting the State*, 203. See also idem, "Constructing a Mainland State in Literature: Perceptions of Venice and its *Terraferma* in Marin Sanudo's Geographical Descriptions," *Renaissance and Reformation* 37 (2014): 5–30.

58. Mallet and Hale, *The Military Organization*, 9.

Part II

Spain's "Diabolical" Friends

Chapter Four

Ferdinand the Catholic's Perception of the Genoese and of Their Role in His Economic Policy

This chapter and chapter 5 trace the political and diplomatic origins of the Hispanic-Genoese system. Relations between Genoa and the Spanish kingdoms in the late Middle Ages and the early modern period were complex and contradictory. The story of how Ligurian merchants and bankers eventually became involved in the Habsburg military strategy and even in Spain's overseas colonies can be told in many different ways. Yet what seems important to illustrate here is, on the one hand, the perception of Genoese economic actors in the mind of Ferdinand the Catholic (1452–1516), and, on the other, the role subsequently played by Genoa within the Habsburg Empire during the reign of Charles V (1500–1558). Through the study of sources that have thus far been overlooked by the scholarship on this subject, this chapter shows Ferdinand's consistent efforts to protect the Genoese trading in his kingdoms. Chapter 5 will then offer an interpretation and contextualization of Genoa's resilient republican tradition as well as an explanation of the role played by private arms in Genoa, thereby helping us to understand the causes and consequences of Charles V's alliance with the Ligurian city-state.

THE GENOESE MOVEMENT EAST-WEST AND THE ARAGONESE ENIGMA

Fifteenth-century Genoese citizens understood *libertà* as the absence of a local dynasty and the lack of obstacles in the path to private enterprise and wealth creation. Genoa's industrious sons were celebrated in the description of the distant cities that had been enriched by the arrival of this dynamic, anonymous literary hero: the Genoese businessman. The colonies and the port were places of encounter and enrichment, the symbols of economic entanglement with many peoples in a cosmopolitan merchant network. This view did not crystallize in a mannered Renaissance court. In fact, Genoa's humanism was singularly pragmatic and proudly unsophisticated. From time immemorial, boys moving from the mountainous countryside of Liguria to the metropolis directed their first, amazed glance to the port. In the early 1460s, a young lad named Cristoforo, whose family was of modest means but whose destiny was to be fateful, had also admired this vibrant place, where foreign travelers, golden grain, colorful cloths, and fragrant spices continuously arrived.[1] The harbor was to the Genoese the best symbol of their civilization, a concentrate of human action, and the space where citizens visibly enjoyed *libertà*, taking part in the intercontinental system of trade and capital market.

The Genoese believed that freedom—especially in the economic sphere—is always freedom to act. However, as men and women engage in increasingly complex economic activities, their freedom, which is to say their action, needs to be met by a non-hostile economic environment and, in ultimate analysis, by the collaboration of other economic actors.[2] This problem is not simple, and it cannot be dismissed with the assumption that where capital, supply, and demand are available, market expansion can easily take place. As we have seen, in Southern England these three components were present, and yet the Genoese investors, notwithstanding the establishment of an important colony in Southampton, were eventually stopped by legislative, social, and political obstacles.[3] The English king was unable to guarantee the rule of law, and this meant that the amount of freedom—the action allowed—was not enough.[4] The historical movement, East-West (a movement of businesses and capital), was nonetheless successful, because of that pivotal characteristic of the Genoese economic culture, diversification of investment, which was possible precisely thanks to the lack of a state-run colonial policy.[5] While some Genoese families were trying to open the English market, others were moving their interests to Rome, Sicily, Northwestern Africa, Portugal, and Spain.[6] That the Genoese were successful in penetrating the Spanish markets is a well-known fact.[7] Even before the crisis of the Catalan commercial empire, the Genoese anticipated their Aragonese rivals and helped the Castilian economy to develop, drawing it into the intercontinental system of trade and bringing in fresh capital (as well as an unquantifiable and yet crucial business experience).[8] The role of the Genoese in Castile is especially important given the feudalist and militaristic culture of this region.[9] However, the Genoese became progressively involved also in the city-ports of their most important economic rivals and political enemies in the Western Mediterranean, the Aragonese.

The Crown of Aragon, composed by three independent entities (Catalonia, Valencia, and the Kingdom of Aragon), had built an impressive overseas empire, stretching from Sardinia to Greece.[10] The clash with Genoa had been the unavoidable consequence of conflicting interests, but by the half of the fifteenth century the economic crisis afflicting Catalonia had become structural, while the Genoese had won the battle for the commercial and financial (though not territorial) predominance in the Western Mediterranean. Moreover, the Genoese had solid trading colonies in Portugal, Castile, and Sicily (that had become part of the Aragonese possessions). These were important considerations at a time when the idea of an alliance with Castile was taking shape and Sicily's need to sell grain was as serious as Genoa's need to import (and partly re-export) it. In sum, the economic and the political situation was propitious (at least, more propitious than it had been in the past centuries) for the establishment of stable economic relations between the Genoese merchant community and the Crown of Aragon. But widespread piracy as well as complex political and diplomatic problems rendered the alliance arduous.[11] In this context, the study of some diplomatic documents preserved in the Archive of the Crown of Aragon can shed some light on the economic policy of Ferdinand the Catholic with regard to the Western Mediterranean and, more specifically, to the Genoese commercial fleet.[12] This chapter will thus focus on Ferdinand's opinion on the Genoese, on his attitude towards their businesses in his territories, and on the possibility of discerning any similarity or compatibility between Ferdinand's economic vision and the Genoese idea of *libertà*.

When Ferdinand succeeded his father John on the throne of Aragon in 1479, the peace between his Spanish domains and the Republic of Genoa was as fragile as ever. The truce of 1478 had been the result of long negotiations and it was constantly threatened by acts of piracy committed by both Catalan and Ligurian corsairs.[13] One could argue that piracy is mainly an economic phenomenon; but in this case we cannot underestimate its political and contingent causes. During the Catalonian Civil War (1462–1472), the rebels besieged in Barcelona were depending on food supplies bought from Genoa and often transported by Genoese vessels; yet, as a consequence of an agreement between John II and the Genoese doge, Ligurian ships were officially forbidden to help Barcelona. So, after the fall of the rebellious city in 1472, many Catalans had rancorous feelings towards the Ligurian merchants (who had in practice been forced by a political pact to starve Barcelona); unsurprisingly, the Catalans intensified their raids against Genoese merchants in the Aragonese ports across the Western Mediterranean—with the tacit consent of John, who did not need the Genoese anymore. These events, in turn, provoked the reaction of Genoa's communal government, which hired private ships for the destruction of Catalonian warships and sometimes issued patents allowing Genoese merchants to rob Aragonese vessels.[14] Admittedly, this rivalry's roots can be traced back to a historical clash of economic interests; during the fourteenth century, Aragon had even formed an anti-Genoese alliance with the distant Venice; and a century later, in 1466, Genoa had taken the exceptional decision to arm a public fleet with which to attack Barcelona.[15] But, by the first half of the fifteenth century, the Spanish territories of the Crown of Aragon were experiencing a profound economic and social crisis; in particular, the Catalonian elite, which since the series of bank failures in the 1380s had ceased to compete with the Genoese in the capital market, was now also withdrawing investments from the Aragonese empire and could not compete with the Genoese private fleet anymore. The entrepreneurial spirit of the Aragonese merchants was suffering from the same fate as the Venetian one, and capital was progressively moved from commercial enterprises to rental investments. This situation was worsened by a demographic crisis that interested the whole continent, but was particularly profound in Catalonia and Aragon; Barcelona, which in 1340 had a population of about 50,000, by 1497 had only 28,500 inhabitants.[16] At this point, for the first time in almost three centuries, economic interests would have favored a fruitful trading and financial relationship between Aragon and Genoa, but political resentments and the problem of lawlessness on the sea seemed to prevent the establishment of a stable peace in the West Mediterranean region.

On September 26, 1482, Ferdinand wrote a letter to the political actor who had been the main architect of the 1478 truce, the king of Naples Ferdinand I (also called Ferrante).[17] In this letter, the king of Aragon communicated to his cousin the decision to scrap the truce with Genoa, lamenting the criminal actions of Genoese pirates against Aragonese subjects and openly accusing the Italian city-state of protecting and supporting these corsairs:

> Your Highness will surely remember the truce that, thanks to the intercession given by you and the Most Serene queen, our dear and much loved sister, like daughter, your wife, we concluded and signed with the community of Genoa, and with how much integrity and observance we have so far kept our promise, while on the other hand they have done so really badly and have used violence; that Polo Baptista, corsair, with the knowledge, help and consent of the aforementioned community, has given and caused, during the said truce, much damage to many of our subjects and vassals.[18]

The letter goes on to declare the truce broken and all the licenses released to Genoese merchants null. The tone of the document is severe, and apparently Ferdinand did not want to leave any space for a diplomatic solution or reconciliation with Genoa. However, it is important to read this source as a political statement, one where appearances are often misleading. It is true that the Mediterranean commerce was being gravely damaged by privateers and pirates, but (as Ferdinand surely knew) many among them were Catalans.[19] What moved Ferdinand to pen this letter was possibly the political pressure coming from some Catalonian nobles and in particular from a key ally of the Crown of Aragon, the count of Cardona.[20] To understand this, one needs to take into consideration a previous letter, written by Ferdinand to the Queen of Naples in August 1482.[21] Here, Ferdinand communicated to his sister some of the political and military events that had recently taken place in Spain, Sicily, and Rome. Among the other news, in a brief but very important paragraph, Ferdinand recounted that two Aragonese galleys that he had requested for the war in Granada had entered the port of Barcelona when a famous Genoese pirate passed through the waters in front of the harbor.[22] The citizens of Barcelona had quickly armed the two warships, hoping to chase and capture the Italian corsair; however, after leaving the port and reaching the enemy, the Catalonian vessels were defeated and one of them, with many soldiers on board—*con mucha gente*—was taken. This captured galley was owned by the count of Cardona, whose family had traditionally been one of the most important Catalonian allies of the Aragonese Crown (even during the Catalonian Civil War). And that this episode was the real reason behind Ferdinand's declaration of war against Genoa seems to be confirmed by the fact that on September 26—the same day in which he wrote the letter to the king of Naples communicating to him the intention to scrap the truce with the Ligurians—he also wrote a letter to the count of Cardona, expressing sadness (*la gran displicentia*) and sympathy for the loss of his warship.[23] Tellingly enough, the tone used by Ferdinand in this document sounds almost regretful, and surely apologetic. In a key passage of the letter, the Aragonese king said: "And what makes us feel especially sorry is that [this damage] was done by the Genoese, which is a nation close to our heart."[24] With this, as well as with the following lines where he promised both the construction of a new galley and military retaliation against the Ligurians, Ferdinand wished to apologize, admitting the close commercial relations between Aragon and the Genoese. The count was a very important ally in the Catalonian political landscape and in the struggle against the Moors, so behind Ferdinand's rhetoric there was a serious concern. But at the same time, by reaffirming that the Crown was fond of the Genoese "nation," Ferdinand indirectly stressed that a solution to the diplomatic crisis could be reached only through him; moreover, a future normalization and a new agreement with the Genoese were not ruled out.

The war against Genoa, therefore, was not due to Ferdinand's economic agenda or to his hostility towards the Genoese. Instead, it was a series of unfortunate episodes of piracy that provoked Ferdinand's reaction. One of these episodes had involved the galley offered to the king by the count of Cardona; and yet through another letter we know for sure that some Genoese pirates had even dared to attack Neapolitan ships, thus enraging a traditional ally of the republic.[25] If the stormy diplomatic relations between Ferdinand and Genoa were caused by an old rivalry, a chaotic situation in the Western

Mediterranean, and a number of incidents damaging key pieces of the puzzle composing the Aragonese dominions, then we need to investigate deeper in order to understand the king's real opinion of the Genoese and his long-term policies towards them. The mere and extemporary suspension of a truce, or a letter written with a severe tone and with a specific political objective, do not constitute proofs of an anti-Genoese feeling. In fact, despite existing enmity, the Catalonian commercial empire was now unable to compete with the Genoese, and the Crown needed Ligurian merchants and bankers to visit its ports, connect its markets, sell its Sicilian grain, furnish capital, and pay tariffs.[26] As we shall see in the next pages, Ferdinand was well aware of this.

If Ferdinand had wished to use the presence of Genoese pirates in the Western Mediterranean as an excuse to start a military conflict, he could have done so before. The same pirate who was responsible for the capture of the count of Cardona's galley had in fact already assaulted Aragonese vessels in the preceding years. But as long as this Genoese buccaneer had not created a diplomatic embarrassment, Ferdinand had tried to solve the problem limiting the political damage. From two letters written in June 1482, three months before the decision to scrap the truce with Genoa, we learn that the king of Aragon attempted to organize an international force, with the aim of policing the sea and capturing Polo Baptista. The fact that two of the galleys composing this fleet were Genoese is revealing. This is unambiguously stated in a letter dated June 11, where Ferdinand ordered to his counselor, Alvaro de Nava, who was captain of two Aragonese warships, to join four galleys, two Neapolitans and two Genoese, with which to chase the two galleys of Polo Baptista.[27] The day after, on June 12, Ferdinand penned a message for the count of Trivento, who was the commander of his maritime forces in Naples, communicating that two galleys captained by Alvaro de Nava would be joining Neapolitan and Genoese ships with the intent to capture a Genoese pirate.[28] What can be learned from these documents is that Ferdinand had a very pragmatic approach to the problem of piracy, one that cannot be detected from his more political messages. He knew that most of the Genoese buccaneers were not acting under the direction of their community, but he attempted to hold the Ligurian city-state at least partly responsible. The idea of an international police force is an example of that sophisticated diplomatic art that places Ferdinand among the shrewdest sovereigns of his time. He seems to have shared with the large majority of the Genoese community the desire to guarantee the rule of law, and this was not something obvious. His father, John II, had not hesitated to unleash his Aragonese and Catalonian subjects (respectively during and after the Civil War) against the Genoese merchants.[29]

BEYOND POLITICS AND DIPLOMACY: FERDINAND'S ACTION TO PROTECT THE GENOESE AND PROPERTY RIGHTS

In order to uncover what Ferdinand really thought about the Genoese and how he perceived their entrepreneurial spirit, it is necessary to look at the more discreet and consistent actions that he took, even in times of diplomatic crisis and (official) war.[30] A few months after he had scrapped the truce with Genoa, Ferdinand wrote an interesting letter to the authorities of Valencia.[31] In this document, the king confirmed his decision, but he ordered that the Genoese resident in Valencia be protected and their safe conducts respected, notwithstanding the previously mentioned revocation of the truce—*non obstante prememorata reuocacione*. This willingness to protect the Genoese merchants while officially blaming their republic for the lawlessness on the sea seems to indicate that Ferdinand considered the Genoese as indispensable economic actors in the commercial system of the Western Mediterranean. And other manuscripts confirm that this was the king's deeply held belief.

In a letter dated December 23, 1483, the sovereign addressed the economic crisis produced in Sardinia by the hostilities between Aragon and Genoa.[32] Ferdinand realized that the Genoese capital and trading networks were vital for the economic stability of his domains; he begun the letter with a historical note, recounting the long tradition of commercial relations between Alghero and the Genoese, "both before and after my happy succession to the reigns of Aragon."[33] But now, the king wrote, because of the revocation of the truce with the Genoese community, "the said Genoese commerce ceased in this town [Alghero], and as a consequence, I am informed, not only this town is damaged and impoverished, but also our royalties and royal customs are much less profitable."[34] After this sort of introduction, Ferdinand continued the lengthy document granting to three Genoese merchants resident in Calvi, Corsica, royal safe conducts with which they (and their representatives) could trade any sort of goods and reestablish the commercial route between Genoa and Alghero.[35] But, once again, it is important to go beyond the political language that Ferdinand was forced to use, due to the delicate position of the Crown within the complex and composite polity that we call Aragon.[36] If we approach this source having in mind the cosmopolitan and entangled network woven by the Genoese across the Mediterranean, and if we hypothesize that Ferdinand understood the multi-market system of which his domains were part, the sudden isolation suffered by the town of Alghero seems only an excuse, almost a rhetorical instrument with which the king justified his defense of international commerce. This hypothesis seems to be confirmed by the geographically limitless permission granted to these three merchants, who were allowed to

> come, from the city *and the coastal territories* of Genoa *or from other lands*, to the mentioned town of Alghero *and to other cities, towns, and places of the said kingdom of Sardinia, and to any among our other kingdoms and lands, both here and overseas*, bringing any sort of goods, foodstuff, cloths, or silver, money, or any other thing, of any nature or kind, and [they can] unload them in the mentioned town *or in any other among our possessions and lands*, and there [they can] sell, barter, or negotiate and trade in other ways.[37]

Then, Ferdinand continued the letter inviting the Genoese to use the profits of such business to buy other goods from the local merchants, go back to Genoa or any other land, and come back again "either once or several times, safely and securely."[38] The rest of the document forbade the beneficiaries to trade with the "infidels" in Granada, and asked them to pay the duty usually paid by the Genoese. The king also warned all the viceroys, the captains, the merchants, the sailors, and the officials of all his reigns not to arrest, rob, or molest in any way these Genoese, under the penalty of 10,000 florins of gold (*pena de deu milia florins d or*).[39] The same day, December 23, 1483, Ferdinand wrote another, identical safe conduct for three other Genoese (inhabitants of Savona and Darax).[40]

When reading these safe conducts, one could consider the economic suffering of Alghero a sort of starting point, the political argument used by Ferdinand to justify his policy towards the Genoese merchants coming to all the ports of the Aragonese empire. Indeed, it would have been impossible to reopen a trading route exclusively between Genoa and Alghero, and not only because this Sardinian city was not a major market. The Genoese businessmen were used to investing in a variety of markets at the same time.[41] As a consequence, a Genoese shipowner or a Ligurian moneylender would have never armed a vessel for a trip calling only at one port or aimed at selling or buying only one specific product. If Ferdinand wanted to keep his domains connected with the many markets controlled by the Genoese—especially in a century when Catalan merchants were withdrawing investments and losing their entrepreneurial spirit[42]—he had to allow them to play by their rules, which meant with as few limitations as possible. Therefore, at least three noteworthy facts seem to emerge from these sources: Ferdinand's acute understanding of the international market; his attempts to secure the rule of law and to protect property rights in both times of peace and war (*axi en temps de pau com de guerra*); and the fact that he perceived the Genoese in terms that were strikingly similar to those with which (as we have seen) they described themselves. That the Genoese civic culture was not rooted in abstract republican ideals or in a literary revival, but rather in a contagiously enriching array of business activities was something that Ferdinand clearly appreciated. Undoubtedly, these diplomatic papers deserve attention for many reasons and could be studied from many other historiographical perspectives. But for the sake of this book, Ferdinand's opinion of the Genoese, the fact that the Genoese were recognized for their economic culture and role, is surely the most interesting finding.

In the subsequent decades, Ferdinand continued to favor international commerce and to protect the Genoese traveling or living in his reigns. In the letters written by the king and his secretaries throughout two decades, the Genoese appear with regularity, as the Crown tried to shield them from diplomatic turbulences and local powers. The most common kind of communication mentioning Genoese citizens among Ferdinand's letters continued to be the safe conduct. Safe conducts were often granted to protect the Genoese entering or leaving his kingdoms, traveling to or from Genoa. These documents typically mentioned that the beneficiaries' families and possessions were also under the protection of the king, and they prove Ferdinand's continuous attention toward the Ligurian merchants living and trading within his domains.[43] On April 30, 1491, Ferdinand used one of these safe conducts to briefly reflect on the economic benefits brought to his kingdoms by the exchange of goods.[44] This document is similar to the previously analyzed letter concerning Alghero, but here Ferdinand's reflection is very short, as he simply noticed how, thanks to the *mercaderia*, guilds, cities, and towns were preserved and could grow, and the revenues coming from duties could increase. Yet, there are other reasons why this document seems particularly interesting. To begin with, the letter contained not just one, but three safe conducts, granted to three members of the Mallo family; moreover, Ferdinand pointed out in the text that he was granting these documents also because he wanted to please his sister, the Queen of Naples, who had pleaded for the protection of these Genoese merchants.[45] The second half of the letter is an effort to mention any possible route and any possible business with the intent to explicitly allow these Genoese to travel and trade, sell and buy whenever they wished and whatever they desired. That the Queen of Naples had bothered to recommend a handful of Genoese to her brother, beside confirming the political and economic ties between Genoa and Naples, is yet another important clue of the fact that the Genoese entrepreneurial activities were not organized, sponsored, or protected by the republican government. Rather, it was up to a single family, or even a single individual, to explore and open new markets; and where business activities were threatened by the absence of the rule of law (embodied in the hostility of local merchants or the bullying of foreign authorities, often emboldened by the official diplomatic conflict between their sovereign and Genoa), the Genoese were ready to use every political connection in order to see their property rights respected. To be sure, even after pleading for protection and asking for safe conducts at the highest political levels, there was no guarantee that the king would grant them. This is why Ferdinand's consistent policy towards the Genoese is significant. The fact that Ferdinand signed this particular letter while being in Real del Gozco, during the feverish and momentous months of the decisive assault on Granada, suggests once more that he truly cared about the positive economic impact of the Genoese colonies across his kingdoms.

The Genoese did not enjoy a good reputation. Ferdinand knew that some of them were lawless robbers, and that all of them were involved in socially and morally deplorable activities (e.g., usury and trade); but he also knew that Spain needed to be part of their commercial network. Ferdinand clearly explained in more than one letter that he was deeply convinced of the necessity to welcome Genoese investments in order to increase state revenues and bring about economic prosperity. It is not far-fetched to imagine that Ferdinand's opinion of the Genoese was confirmed and strengthened in the years after his marriage with Isabella, and in particular as he increasingly passed more time in Castilian territories, where the Genoese had long since been playing a major role as moneylenders and international traders.[46] Just four days after penning the safe conducts for the three businessmen of the Mallo family, Ferdinand signed a document naturalizing the Genoese Uberto Spinola, who since that moment was to be considered as a vassal born in Aragon—*ac si in aliqua ciutate regnorum nostrorum Corone Aragonum natus fuisset*.[47] A few months later, from the encampment in Granada, Ferdinand wrote a friendly letter to thank the Genoese captain Pedro Vivaldo, who had been faithfully serving him, and to grant him the honor to raise the royal insignias on his ship, which would have been since then under the monarch's "special protection" (*sub nostris protectione et saluaguardia specialibus*).[48] The years went by, and fateful events changed the history of Spain and of the world in which Ferdinand lived. But the king continued to help the Genoese and to protect their property rights across his domains, both before and after achieving peace with Genoa in 1493;[49] both before and after the most stubborn and intrepid son of the Ligurian republic brought to his wife Isabella a New World.[50]

CONCLUSION

To the eyes of Ferdinand II, the Genoese were not merely a group of *extranjeros* among many others. In light of the evidence presented above, and considering in particular Ferdinand's exquisitely economic reflections (e.g., in the letter concerning Alghero), we can conclude that the king saw the Genoese as exceptional and ubiquitous creators of wealth. This opinion of the Genoese was strikingly similar to the image with which they had been intellectualizing and describing themselves in literary works such as the *laudatio* and the poems presented in the previous chapter. This is a significant conclusion to draw from the sources analyzed, because, while several scholars (at least in the Spanish-speaking academic world) have written about the Genoese presence in Castile, the same cannot be said with regard to the

Ligurian penetration of Aragon and Catalonia.[51] More importantly, economic historians have until now studied the Genoese colonies in Spain following a "quantitative" methodology; yet, the Ligurian presence in the Spanish kingdoms (and in the Atlantic) had also an intellectual impact. Merchants and bankers, sailors and captains carried with them not only cargoes and capital, but also the colonial techniques and the economic culture that I have described in part I.

Considering the aims of my research, what seems especially remarkable among the findings of this chapter is the confirmation that the movement East-West was accomplished by fifteenth-century Genoese through the private, unplanned exploration of every available market, including the one represented by an old economic archrival and a recent political foe: the Crown of Aragon. In addition, Ferdinand's letters have shown that the king protected the Genoese even in times of stormy diplomatic relations between Aragon and their mother land. He granted them licenses to trade across the western Mediterranean, he employed them in his fleet and rewarded them promptly, and he intervened when their ships, property, and merchandise were seized by Catalan officials. Ferdinand arguably favored the integration of Genoese merchants into the socioeconomic fabric of his kingdoms, going beyond the concept of "complementary enemies"[52] and probably imagining that the Ligurian commune would eventually join his imperial project in Italy and the Mediterranean, as a strategic ally if not as a subject state. This constitutes a significant first step in the direction of the Hispanic-Genoese alliance of the following century, and it therefore needs to be considered in order to contextualize the policy of Charles V towards Genoa, which I will discuss in the next chapter. Ferdinand befriended Genoese families and blessed the expansion of Genoese networks because he shared with them some of the same economic ideas (e.g., rule of law, protection of property rights, connection of markets), but also because he appreciated the outstanding ability of the Genoese to bring prosperity (and therefore, among other beneficial effects, to increase both local and royal revenues). Ferdinand had a remarkable talent for diplomacy, and as a consequence some of his letters must be patiently and correctly contextualized in order to understand what he really planned to do with regard to Genoa and (or even vs.) the Genoese. Nevertheless, Ferdinand's missives remain uniquely revealing, precisely because, due to the composite nature of his Crown and to the creeping political tensions of which the Civil War fought by his father had been a spectacular reminder, he had at certain times to carefully justify his decisions. And in doing so, the monarch allowed us to catch a glimpse of the place reserved for the Genoese in his geopolitical and macroeconomic vision.

NOTES

1. On Christopher Columbus's early life, see Morison, *The Great Explorers*, 354–360; and William D. Phillips and Carla Rahn Phillips, *The Worlds of Christopher Columbus* (Cambridge: Cambridge University Press, 1992), 85–111.

2. "The more complicated an action is the more freedom is needed by the individuals who have to act, and the more one needs the action and collaboration of other individuals, the more freedom is necessary for all of them to act and collaborate as requested." Bruno Leoni, "Two Views of Liberty, Occidental and Oriental(?)," *Libertarian Papers* 1 (2009): 16. Paper originally presented in Tokyo, in 1966.

3. See chapter 1.

4. "The rule of law, in the classical sense of the expression, cannot be maintained without actually securing the certainty of law, conceived as the possibility of long-run planning on the part of individuals in regard to their behaviour in private life and business." Bruno Leoni, *Freedom and the Law* (Indianapolis: Liberty Fund, 1991), 72. First published in 1961.

5. "As a matter of fact, to a much larger extent than the Venetians or the Florentines, the Genoese endeavoured to compensate for the gradual closing of eastern markets and shortage of eastern spices by increasing their share in western markets and western cheap bulky goods." Lopez, "Market Expansion: The Case of Genoa," 455.

6. The Genoese presence in Rome was linked to the production of alum, and later to banking. Charles L. Stinger, *The Renaissance in Rome* (Bloomington: Indiana University Press, 1998), 19; and Maria Luigia Ronco Valenti, "Un angolo di Liguria nel cuore di Trastevere," *Storia* 4 (2004): 70–79. In Sicily, Genoese merchants had been buying wheat since the twelfth century: see Steven A. Epstein, *Genoa and the Genoese, 958–1528* (Chapel Hill: University of North Carolina Press, 1996), 26–28.

7. The pioneering works were Lopez, "Il predominio economico dei genovesi,"; ID., "Alfonso el Sabio y el primer almirante genovés de Castilla," *Quadernos de Historia de España* 14 (1950): 5–16; Charles Verlinden, "Italian Influence"; and Pike, *Enterprise and Adventure*. For a collection of more recent studies (which however deal with a later period), see *Génova y la monarquía hispánica*, ed. Herrero Sánchez.

8. On the early Genoese colonies in Andalusia, see, for example, José Damián González Arce, "El Consulado Genovés de Sevilla (siglos XIII–XV)," *Studia Historica. Historia Medieval* 28 (2010): 179–206. About the growth of Castilian exports in this period, see Hilario Casado Alonso, *Castilla y Europa: Comercio y mercaderes en los siglos XIV, XV y XVI* (Burgos: Diputación Provincial de Burgos, 1995).

9. The Castilian culture of the later Middle Ages was obviously influenced by the experience of the *Reconquista*, a long historical process that had deep social and political consequences in the organization and development of this kingdom. Business activities, and in particular trade, were held in contempt not only by the Castilian aristocracy, but also by lower social groups. See Elliott, *Imperial Spain*, 31–32.

10. For an introduction to the history of Aragon, see Thomas N. Bisson, *The Medieval Crown of Aragon* (Oxford: Clarendon, 2000).

11. On these themes, see Vincente Salavert y Roca, "El problema estratégico del Mediterraneo occidental y la política aragonesa (siglos XIV y XV)," in *Actas y comunicaciones del IV congreso de historia de la Corona d'Aragón* (Palma de Mallorca: Graficas Miramar, 1959), 201–21; Mario del Treppo, *I mercanti catalani e l'espansione della Corona d'Aragona nel secolo XV* (Napoli: L'Arte Tipografica, 1972); and *La Corona d'Arargona in Italia (sec. XIII–XVIII), XIV Congresso di storia della Corona d'Aragona* (Sassari: Delfino, 1993).

12. These documents have been published in six volumes, which, to my knowledge, have never been previously used to illuminate the Genoese presence in the Crown of Aragon and Ferdinand's perception of (and attitude towards) the Ligurian merchants (and pirates). *Documentos sobre relaciones internacionales de los Reyes Católicos*, ed. Antonio de la Torre (Barcelona: CSIC, 1949–1966).

13. The problem of piracy in the Mediterranean world was not limited to the Aragonese and the Genoese. María Teresa Ferrer Mallol, *Corsarios castellanos y vascos en el Mediterráneo medieval* (Barcelona: CSIC, 2000).

14. On the diplomatic relations between Aragon and Genoa during and after the Catalonian Civil War, see the brief but detailed (and unsurpassed) study by Giovanna Petti Balbi, *Le relazioni tra Genova e la Corona d'Aragona dal 1468 al 1478* (Bordighera: Istituto Internazionale Studi Liguri, 1974).

15. On the alliance between Aragon and Venice, see José Vicente Cabezuelo Pliego, "Diplomacia y Guerra en el Mediterráneo medieval. La liga véneto-aragonesa contra Génova de 1351," *Anuario de estudios medievales* 36 (2006): 253–94. The 1466 Genoese expedition against Barcelona is told in the contemporary chronicle written by Antonio Gallo, *Commentarius de Genuensium maritima classe in Barchinonenses expedita*, ed. Emilio Pandiani (Città di Castello: Lapi, 1910).

16. On the Aragonese economic crisis and the decline of Catalonian entrepreneurship, see Elliott, *Imperial Spain*, 37–40; on the demographic crisis in Catalonia and the population decline in Barcelona, see Enrique Llopis, Francisco Comín, Mauro Hernández, *Historia económica de España, siglos X–XX* (Barcelona: Critica, 2002), 34–47.

17. On Ferrante, see Ernesto Pontieri, *Per la storia del regno di Ferrante I d'Aragona re di Napoli* (Napoli: 1969).

18. "Bien se acordara vuestra serenidat la tregua que, por intercession vuestra y de la serenissima reyna, nuestra muy cara y muy amada hermana, como fija, muger vuestra, fezimos e firmamos con la comunidat de Genoua, e con quanta rectitud e obseruancia hauemos fastaqui tenido nuestra fe e promesa, lo que ellos muy mal y con violencia han fecho; que Polo Baptista, corsario, con sabiduria, ayuda e consentimientode la dicha comunidat, ha dado e inferido, durando el tiempo de la dicha tregua, tantos danyos a muchos subditos e vassallos nuestros." *Documentos sobre relaciones internacionales*, vol. 1, letter 66, 277.

19. The Archivio di Stato di Genova preserves numerous fifteenth-century documents that show the attacks of Catalonian privateers; these manuscripts are often copies of letters sent by the Genoese government to John II. But the situation was complicated by the presence of many other corsairs, such as Portuguese and the Aragonese based in Sardinia. Some of these documents are mentioned in Petti Balbi, *Le relazioni tra Genova e la Corona d'Aragona*; see in particular the footnotes on 22. In November 1477, Catalonian vessels had reached the waters in front of the harbor of Genoa, attacking several Genoese ships; see Archivio di Stato di Genova, *Litterarum Comunis Ianue (Archivio Segreto)*, 24 A/1800, c. 78 r.-v., November 10.

20. Joan Ramon Folc III, count of Cardona and Prades (1418–1486).

21. *Documentos sobre relaciones internacionales*, vol. 1, letter 42, 249–251.

22. Ibid., 250–251.

23. Ibid., vol. 1, letter 67, 278.

24. "E lo que mes nos desplau, es per esser stat fet per genouesos, que es natio que tenim tant a cor." Ibid.

25. In December 1482, Ferdinand mentioned this "war" of the Genoese against the commercial fleet of the Kingdom of Naples. In a letter written to the king of Naples, Ferdinand said that he was not surprised by these events, "because we already know well their [the Genoese's] actions." The word used is *praticas*, which underlines the continuous, habitual nature of the Genoese pirate activities. However it is hard to precisely judge when these assaults on Neapolitan ships took place; it is possible that at that point the Crown of Aragon was already officially at war with Genoa (in this same letter Ferdinand assured the king of Naples that the declaration of war had been "published" in Aragon); but at any rate, the Genoese government never authorized privateers to attack Neapolitan cargoes. Once again, we must be aware of Ferdinand's political aim when he wrote this letter; notwithstanding the assaults that his merchants might have suffered at the hands of the Genoese, the king of Naples remained close to Genoa in the diplomatic landscape. Ibid., vol.1, letter 76, 284–85. Quote on 285.

26. In Sicily, the Genoese were a fundamental part of the economic life: "Frequently they [the Genoese] quarreled with Aragon over control of the grain trade, yet their privileged position survived just because everybody gained from it; and although Genoa itself no doubt profited the most, Sicily too benefited enormously in terms of good foreign currency. Not only the King, but also many of the landowners came to rely on the Genoese credit, and so did the town of Messina itself. In some years Genoa took more cereals and cheese from Sicily than did Spain, and the rare occasions when we possess comparable figures suggest that, especially after

1450, their ships sometimes outnumbered Catalan in Sicilian ports." Denis Mack Smith, *A History of Sicily, Medieval Sicily: 800–1713* (London: Chatto&Windus, 1968), 103–4. On the question of grain shortage, a dated but still valuable study is Eduardo Ibarra y Rodríguez, *El problema cerealista en España durante el reinado de los Reyes Católicos (1475–1516)* (Madrid: Instituto Sancho de Moncada de Economía, 1944).

27. *Documentos sobre relaciones internacionales*, vol. 1, letter 25, 231.

28. Ibid., letter 26, 231–32, vol. 1.

29. In particular, after the conclusion of the Catalonian Civil War, John II "turned the corsairs and the Catalonians loose on the sea, so that they unleashed against the Genoese vessels their resentment for not having been helped in time of need." "lasciava ampia libertà di azione sul mare ai corsari e ai Catalani, i quali sfogavano contro le imbarcazioni genovesi il loro risentimento per non essere stati aiutati nel momento del bisogno." Petti Balbi, *Le relazioni tra Genova e la Corona d'Aragona*, 27–28.

30. By "official war" I mean to stress here the fact that scrapping a truce did not necessarily mean that the Crown of Aragon or the Republic of Genoa were going to arm public fleets and organize proper military campaigns against each other. More often, being officially at war simply meant that Catalan captains and merchants could legally assault and rob Genoese ships (and vice versa).

31. *Documentos sobre relaciones internacionales*, vol. 1, letter 27, 314–15.

32. Ibid., letter 90, 365–68, vol. 1.

33. "abans y après de nostra beneauenturada succession en los regnes d Arago." Ibid., 366.

34. "lo dit comerci genoues cessa en la dita vila, per la qual cosa, segons som informats, aquella, no solament ne pren gran dan e diminucio, mes encara nostres regalies e duanes reyales ne valen molt menys." Ibid., 366.

35. The (hispanized) names of these three Corsicans are Santino de Loquino, Gregorio de Gerentino, and Jeronimo de Gerentino.

36. "Above all the King of Aragon ruled by consent; to some extent, he even reigned by consent, for the oath of allegiance of his magnates was expressly conditional on his upholding their customs and liberties. He was trammelled up by a variety of representative institutions; and finally he was hampered by the strength and diversity of local laws, partly customary and partly codified." Felipe Fernández-Armesto, *Ferdinand and Isabella* (London: Weidenfeld and Nicolson, 1975), 52. On the political resistance met by Ferdinand's policies in Aragon, see Fernando Solano Costa, "El reino de Aragon durante el gobierno de Fernando el Catolico," *Cuadernos de historia Jerónimo Zurita* 16–18 (1963–1965): 221–46; and Angel Alcalá Galve, "¿Un rey contra su reino? antiforalismo del rey Fernando en la imposición de la Inquisición a su Aragón," in *Ferdinandus Rex Hispaniarum, príncipe del renacimiento*: [exposición, Zaragoza, Palacio de la Aljafería, Cortes de Aragón, 6 de octubre de 2006 a 7 de enero de 2007], 309–18.

37. Emphasis added. "venir, de la ciutat e ribera de Genoua o de altres parts, a la dita vila de Alguer e alters ciutats, viles e lochs del dit regne de Sardenya, e alters qualseuol regnes e terres nostres, citra e ultra marines, portant qualseuol mercaderies, vitualles, robes, or, argent, diners e altres qualseuol cosse, de qualseuol natura o specie sien e aquelles descarregar en la dita vila e alters qualseuol parts e terres nostres, e alli vendre, permutar o en altra manera contractar e comerciar." *Documentos sobre relaciones internacionales*, vol. 1, 366.

38. "en una o moltes vegades, saluament e segura." Ibid.

39. Ibid., 367.

40. Ibid., letter 91, 368. The names of these three Genoese are Jacometo Gosaldo, his brother Franci Gosaldo, and Gaspar Farar.

41. Here, with the word market I intend both a geographical place and a sector of the international trade.

42. The economic crisis in the reigns of the Crown was not merely due to the Catalonian Civil War, which started only in 1462. According to Jaime Vicens Vives, "from 1432–1434 to 1454, shipping in the port of Barcelona declined by 75 to 80%." Jaime Vicent Vives, *An Economic History of Spain* (Princeton, NJ: Princeton University Press, 1969), 229. For an interesting historiographical assessment on the late medieval economic crisis in the Spanish

kingdoms, see David Igual Luis, "¿Crisis? ¿Qué crisis? El comercio internacional en los reinos hispánicos de la Baja Edad Media," *Edad Media* 8 (2007): 203–23.

43. See for instance *Documentos sobre relaciones internacionales*, vol. 3, letters 190 and 191, 172–73. The same kind of document is also penned by Ferdinand a few months later for Dorino de Grimaldo, letter 62, 225. See also letter 100, 260–61; and letter 143, 449–50.

44. Ibid., vol. 3, letter 45, 398–99.

45. "supplicants per la serenissima reyna de Napols." Ibid., 398.

46. Actually, according to Charles Verlinden, Italians, above all the Genoese, had also been the "founders" of international trade in Catalonia, "a situation which lasted until and indeed reached its height in the twelfth century." Charles Verlinden, "The Rise of Spanish Trade in the Middle Ages," *The Economic History Review*, 10 (1940): 48. But of course during the thirteenth and the fourteenth centuries the Catalans had themselves become active protagonists of the international trade. Thus, reversing his father's policy, practically tolerating Genoa's political untrustworthiness, and favoring the Genoese colonies in the Aragonese kingdoms was truly Ferdinand's conscious decision, and it was probably due to his realistic assessment of the long, insolvable crisis afflicting the once dynamic Catalonian economy.

47. *Documentos sobre relaciones internacionales*, vol. 3, letter 50, 401–2. Quote on 401.

48. Ibid., vol. 3, letter 144, 450.

49. The peace between Aragon and Genoa was signed in August 1493. See ibid., vol. 4, documents 221, 222, and 223, on 267–69. The letter 223 is particularly significant, since here Ferdinand explicitly mentioned his intention to favor free commerce by land and by sea. In the previous summer, Ferdinand had written to his captain general, Bernardo de Vilamarí, to condemn the actions of some of his galleys, which had seized Genoese vessels navigating around Sardinia; the king even threatened to order the confiscation of Vilamarí's property as punishment. Ibid., vol. 4, letter 70, 49. Another example of Ferdinand's continuous protection of the Genoese before the peace of 1493 is the letter written by the king to the governor and the general lieutenant of Mallorca in December 1492, where he ordered them to ignore an earlier decree and not to seize the property of the Genoese Luca de Mar and Nicoloso de Morten. Similar documents are numerous; see for instance letter 108, 187. After the peace of 1493, Ferdinand continued to sign safe conducts for Genoese merchants (document 340, on 339) and to defend the Genoese doing business in Catalonia (letter 28, on 414–15; letter 157, 491–92; letter 164, 110 in vol. 5, where Ferdinand orders to swiftly arrest one of his subjects who had dared to assault a vessel armed by a "Francesco Spinola and other Genoese"; and letter 186, on 124).

50. Columbus arrived in Seville on 31 March, 1493. He celebrated the Holy Week surrounded by the local authorities and waiting for a letter from the monarchs. The letter came, and it was addressed to "Don Cristóbal Colón, their Admiral of the Ocean Sea, Viceroy and Governor of the Islands that he hath discovered in the Indies." This hour of triumph was Columbus's apogee, but it also rewarded the Spanish kingdoms for their discontinuous, tormented, at times violent, and yet profound friendship with the Genoese. Letter quoted in Morison, *The Great Explorers*, 429.

51. Perhaps this is partly due to the complex, contradictory and often conflicting political relations between Genoa and the Crown of Aragon. More research is needed to uncover the economic significance of the Genoese colonies in Barcelona, Valencia, and other cities of the Crown of Aragon. Yet, this is not the place for such endeavor.

52. The expression "complementary enemies" was used by Fernand Braudel to describe the commercial alliances of the Mediterranean world. Fernand Braudel, *The Wheels of Commerce: Civilization and Capitalism 15th–18th Century*, vol. 2 (New York: Harper and Row, 1982), 163.

Chapter Five

Rejecting the "Machiavellian" State

Genoa's Regimes from the French Fury to the Second Hispanic–Genoese Alliance

This chapter continues to investigate the origins of the Hispanic-Genoese system, focusing on an array of documents that show the resilience of medieval, traditional forms of civic and military organization in Genoa, even at a time of profound political crisis. Genoa's republican conservatism is here presented as the context in which several changes of regime and the eventual rise of Andrea Doria must be understood. Charles V's expectations, policies and attitudes towards Genoa are also considered, stressing the progressive, mutual understanding between the Ligurian republic and the emperor. As we have seen in the previous chapter, Charles was not the first Spanish monarch to appreciate Genoa's strategic role. Yet the formal alliance between him and Andrea Doria signals a momentous event, not only for the fate of the Italian Wars and for the establishment of a Hispanic-Genoese system with ramifications in the Americas, but also because it contradicts the idea that a movement towards a centralized and militarized Machiavellian state was the only possible way in which sixteenth-century Italian polities could maintain their freedom.

THE END OF A WORLD?

> In Italy, accustomed for many years more to the depictions of wars than to true wars, there was no nerve to resist the French fury.
>
> Francesco Guicciardini[1]

On February 22, 1495, Charles VIII, the king of France, entered Naples holding one of his hunting hawks, to signify that conquering Italy had been as easy and amusing as a ride across one of his royal estates.[2] This was the final act of a historic march from the Alps. Charles's invasion brought to an end the world of the city-states and the age of civic humanism. Admittedly, his stay in Naples would be short-lived, as his enemies on the Italian peninsula quickly reorganized and threatened to cut his supply lines. He had to withdraw and fight his way back to France, preserving his knightly aura, but losing his booty and his conquests. Nonetheless, the political consequences of Charles VIII's military campaign of 1494–1495 were enormous. With his rapid southern march, he demonstrated the weakness of the Italian political system of republics, *signorie* and regional kingdoms, thus starting a long series of conflicts fought by foreign powers over the spoils of the peninsula.[3] The Italian Wars (1494–1559) radically changed the political landscape of Italy, but they also challenged the civic culture, the tradition of competing jurisdictions, and the sophisticated understanding of liberty that had flourished particularly in its proud republics.[4] These republics now appeared tragically small, like tiny relics on the map, soon to be wiped away by the destructive power of a foreign army.

It was the very idea of city-state that came to be under assault. Charles VIII had proven that a relatively centralized kingdom, with its large territories and its vast financial resources, could mobilize a great army, equipped with frighteningly destructive artillery.[5] The "French fury" was precisely this impressive concentration of political and military power: the French king could at any moment decide to quickly level a town to the ground and massacre all its inhabitants. This was the cruel fate of Fivizzano, a fortified village that dared to close its doors at the passing of Charles's troops.[6] For a long time, warfare in Italy had not been such a devastating, bloody affair.[7] So in 1494, terror quickly filled the hearts of the Italian populace and of its rulers. Among them, Piero de Medici, shocked by the events of Fivizzano, rushed to Charles, offering the keys of all his Tuscan fortresses and meekly agreeing to open the port of Livorno to the French fleet.[8] Even after Charles VIII's retreat (and death) in 1498, nothing could ever be the same. Not only Charles's heirs, but also Swiss mercenaries, Spanish generals, and German troops would continue to fight in Italy for sixty years. This was the moment when the inadequacy of the city-state *vis-a-vis* national and imperial forces became (apparently) undeniable. Italy's medieval and humanist political formulas and institutional arrangements were thrown into crisis. Recounting these events in the late 1530s, Guicciardini stated: "the year fourteen ninety-four . . . most unhappy for Italy, and truly the first of the miserable years, because it opened the door to innumerable, and horrible calamities, from which we may say that in different ways has suffered a great part of the world."[9]

Facing a crisis of these proportions, the Italian states elaborated diplomatic and political answers that ranged from expedient alliances with French and Spanish kings to bolder policies of neutrality and a more systematic assertion of power over their territories—a trend that Venice, Florence, and Siena had already started well before the fifteenth century.[10] However, the political crisis did not spark only political change. The intellectual debate concerning *stato* and *libertà* was also reshaped. This altered both the boundaries of the humanist vocabulary and the focus of political reflection.[11] The new attention given to the territorial state is exemplified notably in some of Niccolò Machiavelli's works.[12] As convincingly shown by Elena Fasano Guarini, themes such as the centralized state, the assertion of power over a large territory, and the necessity for a republic to conquer (*acquistare*) nearby towns and enlarge (*ampliare*) its possessions are pivotal in Machiavelli's less known writings (e.g., in his *Ritratto di cose di Francia*), but also in the *Prince* and the *Discourses*.[13] Therefore, in the political philosophy of sixteenth-century Italy, other models—centralized empires, great monarchies, and entities embracing several cities—progressively replaced the city-state. At the same time, the authority of the state became more important than (and even antithetical to) the humanist approval of private wealth. Due to the specific aim of her essay, Guarini does not investigate more in detail the position of Machiavelli in the *Discourses* with regard to wealth. But I would like to point out that Machiavelli went as far as imagining (and praising) a republic where the citizens were poor while the state was wealthy.[14] This public wealth and authority, in the post-1494, "Machiavellian" political recipe, had to be embodied first and foremost in a large, disciplined standing army: "the chief foundations of all states, new as well as old or composite, are good laws and good arms; . . . there cannot be good laws where the state is not well armed."[15] Whether we interpret this blossoming of the idea of a territorial, militarily powerful state as a consequence of French and Swiss armies pillaging Italy or rather as the final steps of an intellectual process that had already begun at an earlier stage, we have to admit that it is hard to imagine any concept further removed from the model of a communal maritime republic with a small territory and without a public fleet—that is to say, from the model of Genoa.[16]

Not surprisingly, the "French fury" and the Italian Wars provoked a political crisis also in the Ligurian republic. And yet, after three decades of tumultuous events, foreign invasions, and economic depression, Andrea Doria led Genoa towards an institutional solution and a diplomatic realignment that involved neither territorial expansion, nor the militarization of the *stato*, nor the creation of a local dynasty. Genoa—the great absentee in the historiographical debate on medieval and Renaissance republicanism—was arguably (and quite ironically) the only Italian polity that stayed true to its late medieval republican belief system, in the midst of a geopolitical storm.[17] This is not to say that Genoa's institutions were not altered, or that Liguria completely lacked intellectual dissenters and "Machiavellian" writers voicing dreams of a territorial, authoritative, and centralized state, which markedly departed from the late medieval, communal concept of *stato*. In fact, later in this chapter some space will be dedicated to one of these "dissenters," namely Uberto Foglietta. Yet, Genoa's territorial possessions (that narrow strip of land called *Riviere* and the shaky dominion in Corsica) would eventually remain the same;[18] the republic's political influence over its neighbors would not be enhanced by a public fleet; contingent economic considerations would continue to drive Genoa's political and diplomatic decisions; and at the end of this period, the figure of the doge would be even weaker. The reforms of 1528 did not revolutionize the Genoese constitutional framework: they reorganized it, confirming its ideological premises and retaining its traditional dispersion of power. As I will argue in this chapter, in spite of the Italian Wars, the Genoese still understood *libertà* as dispersion of power, financial self-government, and economic freedom. This distinct form of *libertà* had not been wiped away by coups and foreign armies. And such a resilient republican spirit had a remarkable impact on both Hispanic-Genoese relations and the way in which the Spanish came to perceive Ligurian businessmen within the Castilian empire. Both Genoese and Spanish sources confirm the impression that Genoa maintained its independence and its late medieval civic culture, precisely because its wealth, its galleys, and its arms were in private hands—constituting a threat and a destabilizing force, which prevented anyone from centralizing political power and plundering local resources. Andrea Doria exemplified and masterfully took advantage of this reality; at the same time, he placed Genoa on the Spanish side, thus deciding the fate of the Italian Wars, and giving to his countrymen the possibility to legitimize and widen the Ligurian presence within the Spanish Atlantic.

"PASSIONS AND PARTIALITIES AND REVOLUTIONS":[19] THE SLIPPERY NATURE OF POWER IN GENOA, 1513–1527.

The political history of the Genoese republic between the beginning of the Italian Wars and 1528 is violent, extremely complex, and at times mysterious.[20] Genoa entered the long conflict on the French side, and there it remained, unstably and riotously, until 1522.[21] During this period, the factionalism that had characterized the history of Genoa since the Middle Ages became an even more dangerous game of conflicting alliances with militarily powerful foreign rulers. The coups taking place in Genoa were often the reflection of broader military and geopolitical events. In 1512, Giano II Fregoso, with the help of Pope Julius II (himself a Ligurian countryman), guided a rebellion against the French governor and was able to hold the dogeship for one year, before the French troops, accompanied by the armed forces of the Adorno and Fieschi families, retook the *Riviere* and entered Genoa on May 25, 1513.[22] But the new governor, Antoniotto II Adorno, did not enjoy the fruits of his machinations for longer than ten days, as the French defeat in the battle of Novara (on June 6) galvanized the Fregoso faction, which quickly regrouped and counterattacked.[23] Ottaviano Fregoso, with the support of Spanish troops, organized a military expedition in the *Riviere*, entered Genoa, and was named doge. Ottaviano decided not only to put under siege the French garrison guarding the port, but also, after the surrender of the soldiers within it, to destroy that threat to the city's maritime connections once and for all.[24]

Ottaviano was a gifted leader and a shrewd political actor.[25] Although he had become doge ousting the French faction and partly thanks to Ferdinand II, he understood that in the post-1494 geopolitical landscape, Genoa could not hope to maintain the status quo. The republic needed to take advantage of its wealth and of its strategic position to reach a favorable bargain with the strongest monarch. When in 1515 Louis XII died and Francis I, the new king of France, declared himself lord of Genoa, Ottaviano reassured his Spanish allies while secretly reaching an advantageous agreement with Francis.[26] The French were going to reenter Liguria, and they could send a garrison to take possession of Genoa's castle (*Castelletto*); but Francis had to keep Ottaviano as his governor and respect all the privileges of the city that Louis XII had honored before the rebellion of 1507. Ottaviano had not been forced to switch sides, as some historians have incorrectly stated.[27] In a sixteenth-century manuscript preserved in Genoa, a Genoese sympathizing with the French admits that it was not Francis's armies that had retaken Liguria; rather, Ottaviano Fregoso had willingly decided to change his alliances with a bold move:

> Ottaviano Fregoso was made Doge by the fury of his faction and by other citizens, on June 10. And having prudently acknowledged that his forces were unstable and his enemies powerful, through certain pacts he brought the city under the protection of Francis of Valois, King of France, and by him [Ottaviano Fregoso] with title of royal governor the city was ruled until the year 1522.[28]

In his thinking as well as in his political action, Ottaviano Fregoso has been a precursor of Andrea Doria; he understood that stability could be obtained only if Genoa chose her protector and proposed an agreement with favorable terms. A foreign invasion or an unfavorable agreement imposed on the city were simply going to spark discontent, strengthening the ousted factions, and paving the way for new coups.

Fregoso's strategy was initially successful, and Genoa lived in peace under his rule for almost nine years—a remarkable lapse of time. However,

Ottaviano did not have the political strength to impose a reform of the Genoese institutions, so a large group of internal enemies and exiled nobles continued to patiently plot against him, waiting for a chance to overthrow his government, possibly with the help of foreign troops. When the French army was vanquished by Spanish and papal forces at the battle of Bicocca, on April 27, 1522, the Adorno knew that their revenge was at hand.[29] The siege of Genoa lasted for ten days; two documents dealing with this tragic event seem worthy of consideration. The first one is a letter written by Ottaviano Fregoso to his ambassador at the court of Francis.[30] The desperate doge wanted Cattaneo Lomellino to urge the French king to quickly send troops in order to break the siege and save the city. What seems especially relevant here is the description of the city given by Ottaviano in this text. Genoa, according to the doge, was different from any other state, because its wealth was constituted primarily by mobile capital. Other city-states, continued Ottaviano, would maintain their territories even after a sack, so that they could rebuild their revenues; Genoa, on the other hand, possessed only private wealth, and the consequences of a military defeat would have been disastrous. In a key passage of the document, Ottaviano wrote: "our way of being and our life are the most different from the other cities, which even when losing their mobile riches still hold the territories and the possessions that belong to them."[31] Obviously, this letter is interesting for a number of reasons; but here it is enough to underline the self-perceived uniqueness of the Genoese republic, which coincided with (and stemmed from) the Genoese economic praxis, colonial experience, and political constitution. Ottaviano's analysis was in line with Genoa's history and identity. Yet, more importantly, although his depiction of the Genoese city-state was correct, his conclusions were patently mistaken—and he probably formulated them in this way deliberately, only because of the specific, peculiar (and desperate) aim of this letter. In fact, precisely because of the two main characteristics of the Ligurian republic correctly depicted by Fregoso—its limited territorial possessions and the great wealth and power of its private citizens—Genoa could neither be stably ruled by one of the local families struggling for the dogeship, nor thoroughly conquered and pacified by a foreign prince. To confirm this thesis we shall now consider the second manuscript dealing with the Spanish conquest of Genoa.

In an eighteenth-century volume recounting the history of Genoa, and probably written by Francesco Maria Accinelli (1700–1777), a long paragraph, at the beginning of chapter twelve, is dedicated to the events leading to the sack of 1522:

> The French continued to hold Genoa, when the Adorno and the Fieschi, powerful families, conspired against them and against the faction of the Fregoso, trying to accomplish their purpose at the time in which to Maximilian had

> succeeded Charles V, son of Philip king of Spain, and grandson of the said Maximilian.[32]

Since these first lines, the reader's attention is drawn to the internal factions plotting against the French and the Fregoso. The battle of Bicocca is not mentioned, and the Spanish seem to have become involved in the plan to conquer Genoa only at the Adorno's and Fieschi's insistence:

> [the Adorno and Fieschi] induced the new emperor to attempt this enterprise against the City, so that he could drive away his enemies, and they could take over the Dogeship. Charles ordered Prospero Colonna, the Duke of Milan, and the Marquise of Pescara, who were his generals, to go with the army to Genoa and because His Majesty knew the truth in the proverb that unless Genoa conquers Genoa not even the whole world can conquer Genoa, he ordered his generals to take advantage of the Adorno faction and in particular to obey Gerolamo Adorno during this endeavor.

Accinelli continues:

> Twenty-thousand men besieged the City, and its Citizens resisted with republican courage, but prevailing during the night the Marquis of Pescara entered through a gate called of Saint Michael (today, Saint Thomas) with soldiers shouting "Adorno" and "Spain," Genoa was brutally sacked and Ottaviano Fregoso was captured, so that it could be said in truth that Genoa, and not the enemies, took Genoa. Antoniotto Adorno was elected Doge, and the army went back to Lombardy.[33]

To be sure, we cannot read this document uncritically. The volume was penned with the title *Libertà e indipendenza della città di Genova*, so its main objective was to show how Genoa had always remained substantially independent throughout its history (an objective that, incidentally, is itself quite revealing of the continuous interest and attitudes of Genoese culture towards the humanist themes of a city's self-government and *libertà*). But that the details gathered by this eighteenth-century account are reliable seems to be confirmed by the numerous documents that link the Adorno family, and in particular Gerolamo, with Charles V. These documents—preserved at the Real Academia de la Historia in Madrid—uncover a patient strategy of mutual cooperation. Gerolamo worked several years for Charles V, serving as diplomat, general, counsellor, and informer.[34] Therefore, it is plausible that Gerolamo, having already built for himself a successful career as general in the Spanish army deployed in Italy, was put in charge of the military operations in Liguria. Although it is undeniable that after the Spanish victory at the battle of Bicocca, Genoa had become an almost obvious military target for the imperial forces, nonetheless the insistence, the preparation, and the support of the Adorno faction was fundamental both for the rapid success of the military expedition and for the establishment of a legitimate government, headed by a Genoese figure. The very fact that Antoniotto Adorno, and not a Spanish aristocrat, was immediately named doge indicates the role played by this family (and their *nobili* allies, the Fieschi) in the fulminous coup. More importantly, Genoa's unruliness and resistance to any centralized authority (be it a local doge or a foreign predatory governor) are reflected in contemporary Spanish sources.

Antoniotto Adorno was the doge of the Genoese republic from 1522 to 1527.[35] During these five years, Genoa was part of the international alliance led by the emperor Charles V, but the political relationship between the Ligurian government and Spain is not clear. Thomas Kirk has written that in this period "Adorno had little autonomy, and Genoa was a subject state."[36] However, in spite of the important role played by the Spanish ambassador Lope de Soria in the political life of the republic, the Genoese constitution and private arms represented instruments of resistance to the fiscal and military policies recommended by Charles. Liguria did not embody an exception within the Habsburg system of governance. Rather, the five years of the first Hispanic-Genoese alliance represented a key period during which the Genoese became acquainted with the typical features of Charles's empire. I am surely not the first one to reflect on the differences in governance between Valois and Habsburgs in Liguria: Manuel Herrero Sánchez has written an illuminating essay on this subject.[37] As I will show in the following pages, early Cinquecento Genoese found the (relative) looseness of the Habsburg system and its respect for local liberties convenient or at least acceptable—especially when compared to the tactics and policies traditionally followed by the French Crown. The Spanish were obviously ready to seize an opportunity for the establishment of a more "direct" and predatory form of government in places like Milan, where the political history, the civic culture, and even the geographical conditions allowed it. But Charles quickly understood that the situation in Genoa was remarkably different, and that anyway he could achieve many of his objectives (e.g., transporting troops; controlling routes in the West Mediterranean; accessing the capital of private bankers) while accepting Genoa's constitutional tradition. This first period of collaboration was therefore fundamental, for the Genoese learned that their communal order and their property rights were more secure under the Habsburg banner than under the Valois's, and at the same time Charles came to value the strategic importance of Genoa while becoming aware of the power of its private arms and of the peculiarities of its economic praxis and political culture.

In a letter written on February 24, 1524, the emperor was informed by Lope de Soria about the military situation in Northern Italy. In this text, the ambassador also described two issues that were creating tensions within the

Figure 5.1. Charles V. ©iStock.com/ZU_09.

Genoese republic: taxation of the capital market and disagreements between Genoa and Savona. On the former problem, the ambassador wrote:

> The Doge and the Community of Genoa have now decided to establish a new fee on those who buy and sell the bonds of Saint George, which is five *sueldos* of this coin for each [bond], so while before they had to pay ten *sueldos* for each [bond], now they have to pay fifteen *sueldos* . . . and in this place you have no other way to collect money other than charging new fees, and this

> Community is already so much taxed that in the future it will be hard to obtain such great amount of money and it will be necessary that God and Your Majesty find a remedy because otherwise it will be impossible to avoid some uproar of the people considering the numerous fees and burdens that one can find in this land.[38]

This letter shows all the discouragement and the frustration felt by Charles's ambassador. First of all, it is important to notice that fiscal power in Genoa was held neither by Lope de Soria nor by Antoniotto Adorno on their own, but rather by the latter "and the Community," an expression that indicates and summarizes the complex institutional and juridical structure put in place by the *regulae* of 1363.[39] Not even the doge who had been named in the aftermath of the devastating sack of 1522 and with the support of the most powerful monarch of the European continent could autonomously decide to raise taxes in Genoa. So much so that the *derechos* described here by Lope de Soria, the fees paid by those who sell and buy the bonds of St. George, were the only artifice through which the republican government could raise any revenue. The Spanish diplomat certainly admitted this fact, when he wrote that "in this place you have no other way to collect money." Such affirmation is only apparently in contradiction with what Lope de Soria then emphatically repeats twice: that the Genoese people are burdened with taxes. Indeed, at this point, one could ask: if there is no way for the doge to collect any fiscal revenue other than charging the exchange of public bonds in the secondary market, and yet the Genoese people are being considerably taxed, then who is exactly taxing them? The answer (which Charles knew quite well) is the Genoese businessmen themselves, who had progressively privatized the fiscal apparatus of the Ligurian *stato*—a process hastened and perfected by the Bank of St. George.[40] In Genoa, self-government meant primarily financial self-government.[41] In this context, Lope de Soria overstated the fiscal burden placed on the Genoese citizens, because he knew that Antoniotto Adorno had almost no space for political maneuver: it was virtually impossible for the Genoese head of state to increase the revenues, since he could not administer the *gabelle* and thus he could not have access to the Genoese people's capital.[42] The Spanish diplomat candidly emphasized in his letter that it would have been impossible in the future to receive more funds from the community of Genoa. Therefore, a careful analysis and contextualization of this passage, though of course not by itself exhaustive, already suggests that Genoa between 1522 and 1527 was not a "subject state," that all the communal institutions devised in 1363 to divide power were still in place, and, more importantly, that the spirit of Genoa's laws was still effective, preventing the doge from increasing its revenues and embarking in military campaigns or in the construction of a large public fleet.[43] As a final reflection on this paragraph, it seems quite telling the fact that the Spanish feared an uprising and a violent revolt in Genoa, less than two years after the sack, and with their troops being already on the ground in Northern Italy; as we shall see, other letters corroborate the fact that the Spanish perceived Genoa as a testy and untrustworthy polity.

The second theme treated by Lope de Soria in this letter is the tension between Savona and Genoa. Savona, which was part of the traditional possessions called by the Genoese *Riviere*, was a natural competitor of Genoa, having a large harbor and being well connected to France, Monferrato, and Milan. The Genoese had always tried to prevent this city from becoming an international hub, forbidding the transit of certain goods and demanding high tariffs on products like salt.[44] Lope de Soria's paragraph dedicated to this quarrel begins with these words:

> The said Community of Genoa and the people of Savona are deeply in discord about the dominion, because the Genoese demand the supreme and entire sovereignty over Savona in the same way in which they exercise it over all the other places that are subject to them.[45]

Despite their traditional skepticism towards communal military adventures and territorial expansion, the Genoese continued to consider their control of the *Riviere* a non-negotiable privilege. This position was based neither on a patriotic lucubration, nor on a post-1494 defensive strategy, but, as made clear by Lope de Soria, rather on purely economic considerations: "and based on this they [the Genoese] keep Savona very subjugated and almost destroyed, as they do not let it do any business and they prevent any commercial good and any ship from entering or leaving the port."[46] Notwithstanding the tragic events of 1522, and despite the Spanish influence on Liguria, in 1524 Genoa was still retaining its territorial possessions, and Charles was respecting its privileges as well as the unity of its dominion. But for the people of Savona the Hispanic-Genoese alliance represented an opportunity to change this sad state of affairs. Thus, they astutely proposed to overlap the Genoese and the imperial jurisdictions, in order to place their city under the protection of Charles:

> And the inhabitants of Savona simply ask to have the possibility to petition and appeal to your Cesarean Majesty in case they may have any dispute with the Genoese, and this is the only thing on which they disagree, because the people of Savona are glad to observe all the treaties and agreements that they have with the Genoese and if this is not enough they are ready to write down the treaties once again with all that is claimed [by the Genoese] and they will accept them, but they want that only in case any unforeseen disagreement arises between them your Cesarean Majesty will be the judge and they can plea to him, however the Genoese do not want this as they want to be the judges in any dispute and they do not want them [the people of Savona] to plea to your Cesarean Majesty.[47]

Perhaps, the Spanish diplomat was here simply reporting almost word by word what the representatives of Savona had told him. But there is no doubt that if Charles had accepted Savona's proposal he would have soon been overwhelmed by petitions and he would have compromised the Adorno regime in Genoa. That the inhabitants of Savona could bend their Ligurian identity to the extent of rejecting a key component of their state's sovereign powers represents in itself a really interesting, non-Atlantic case of entangled communities.[48] The very concept of state, when uncritically used in the study of early modern Italy, is called into question by this episode and, more generally, throughout this book. But considering the aim of this chapter, what seems remarkable here is that after almost two years of Spanish "rule," Charles had never tried to take advantage of Savona's port or to intervene in quarrels between Genoa and its Ligurian possessions. Savona's issue was raised for the first time by the inhabitants of Savona themselves. So, in 1524 the metropolis was still exercising—both officially and *de facto*—its authority over the Ligurian dominion. In sum, the study of this manuscript dated February 25, 1524, suggests that during the first Hispanic-Genoese alliance (1522–1527) Genoa maintained its constitutional order, as well as the dominion in the *Riviere*. Charles did not disrespect Genoa's privileges or break the Ligurian territorial unity, because private capital, as well as private arms, were ready to be used to overthrow Adorno's government, had this been perceived as too servile or unable to guarantee Genoa's *libertà*—a concept of which, as we have seen here and in previous chapters, economic prosperity was a key component. In 1528, the Genoese were going to prove how much they cared about the economic subjugation of Savona, but I will return on the importance of economic considerations for the Genoese when treating the momentous events of that year. Now, we shall focus on other diplomatic communications penned by Lope de Soria, in order to support with more evidence the twofold thesis that the Spanish were not ruling Genoa and that they were seriously worried about Genoa's factions and private arms.

On March 6, 1524, Lope de Soria wrote a letter to Charles to express his opinion with regard to a negotiation that was underway between the viceroy Carlos de Lannoy and members of the Fregoso faction. As explained in the document, the Fregoso, who had been exiled since 1522, had first contacted the Duke of Urbino, and through him they had been able to begin informal talks with the viceroy.[49] The Fregoso were asking for the permission to return to Genoa and were promising in turn to do great things (*grandes cosas*) for the Hispanic-Genoese alliance. But news of this plan had reached Genoa, and Lope de Soria thought that such talks were a reckless diplomatic move, because allowing the Fregoso to enter Genoa could have terrible, unpredictable consequences. Even the fact that the viceroy had accepted to communicate with the Fregoso was already jeopardizing the Spanish faction within Genoa. In particular, the ambassador wrote: "I do not know what the viceroy has answered to them [the Fregoso], but this doge [Antoniotto Adorno] and this community [Genoa] have been and still are quite angry about this negotiation, even though they are sure that the viceroy will not agree."[50] Lope de Soria explicitly stated that he feared an explosion of violence in Genoa, given the characteristics of the Genoese people. According to the ambassador, the viceroy must not respond, because "it would not be good for your Majesty if it was said that these negotiations are going on, especially considering the quality of this city [Genoa], which is *mother of passions and partialities and revolutions*, I believe that the said viceroy has not lent an ear and until now he has not agreed."[51] This key passage sparks two significant reflections: it opens a window on the way in which the Spanish perceived the Genoese polity; and it shows one of the reasons why the Genoese could resist the post-1494 change in the categories of Renaissance political thought, holding on to the model of the medieval commune and retaining their republican civic cosmology. On the first point, Castilians and Aragonese had known the Genoese for centuries as merchants and bankers, sailors and pirates; Ferdinand II had protected them, understanding their fundamental role in the economic life of the Iberian Peninsula and of the Western Mediterranean.[52] The Genoese abroad were indeed perceived in a way that was strikingly similar to the self-perception and celebration emerging from Genoese sources.[53] However, as the Spanish soon discovered, the political life of Genoa was dangerously complex. Lope de Soria understood that the Fregoso family could not be reintegrated into the community, because it maintained an armed faction and friendships with *nobili* families who could gather little armies in the countryside. In other words, what the Spanish learned about Genoa in the years 1522–1527 made them grasp the volatility of any regime in this polity and prepared them to appreciate the solution later proposed by Andrea Doria.

The second reflection sparked by this episode has to do with the resistance (and resilience) of Genoa's republican conservatism in the hostile political climate of the time. A true pacification—and thus a true conquest—of Liguria remained an impossible task, not only for the lack of a strong central authority commanding a standing army or a public fleet, but also for the wealth and power of private citizens. A foreign ruler could not simply decapitate the Genoese structure and take control of it, because, in a sense, Genoa had no structure at all. The "structure" in place was the *regulae* of 1363, whose main objective was to deliberately disperse power.[54] But the lack of a structure did not imply the lack of any financial resource, political network, or even military force on the ground. Therefore, in Genoa the availability of private armies, fleets, and funds rendered the threat of subjugation (either by Spain or France) more remote and the crisis of city-state republicanism less deep. This helps to explain why a "Machiavellian" solution (with centralizing reforms and territorial acquisitions) appeared to a majority of Genoese businessmen not only unpalatably authoritarian and expensive, but also quite unnecessary.

During the first months of 1524, the troops of Francis I had not only renounced their attack on Milan, but also begun a long retreat toward France.[55] Even before the battle of Sesia (April 30), Charles V was making plans to launch an expedition against the ports of Provence, while his generals would invade France. In fact, on the very day of the victory, Lope de Soria, from Genoa, was already penning a letter concerning the preparation of the naval force.[56] From this letter, we learn that Charles wanted the Genoese to participate in the expedition, furnishing as many galleys as possible. His ambassador had indeed diligently and forcefully presented this request to the Genoese republic and wrote: "I have put pressure on the said doge of Genoa to get him and the people of this republic to arm as many ships as possible."[57] However, the ambassador continued:

> he [the doge] says that in case it will be necessary for the expedition to Provence, he will arm here all the ships that is possible, but they [the Genoese] will not do it simply to accompany the galleys of your Majesty to assault the coast of Provence, because this would have damaging consequences for this community [Genoa].[58]

Lope de Soria concluded the letter trying to reassure his monarch about the number of ships that would eventually be gathered under his flag, but Genoa's response remained unequivocal. Adorno's words were surely not those that one would expect from the representative of a "subject state." First, the doge put into question the very need for Genoese vessels, reserving his (or better, the Genoese galley owners') right to judge whether this existed or not; then, he clarified that, even if Genoa had furnished some warships, the Genoese would not have consented to use them to get actively involved in an attack that could jeopardize their interests.[59] In sum, no one could order the Genoese people to fight, or to give up their private galleys. Political power in Genoa remained fragmentary, slippery, and, from the perspective of the doge (and of those who hoped to influence him), nearly insubstantial. The governmental structure was simply too weak to rapidly mobilize military forces or to seize private assets. Private citizens and nongovernmental entities like St. George remained in control of most of the arms and wealth in Genoa. In July, the imperial army entered France, while a Spanish naval posse attacked the coast of Provence. Not even one Genoese ship took part in this expedition; Antoniotto Adorno sent seven galleys out to sea, but they simply guarded the Ligurian Sea and the port.[60] The only Genoese warships intervening in Provence were those of the private fleet of the Doria family, which fought for the French.

DORIA'S WAY: THE POWER OF PRIVATE CITIZENS AND THE SURVIVAL OF THE GENOESE ECONOMIC CULTURE

Andrea Doria (1466–1560) was born in a *nobili* family, but, as we have seen, this did not mean much in Genoa, where business success and personal wealth were more decisive than anything else in determining the social status and the political profile of a citizen. Moreover, Andrea's branch of the family was a secondary one, and we know that his financial means were initially very modest (at least when compared to those of other young aristocrats, both *nobili* and *popolari*). While very few historians have told the story of the first Hispanic-Genoese alliance, the literature on Doria, his military endeavors, and his coup of 1528 is quite abundant.[61] Thus, here I will primarily consider what motivated Doria (and his countrymen) to switch sides in 1528, inaugurating a second Hispanic-Genoese alliance and deciding the fate of the Italian Wars. Subsequently, I will briefly present the most important pamphlet of Uberto Foglietta, whose frustration shall help us to understand how Doria's reforms did not represent a break away from Genoa's late medieval and republican culture.

The first Hispanic-Genoese alliance ended in 1527, when a French army (helped, as usual, by Genoese exiles and nobles) entered Genoa, while Andrea Doria, who was fighting the Italian Wars on the French side, supported the expedition by sea. Antoniotto Adorno and Lope de Soria had to flee across the mountains. What happened in the next months has rarely been investigated with due attention. The new French governor, a non-Genoese Italian noble, was unexpectedly ousted, just one year later, by a coup led by none other than Andrea Doria. Doria's startling decision to abandon the French king and to enter the service of Charles V has been usually seen as mainly due to the jealous character and the clumsy, arrogant attitudes of Francis I (which are admittedly hard to deny). Another factor which has been given much importance is Charles's promise to Andrea to respect Genoa's independence—an opinion based on a somehow anachronistic view of what "independence" meant to the Genoese, as well as on a mistaken conviction that Charles could have in fact easily conquered and pacified the Ligurian republic. Yet, several key documents and chronicles demonstrate that contingent economic considerations and a progressive appreciation of the differences between Valois and Habsburg governance motivated both Andrea Doria and the Genoese elite.

Agostino Mascardi (1590–1640) was a Jesuit, historian, and poet born in the town of Sarzana, at the outskirts of the Genoese territory. A typical humanist intellectual, he lived and worked in several Renaissance courts across Italy, producing during his lifetime an impressive amount of books, pamphlets, and poems.[62] One of his most intriguing literary endeavors is *Congiura del conte Gio Luigi Fiesco, seguita l'Anno 1547*, a historical account of the conspiracy that had famously shaken Genoa and Andrea Doria's new constitutional arrangement in 1547.[63] The bloody revolt (and subsequent repression) of that year is not the topic of this chapter; yet, at the beginning of his book, after an opening statement, Mascardi offers a summary of the events that had led to Doria's coup of 1528:

> The war raging in Italy between the emperor Charles V and Francis I king of France, Andrea Doria, an experienced commander in sea-affairs, follow'd the banner of the French . . . But, as it is the fatal infelicity of princes not to esteem eminent persons whilst they are engaged in their service, the king, by ways little discreet, exasperated the mind of Andrea, a minister so necessary to him at this time. He did not pay him his assign'd stipend; and, after he had taken from him the prince of Orange, his prisoner of war, and set him at liberty, thereby defrauding him of his due ransom, he demanded with importunity and insolent threatnings the marquis Vasto, and Ascanio Colonna, taken in fight by Philippino Doria, lieutenant to Andrea. But that which most pierced the soul of the good old man, was the small faith of the king in complying with his promise, touching the interest and the reputation of the Genoese. The city of Savona had withdrawn itself from the obedience of the common-wealth; expecting under the protection of France, to better its condition by the commodiousness of the port, which furnished them with extraordinary emoluments, to the irreparable damage of the city of Genoa.[64]

Doria complained to his royal patron about all these issues, and in particular about the economic threat constituted by Savona. However, Francis did not immediately perceive the danger of losing his best admiral and, even worse, to see him entering the service of his archenemy.

> He [Francis] had seen by experience how inconstant the Genoese were, and how little he could depend upon that common-wealth for his war in Italy. . . . [T]herefore esteeming it necessary for his designs to have a port at his devotion commodious for the affairs of Lombardy, he chose Savona, and gave the charge of it to Momorancy. Conceiving, that with this determination he had at once bridled the inconstancy of the Genoese, and greatly advantag'd the course of his enterprize; because the city of Savona being near to Piedmont, Montferrat and Lombardy, it became an opportune scale, no less for merchandise than for war: hence 'twas fear'd, that in a few years growing in reputation and riches, it might not only divert the trade from the port of Genoa, but rival it with them for the principality of the sea. Of this Doria, as a singular lover of his country, sharply complain'd: but at last seeing it was in vain, he turns his mind to other counsels.[65]

Thus, Andrea Doria left the French side, and his galleys became an invaluable military asset for the emperor Charles V.[66] The Genoese *condottiero* entered Liguria, and immediately his countrymen rose against the French governor, the Milanese Teodoro Trivulzio. Genoa once again shook off a foreign government, and as Andrea refused to become a dictator, he welcomed the title of liberator, while preparing to reform the constitutional order of his city-state.

Before analyzing Mascardi's words, it is opportune to juxtapose an earlier document, which was written by the cousin of Andrea Doria. The book entitled *Compendio d'Antonio Doria delle cose di sua notitia, et memoria occorse al mondo nel tempo dell'imperatore Carlo Quinto* was published in Genoa in 1571.[67] Its author was an extraordinary man, whose adventurous life has been overshadowed only because of his more famous relative. Antonio Doria was born in a *nobili* family, but when young he had traveled to Spain to learn the profession of merchant; later, he had joined the family fleet, where he fought under Andrea's command.[68] Antonio quickly became an experienced and talented captain, in charge of two galleys of the French fleet. When, in 1528, Andrea Doria abandoned the French king to join the imperial side, Antonio did not follow him.[69] Only in 1531, after months of unpaid work, did Antonio rejoin Andrea, switching sides and joining the imperial fleet in the Mediterranean.[70]

In his *Compendio*, while recounting the conflict of 1521–1527 (a series of military clashes, which were part of the Italian Wars), Antonio Doria spent some pages to detail the fall of the Adorno regime, and the end of the first Hispanic-Genoese alliance. As confirmed by this source, there is no doubt that Andrea Doria and his entire military force (both the galleys directly commanded by him and the infantry led by Filippino Doria) actively participated in the French conquest of Genoa.[71] This is not to say that until 1527 the relationship between Andrea Doria and Francis had been spotless or unproblematic. However, delays in the payment of troops and *condottieri* were a recurring feature of the Italian Wars, and to assume that Andrea was already planning to join the imperial side and that he had begun to withdraw his support from the French military operations would be an unfair and unsubstantiated claim. He fought for Francis as late as August 1527, and his galleys' contribution was decisive to conquer Genoa.[72] What was, then, Andrea's reason for subsequently abandoning the French side? In other words, what events taking place in the months after the instauration of Trivulzio as French governor of the Genoese republic did cause a dramatic deterioration of Andrea's relationship with the transalpine monarch?

On page 36 of his book, Antonio Doria begins to describe the chain of events that led to his relative's (and commander's) decision to "free" Genoa, entering the service of Charles V. After the conquest of Genoa and other clashes in Northern Italy, the main battlefield of the war moved, at the beginning of 1528, towards Naples. Here, during a clash between French forces and the imperial army, Count Filippino Doria was able to capture Ascanio Colonna and the Marquis of Vasto, who were two of Charles's *condottieri*. When Francis heard of this capture, he ordered Andrea to give him the two imperial commanders. Yet,

> because a few years earlier he had given to him Philibert Prince of Orange but he [Francis] had never paid the promised reward, he [Andrea] refused. Moreover, both he [Andrea] and the citizens of Genoa being upset with the king, because of the occupation of Savona, where he [Francis] collected the taxes and allowed the trade of salt which was forbidden by the conventions, he [Andrea] tried to take advantage of these events in order to bring them to unity and to abolish all those partialities that for so many years had divided them, and he obtained this easily.[73]

Through his prisoner, the Marquis of Vasto, Andrea approached the imperial side and reached an agreement with Charles V. Thus Andrea Doria went to Naples with his fleet and broke the siege that just a few months earlier he had helped to lay. The Genoese admiral chased the French ships that, having abandoned the siege of Naples, were swiftly moving towards Liguria. But the French governor Trivulzio, rather than organizing the defense of Genoa, preferred to close himself inside the fortress called *Castelletto*. Seeing that Genoa's port was not a safe harbor (but rather a potential trap), the French vessels tried to seek refuge in Savona, but Doria reached them and, after a short battle, was able to capture three of them.[74] Then, Andrea went back to Genoa and

> entering the city with his troops, raising the cry for *libertà* and calling all the citizens from the villas where they had taken refuge because of the plague, he was followed by all with great enthusiasm, and laid a siege to the *Castelletto*. . . . Trivulzio, desperate for help, soon surrendered the *Castelletto*. And in this way, that Republic that for so long had suffered, with few forces and in a dangerous moment, being the enemy army close, remained in *libertà*, thanks to the unity and concord of the citizens, who having organized quite quickly an army, which was mostly composed by their own people, and having named the Count Filippino Doria as its Captain, they sent it to reconquer Savona.[75]

But what was the relation between the Genoese idea of *libertà* and the submission of Savona? Antonio Doria unraveled this question, as on the next page he wrote:

> And in order to prevent that city from damaging the Republic, through the commodiousness of its port and the place where it was founded—and this would have surely happened if it had been allowed to remain separated from its [Genoa's] dominion for longer, because being possible to bring merchandise and salt through that way easily to Lombardy, it would have taken away even more business from Genoa. . . . [The Genoese] had the port completely filled, as they had completely destroyed a beautiful pier a few years earlier, for

> the same reasons. They also levelled the bastions and the fortifications that the Count of Navarra had built for the defense of that city.[76]

Another author who recounted the coup of 1528 is the Renaissance historian and intellectual Carlo Sigonio (1520–1584).[77] In his *Della vita et fatti di Andrea Doria*, Sigonio adds a remarkable detail to the reconstruction of the events that led to the Genoese admiral's decision to abandon his alliance with the French monarch. According to this writer, the relations between Andrea and Francis were intentionally ruined by a group of jealous ministers surrounding the king.[78] More importantly, Sigonio claims that the issue of hostages and ransoms was not as decisive as the political issue regarding Savona; by the time Francis demanded the captives and Doria refused, the relationship had already deteriorated. Yet the truly noteworthy information delivered by Sigonio's book is that, beside Savona, there was a second political issue that contributed to create tension between Doria's faction and the transalpine court:

> while the King had often given some hope to Doria that he would give back to Genoa its *libertà*, [the French] continuously put pressure on him [the King] to put it [Genoa] under an even more severe state of subjugation, and among other things they persuaded him to fortify Savona taking it away from Genoa's dominion, and to impose in the future more burdens on the city, and in order to do that they sent to Genoa the Viscount of Turena to ask a certain sum of money in the name of the King; and by all these things the heart of Doria was enormously offended.[79]

Sigonio's account goes on describing how Andrea, after learning the request made by Turena, and hearing the pleas of many Genoese citizens, rushed out of his villa riding a horse and entered the Ducal Palace where Trivulzio and the French envoy were still talking. There, Doria confronted Turena and plainly stated that the Genoese people could not and would not pay any money to the king. The French noble, according to Sigonio, was so startled that he left the palace without uttering a single word.[80] This episode is significant not only because it adds another piece to the puzzle of the deteriorating relations between Francis I and Andrea Doria, but also because of the nature of the diatribe, which is, once again, economic. As in the case of Savona, Francis was disrespecting Genoa's constitutional order, thus jeopardizing Genoa's privet profits and wealth. This—not the French garrisons in Liguria, not a foreign governor in the Ducal Palace—was unacceptable to Doria as well as to the Genoese people.

Mascardi's historical summary, Antonio Doria's account, and Sigonio's biography allow us to draw some interesting conclusions. Part I of this book has uncovered a peculiarly Genoese economic culture, characterized by adaptability and private entrepreneurship, and mainly focused on trade; this culture was both influencing and influenced by a political order based on the division of offices among groups of citizens, to the detriment of the doge's prerogatives. During the late Middle Ages, Genoese businessmen had privatized public finance, reformed the fiscal and constitutional structure of the republic to protect the accumulation of private wealth, and prevented military adventures or the organization of a public fleet. This chapter has posed the question whether such Genoese model of republican city-state resisted to the challenge brought into the Italian world by the descent of Charles VIII. The study of Genoa's political history and the analysis of the documents presented above indicate that during this period no one was able to reshuffle the Genoese *stato* and to impose a centralized authority (be it local or foreigner). After 1494, economically successful private citizens and cross-class political factions continued to be politically and militarily influential. Overall, Genoa's civic culture (business-oriented and skeptical towards anything resembling the Machiavellian territorial state) survived the crisis of the Italian Wars. Genoa continued to be what George Gorse has called "a city of private family wealth and power over public communal authority and space, the antithesis of Venice."[81]

Andrea Doria loyally fought for the French monarch as long as it was remunerable for him to do so, and as long as Francis did not implement tactless policies that risked the impoverishment of his city. Not by chance, the sources confirm that the only two political complaints over Genoa that Andrea Doria made to Francis were of a purely economic nature. The first of them regarded Genoese property rights, and in particular the impossibility to arbitrarily demand money from the Genoese citizenry; the second had to do with Savona, and the privileges of Genoa over that potentially rival city port. In the summer of 1528, Doria wisely entered Genoa as a liberator, not as a new ruler. His call for unity and *libertà*, as recounted by his relative Antonio, hinted at the reestablishment of the traditional economic imperialism over the *Riviere* and the thalassocracy in the Western Mediterranean. Savona, thanks to the French king's protection, was threatening what Mascardi called Genoa's "principality of the sea."[82] According to Arturo Pacini, "Francis I had even attempted to divide Liguria in two. Claiming for himself direct jurisdiction over Savona, he had tried to build a political, economic, and strategic-military alternative to Genoa, in order to control the Western Riviera and obtain a safe access from the sea to the high Po valley."[83] Only this serious and manifest threat could "unite" all the Genoese factions, and therefore Doria's first act as "liberator" was precisely to reconquer and punish Savona, not with a bloodbath, but rather with the complete destruction of its economic heart, the harbor.[84] And it would be a mistake to imagine that Savona was just a symbolic prey arbitrarily chosen by Andrea. On the contrary, one year earlier, with the city surrounded by land and by sea, Antoniotto Adorno had sent a representative to the French general Lautrec, in order to negotiate a pacific surrender of Genoa. On this occasion, the only request presented by the Genoese delegation had been the respect of Genoa's dominion over Savona. When Lautrec refused to give his word, saying that he had no authority on that matter and did not know the intentions of his king, the Genoese were so outraged that they decided to (re)take up arms and fight until the end.[85]

All these events show the resilience of a mercantile, commercial culture and of an idea of freedom understood in economic terms among the Genoese people. In Genoa, putting the republic under the nominal protection of a foreign ruler who respected its constitution had always continued to be a legitimate option, because Genoa had never resolved the problems of internal factionalism and external threats by centralizing power (either through the establishment of a *signoria* or, like in Venice and Florence, through territorial expansion). But Genoa's civic cosmology was not merely an ideological remnant. It is important to acknowledge the impact that the first Hispanic-Genoese alliance had on both the Spanish and the Genoese. In 1527, Genoa came from five years of collaboration with the Spanish ambassador. During those five years, notwithstanding Savona's appeal, Charles had prudently abstained from interfering with Genoa's dominion over Liguria. Thus, the Genoese merchant elite learned that under the imperial banner it was possible to maintain a certain level of economic prosperity and independence—medievally intended as respect of the 1363 constitution and of Genoa's authority over the Ligurian *Riviere*.[86] Charles, on the other hand, had learned that while the Genoese had no problems in being ruled by a doge who had been chosen by him, they appeared extremely irascible when asked to do something that might have jeopardized their economic interests. In a letter written on May 26, 1527, Lope de Soria had expressed all his frustration for Genoa's volatile and testy political atmosphere; the Spanish ambassador had called the Genoese *gente del diablo*—"diabolical people."[87] Yet, thanks to the experience accumulated by Charles and the Spanish diplomats during the first Hispanic-Genoese alliance (1522–1527), and thanks to Andrea Doria's timely decision to join the imperial side, this riotous, untrustworthy, greedy, and "diabolical" merchant people would have become Spain's best friend, both in the Mediterranean and in the Atlantic. In the Mediterranean, the Hispanic-Genoese alliance continued well after the defeat of France, because Charles needed financial and naval support to defend the Christians who were increasingly the target of Ottoman raids. As put by Dauverd, "although much smaller than the Ottoman fleet, the Genoese fleet, posted in Naples and Messina, continuously volunteered to protect the western Mediterranean waters from random Turkish assaults."[88] In the Atlantic, as we shall see in the next chapter, the Genoese soon participated in the Spanish effort of empire building.

THROUGH THE EYES OF A DISSIDENT: DORIA'S GENOA AND THE SURVIVAL OF A CITY-STATE

The Genoese had tried to outline political reforms that could maintain the partitioning of political power while breaking the *Cappellazzi* system since at least the beginning of the century.[89] In 1527, the Genoese once again debated what kind of reforms were necessary to limit the excesses of factionalism and achieve political stability. Some of the ideas that emerged in this occasion would be realized one year later, through Doria's reforms. But it would be a mistake to see in this desire for "unity" the success of Machiavelli's political theories in Genoa. The Genoese were not rejecting the idea of a partitioned, weak government; rather, they were aiming at perfecting it, replacing the old, medieval social groups among which offices had been shared until then with new, cross-factional groups (the famous twenty-eight *alberghi*). In the process, the power of what we may call the executive branch was not enhanced, but humbled even further.[90] When Andrea Doria reformed Genoa's political constitution in 1528, he had two main goals: breaking the *cappellazzi* system that had placed the dogeship in the hands of the Adorno and the Fregoso; and eliminating the rivalry between *nobili* and *popolari*. Notwithstanding Charles V's support, Doria did not want to become *signore* of Genoa, both because he knew that Genoa lacked a fiscal and military structure with which he could impose his authority over other wealthy and armed nobles, and because—in perfectly Genoese fashion—he preferred to obtain economic (rather than political) compensations from the emperor.[91] But while Doria's objectives were clear, they were also quite general, and they could be accomplished in several different ways. Genoa could (in theory) have been transformed into a centralized political entity, with a public fleet, a standing army, and a strengthened executive branch; Liguria could have become a territorial state, able perhaps to more adequately face the challenges of a new era. Yet, this Machiavellian turn never materialized.[92] Andrea Doria's reforms changed much in the political institutions, the electoral system, and even the internal alliances and factions within the city; but they did so without altering the spirit of Genoa's republicanism, nor the "pre-1494" peculiarities of the Genoese model.[93] The figure of the doge became even weaker, as his tenure was reduced to two years, without the possibility of a reelection. Indeed, Arturo Pacini has stressed that one of the main objectives of the reforms was to further divide and weaken the political power of the communal government—in line with the medieval political tradition.[94] Genoa remained a republic of private businessmen, who intended *libertà* as freedom to do business, and self-government as St. George's power to collect taxes and grant loans to the government, therefore deciding which policies it would back and finance, and which it would not.

That this was one of the end results of Doria's coup is confirmed by those Genoese who dissented with such a moderate, traditional approach. The writer and polemicist Uberto Foglietta (1518–1581) was surely among these "Machiavellian" thinkers.[95] In his 1559 book *Delle cose della Repubblica di Genova*, the Genoese intellectual imagined a dialogue taking place in Amsterdam, between two Ligurian friends. The main themes of the work are the arrogance of the *nobili* and the internal division that, according to the author, is still tormenting Genoa. However, in several passages throughout the text Foglietta explicitly referred to other, more specific issues that rendered Doria's reforms unsatisfactory and inadequate. In the first part of the dialogue, one of the characters laments the loss of Corsica, and in this way he introduces the broader topic of the numerous territories that the Genoese republic has lost in the Levant.[96] While in this case the author does not specifically mention the need for a powerful public fleet, the foundations for this subsequent argument are laid already here, at the beginning of the dialogue. Moreover, it is significant that in lamenting these territorial losses Foglietta did not stress the economic consequences of these events, choosing instead to strike a patriotic cord by writing that "[our Patria] has lost the dominion over many lands in the Levant that had been taken by our ancestors' virtue and efforts; and together with the dominion [we lost] also the good reputation and the honour of our name."[97]

Foglietta's interest in a territorial state and in military expansion emerges more unmistakably when his characters talk about missed historical opportunities. According to the author, in the previous centuries Genoa could have conquered part of Lombardy, Pisa, and even the rest of Tuscany:

> And with regard to territorial expansion, it could have been easier for the Genoese than for the Venetians to conquer a part of Lombardy, because at that time they would not have found united against them a power such as a Milanese state, since at that time Lombardy was divided in many different states, as many as the cities of that weak Province; and no one among them would have resisted the wealth and the strength of the Genoese, if the Genoese had proceeded in this territorial expansion with that virtue, and industry with which every people that makes its neighbours subject proceeds. . . . Neither did the Florentines need more virtue or more industry, nor did they have much strength at that time, when they conquered large parts of the Lands of Tuscany and Pisa itself, which we could have better conquered than the Florentines if, at that time two hundred years ago, we had proceeded properly. . . . And that achievable conquest of Pisa would have opened for us the road to extend our empire over Tuscany.[98]

But, of course, the Genoese would have never allowed a doge (or a *podesta*) to raise the revenues, to command the troops, and to seize the galleys that were necessary to invade Lombardy and subject the Tuscan coast. So, with these remarks, Foglietta was consciously turning upside down Genoa's civic culture. As we have seen in the previous chapters, during the late Middle Ages the Genoese had usually avoided territorial expansion and state-run military expeditions.[99] In fact, the city's fiscal reforms and communal constitution prevented the doge from taking any significant initiative. And this peculiar kind of polity was mirrored in Genoa's self-perception, as expressed in literary works and poems celebrating anonymous Genoese businessmen, their business activities, their private wealth, their seafaring skills, and their life in distant ports.[100] As we have seen, at times the Genoese were even openly praising their restraint in military matters and their respect for foreign dominions. Therefore, Foglietta's political proposal, as well as his shattered dreams and his bitter considerations, were nothing less than a frontal assault on Genoa's resilient republican model.

Doria had carried out institutional reforms in the name of unity, but Foglietta argued that true unity was impossible as long as private armies were not disbanded and private interests were not subordinated to the higher interests of the state. What Foglietta dreamed was a "Machiavellian" state, where political power was not divided, but centralized. This united, powerful republic would have been able to defend its *libertà*, now intended as positive liberty through political participation, freedom from foreign lords, and ability to increase (in Machiavelli's words, *acquistare* and *ampliare*) territorial possessions. A public army and a public fleet were, unsurprisingly, key components of this political recipe. And this issue was precisely what, more than anything else, rendered Doria's reforms unsatisfactory in the eyes of Uberto Foglietta:

> If such important dangers threaten the Patria, why does not Prince Doria—who is wise and who therefore shall be aware of them, and who is so good that he loves more the Patria than the private greatness of his family, as we have seen—take action? Why does he not act, holding so much authority? And why does not he take away the Galleys from his heirs to offer them to the Patria?[101]

What we see here is a blatant rejection of the themes and ideology celebrated by the Genoese poets of the previous century; likewise, the irreconcilable contraposition between "Patria" and "private greatness" was up to this point completely alien to the Genoese culture. Such contraposition between private wealth and military prowess was, on the other hand, quite familiar to anyone who had read Machiavelli's writings. In the first book of his dialogue entitled *The Art of War*, Machiavelli summarized the characteristics of the ancient Roman republic that he wished to reintroduce in the Italian states. Four of the listed (mythical) Roman attitudes seem eye-catchingly incompatible with the Genoese civic culture: "not to have contempt for poverty, to esteem the modes and orders of military discipline, . . . to live without factions, to esteem less the private than the public good."[102] Interestingly, they are all manifestly part of Foglietta's political ideals and agenda.

In the last section of the book, Foglietta reiterated that giving all his galleys to the republic was the only way for Doria to prove that his glorious actions had been accomplished for the public good, and not for his private interests. The author also defended more in general the idea of a public fleet, able to secure Genoa's power, to guarantee an occupation to the city's youth, and more importantly to command the respect of Italy "and of all the other Princes."[103] Foglietta's "Machiavellian" mentality was the consequence of the shock represented by the Italian Wars, as described at the beginning of this chapter. The following passage is fundamental to understand how after 1494 the (self-)perception of many Italians—though not of many Genoese citizens—had dramatically changed:

> while in the past Civic discords often forced us to seek Foreign governments, at that time there were certain conditions, in which the Citizens had the means to expel them every time they wanted, and in fact, with their governments they have always done so. But now, everyone can see, that things have changed so much, that having to fall prey of *only enormously powerful Princes*, and knowing the one who takes it how useful is Genoa for his ploys but also how often it rebels and changes foreign governments, he would control it [Genoa] in such a way, that we could not play with it, and he would reduce us, both with fortresses and with countless other burdens, in a state of servitude, from which may God save us.[104]

In this context, Foglietta believed that also the Genoese concept of *libertà* needed to evolve.

The Genoese republic had proved, between 1494 and 1528, that it could survive foreign invasions and avoid utter submission to a foreign prince precisely thanks to its unruly armed factions and the absence of a standing army and a state-controlled fleet. Foglietta insisted nonetheless that the age of city-states was over, that Genoa must change, and that the only way to save Genoa's political liberty was to eliminate the power of individual citizens.[105] These "un-Genoese" ideas were sugar-coated with the myth of a unified and militarized Genoa that had supposedly existed two centuries earlier; at the same time, Machiavelli's favorite republic, Rome, was presented by Foglietta as a model of polity able to conquer large territories and live in a state of harmonious internal unity. Unsurprisingly, the republic hailed by the characters of the dialogue to be "the greatest republic of Italy" at the time is Venice; and hence, as Foglietta nonchalantly equates greatness with mere territorial extension, he completes the utter overturning of the traditional Genoese mindset and political culture.[106] The entire book can be read as an invitation to centralize political power and create a strong public fleet. However, Doria's acclaimed reforms, Foglietta's undisguised dissatisfaction (as well as the lamenting tone of his whole pamphlet), and the reaction of the republic's government—that after the publication of this dialogue exiled the author—show that the majority of the Genoese elite disagreed with Uberto Foglietta. Genoa could be (and indeed had been) saved without betraying its vocation of city-state and without altering its late medieval and economic definition of *libertà*—freedom to do business guaranteed by the fragmentation of political power.

NOTES

1. "in Italia assuefatta per molti anni più alle immagini delle guerre, che alle guerre vere, non era nervo da sostenere il furore Franzese." Francesco Guicciardini, *Istoria d'Italia* (London: Dove, 1822), 110.

2. Marco Pellegrini, *Le guerre d'Italia: 1494–1530* (Bologna: Il Mulino, 2009), 48.

3. See David Abulafia, *The French descent into Renaissance Italy, 1494–95: Antecedents and Effects* (Aldershot: Ashgate, 1995); and *Italy and the European Powers. The Impact of War, 1500–1530*, ed. Christine Shaw (Boston: Brill, 2006).

4. On the Italian Wars, a recent and indispensable contribution is Pellegrini, *Le guerre d'Italia*.

5. A contemporary French account of Charles's expedition is Guillaume de Villeneuve, *Mémoires, 1494–97; contenant la conqueste du royaume de Naples par Charles VIII, et la manière dont les François en furent chasses*, in *Collection complète des mémoires relatifs à l'histoire de France* (Paris, 1826).

6. To be precise, Fivizzano was chosen by Charles in order to show the power of his artillery and to punish the fortress of Sarzanello. This fortress protecting the town of Sarzana was a little masterpiece in the defensive system of the Florentine republic; its walls were not very high, but they were thick and reinforced at their bases. The French king, annoyed at the prospect of a long siege, decided to unleash his army's fury against the nearby village of Fivizzano, which was surrounded by medieval walls (high but quite thin, and thus unable to resist intense bombardment). After a breach had been opened by their cannons, the French troops entered the village and massacred all the inhabitants. Pellegrini, *Le guerre d'Italia*, 33–34.

7. To be sure, Venice, Florence, and Milan had expanded their territorial possessions, but none of the political actors in Northern Italy had the means to crush the others. And as demonstrated by the Peace of Lodi (1454), Italian rulers had a shared interest in maintaining this balance of power. See Franco Catalano, *La politica dell'equilibrio nell'Italia del Quattrocento* (Milano: La Goliardica, 1970); on the military and political history of these years, a voluminous but unsurpassed study is Piero Pieri, *Il Rinascimento e la crisi militare italiana* (Torino: Einaudi, 1952).

8. Guicciardini, *Istoria d'Italia*, 135–39; Pellegrini, *Le guerre d'Italia*, 35–36.

9. "l'anno mille quattrocento novantaquattro . . . anno infelicissimo all'Italia, e in verità anno primo degli anni miserabili, perchè aperse la porta a innumerabili, e orribili calamità, delle quali si può dire, che per diversi accidenti abbia di poi partecipato una gran parte del mondo." Francesco Guicciardini, *Istoria d'Italia*, 71.

10. On Venice, see chapter 1. On Florence, see Viroli, *From Politics to Reason of State*, 81. On Siena, a good discussion is offered in William Caferro, "City and Countryside in Siena in the Second Half of the Fourteenth Century," *Journal of Economic History* 54 (1994): 85–103.

11. This change is clear in Guicciardini, a politician, historian, and acute observer who did not believe anymore in classical formulas and humanist receipts for successful governments. Beside Guicciardini's *Istoria d'Italia*, see also his *Ricordi politici e civili* (Milano: Rizzoli, 1977).

12. The interest in ancient city-states declined, and the new model adopted by Machiavelli was Imperial Rome. Yet, this was not an easy and unsophisticated adjustment. Large states and

powerful cities were not always praised; in fact, Machiavelli proposed a dichotomy between Rome and Venice, implicitly urging Florence to follow the example of the former. See Catalin Avramescu, "Machiavelli and the Theory of Exemplary Constitutions," in *Niccolò Machiavelli: History, Power, and Virtue*, ed. Leonidas Donskis (Amsterdam: Rodopi, 2011), 67–76.

13. Elena Fasano Guarini, "Machiavelli and the Crisis of the Italian Republics," in *Machiavelli and Republicanism* (Cambridge: Cambridge University Press, 1990), 17–40. It may seem ironic that one of the editors of this book was Quentin Skinner, whose semantic analysis of late medieval and early modern political texts has usually tended to stress continuity rather than change; see, for example, his contribution in the same volume, "Machiavelli's *Discorsi* and the Pre-humanist Origins of Republican Ideals," 121–42.

14. In book 3, chapter 25 of the *Discourses*, he used the example of Rome to claim that poverty strengthens freedom while riches ruin cities and states. See *The Discourses* (London: Penguin, 2003), 475–77.

15. Niccolò Machiavelli, *The Prince* (Adelaide: The University of Adelaide Library, 2008), chapter 12.

16. "Genoese power came from trade, from the capital resources of its citizens, not from territorial power or the deployment of armies by the state." Shaw, "Genoa," 229.

17. The consistency (or even the obstinacy) with which Genoa has been ignored by historians dealing with civic humanism and Renaissance republicanism may be linked to the peculiar characteristics of the Ligurian polity, which constituted what Rodolfo Savelli has described as the "anti-myth" of Renaissance Italy. Rodolfo Savelli, "Il rovescio e il diritto. Immagini e problemi della storia di Genova in età moderna," in *El siglo de los genoveses*, ed. Piero Boccardo and Clario Di Fabio (Milano: 1999), 15–21.

18. On the Genoese presence in Corsica, see Maria Pia Rota, "Insediamenti genovesi e corsi nella Corsica del Cinquecento," in *Atti del Congresso internazionale di studi storici Rapporti Genova-Mediterraneo-Atlantico nell'eta' moderna—1982*, ed. Raffaele Belvederi (Genova: Università di Genova, 1983), 65–79.

19. See footnote 368.

20. One of the best monographs on this period is Taviani, *Superba discordia*. On the Genose factionalism and on the republican division of offices between the end of the fifteenth and the beginning of the sixteenth century, see Arturo Pacini, *La tirannia delle fazioni e la repubblica dei ceti*. See also Claudio Costantini, *La repubblica di Genova nell'età moderna* (Torino: UTET, 1991); Rodolfo Savelli, *La repubblica oligarchica: legislazioni, istituzioni e ceti a Genova nel Cinquecento* (Milano: Giuffrè, 1981); and Id., *Dalle confraternite allo stato: il sistema assistenziale genovese nel Cinquecento* (Genova: Società Ligure di Storia Patria, 1984).

21. Between 1488 and 1499, Genoa was ruled by Milanese governors. See Cristina Belloni, *Ludovico il Moro, il protonotario Obietto Fieschi ed il cardinale Paolo Fregoso*, in *La Storia dei genovesi*, XI (Genova, 1991); a manuscript containing the agreement signed by the duke of Milan and the Genoese republic in 1488 is preserved at the Archivio di Stato di Milano, in *Registri Ducali*, 50. When Ludovico il Moro, the usurper of the dukedom of Milan, invited Charles VIII to invade Italy, Genoa and the *Riviere* became one of the first theaters of war. In 1494, Aragonese forces, helped by a number of Genoese families, attempted to attack Genoa's harbor, but, finding it well defended, decided to disembark near Portovenere, where they clashed with an army of Milanese, Genoese, and Swiss soldiers. A Milanese governor and a commissioner continued to represent Genoa's heads of state until 1499. When, in the summer of 1495, Ludovico betrayed the French cause, Genoa left for a brief period of time the French side. But in 1499 Genoa passed directly under French rule, even though, as usual, the Genoese political institutions remained intact. Until 1507, Genoa was ruled by French governors, and in 1502 Charles VIII's heir, Louis XII, himself visited the Ligurian city-state. See Emilio Pandiani, *Vita privata genovese nel Rinascimento* (Genova: Tipografia Nazionale di L. Sambolino, 1915), 188–89; see also a primary source that is not used by Pandiani, the *Descriptio adventus Ludovici XII Francorum Regis in Urbem Genuam, Anno MDII, authore Benedicto Portuensi Reipublicae Genuensis Cancellario*, a document published in Atti della Società Ligure di Storia Patria, volume XII, fasc.V (Genova: Tipografia del R.I. de'Sordo-muti, 1884), 915–29. In 1507, a Genoese revolt expelled the French from Genoa and the Fieschi from the *Riviere*; the

dyer Paolo da Novi became doge, but his regime lasted briefly, as a large coalition of Genoese nobles helped the French king to storm into the city, capture and execute Paolo. The indispensable reading on the revolt is the already mentioned Taviani, *Superba discordia*. See also a brief but insightful account of these events in Gianfranco Bettin Lattes, *Un caso d'amour fou nella società aristocratica Genovese del secolo XVI* (Firenze, Firenze University Press, 2011), 137–52; see in particular 150–51. See also Pandiani, *Vita Privata*, 191; and Mariano Bargellini, *Storia popolare di Genova* (Genova: Monni, 1836), 516–22.

22. The Adorno orchestrated this pro-French coup together with some *nobili* families, among which were the Fieschi. The simplistic historiographical narrative depicting well-defined social classes in Genoa and explaining instability merely through the hatred dividing *nobili* and *popolari* is thus (once again) at odds with facts. For a more complete reflection on this point, see the introduction, on pp. x–xii. See also an extraordinary document proving a secret political alliance established between several *nobili* and *popolari* families in 1501, which was recently discovered by Carlo Taviani and presented in his *Superba Discordia*, 46–48.

23. On the military clashes taking place in Northern Italy between April 1512 and October 1513, see Marco Pellegrini, *Le guerre d'Italia*, 129–33.

24. The "Briglia," as it was called, had been built by the French (in 1507), in order to control the entrance of the harbor.

25. Ottaviano Fregoso was praised by several contemporary intellectuals as a cultured and intelligent man. See, for example, his presence throughout the text of Baldassarre Castiglione, *Il Cortegiano* (Firenze: Sansoni, 1894); and Pietro Bembo, *Opere in Volgare* (Firenze: Sansoni, 1961).

26. The most detailed account of these events is in Bargellini, *Storia popolare*, 539–40.

27. For example, Theodore Bent wrote that Francis's "victorious troops in Italy soon obliged Genoa to recognize a French master." Bent, *Genoa*, 196. Yet, Ottaviano concluded his alliance with France before the French victory at the battle of Marignano (September 13–15, 1515).

28. "Ottaviano Fregoso fu egli dal furor della sua fatione e da altri cittadini creato Duce a 10 di giugno. Il quale visto con prudente discorso le proprie forze poco stabili e suoi nemici potenti con alcuni patti ridusse la città sotto la protezione di Francesco Valesio Re di Francia dal quale con titulo di governatore regio fu governata la città fino all'anno 1527." Archivio Biblioteca Civica Berio, m.r., VI, 5, 19, f. 3. The manuscript is entitled *Sommario della storia di Genova fino al 1527*. That the anonymous author was an advocate of the French cause is indicated by the last line of the document, where he claimed that Teodoro Trivulzio (*Theodoro Trivultio*)—a much despised Milanese nobleman who was appointed as governor by Francis in 1527 and whose brief rule was characterized by economic depression and plague—had governed the city "with much humanity" (*con molta humanittà*); see ibid., f. 4.

29. The estimated 3,000 men lost by the French army at the Bicocca were mostly Swiss mercenaries. Nonetheless, this battle forced the French to momentarily abandon Lombardy, thus allowing the Spanish-Imperial forces to occupy several cities and to move towards Genoa. On these events see Marco Pellegrini, *Le guerre d'Italia*, 165–67.

30. Archivio di Stato di Genova, AS, 2707 C, letter 132.

31. "l'essere et il vivere nostro è alieno da le altre cità, quale se ben perdono il mobile loro li restano li fundi e le possessione che non gli possono mancar." Ibid.

32. "Continuava Genova sotto li Francesi, gli Adorni, e Fieschi famiglie potenti congiurarono contro questi e contro la fazione Fregosa, ne tentarono il cimento nel tempo in cui era succeduto a Massimiliano Carlo V, figlio di Filippo re di Spagna, e nipote di detto Massimiliano." Archivio di Stato di Genova, Ms. Bibl., 168.

33. "[gli Adorni e Fieschi] eccitarono il novello imperatore all'impresa contro la Città, questi per discacciarne i suoi nimici, e quegli per impossessarsi del Ducato. Ordinò Carlo a Prospero Colonna, al Duca di Milano, e al Marchese di Pescara suoi Generali di passare coll'esercito a Genova e sapendo sua Maestà, la verità del proverbio, che se Genova non prende Genova, tutto il mondo non piglierà Genova, comandò a detti suoi Generali di prevalersi della fazione Adorna e di ubbidire particolarmente nell'impresa a Gerolamo Adorno. Passarono XXmila uomini all'assedio della Città, quale con repubblicano ardire faceano i suoi Cittadini resistenza alli nimici, prevalendo la forza di questi, entrò di note tempo il Marchese di Pescara

per una porta detta di S. Michele (ora di S. Tommaso) co' soldati gridando Adorni, e Spagna, venne barbaramente saccheggiata Genova e fatto prigione Ottaviano Fregoso, onde potè dirsi con verità che Genova prese Genova, e non li nimici. Fu fatto Doge Antoniotto Adorno, e il campo se ne tornò verso Lombardia." Ibid.

34. See, for example, a letter dated August 27, 1521, where Gerolamo Adorno is mentioned as the general who has taken command of seven thousand German soldiers (Real Academia de la Historia, *Colección Salazar y Castro*, ms 2668, A-21, f. 138–42). About six months before the expedition against Genoa, Gerolamo visited the imperial court; see the letter dated October 1, 1521, where Charles's ambassador in Rome says that Gerolamo Adorno has left Italy and is heading for the Court (RAH, *Colección Salazar y Castro*, ms 2686, A-21, f. 197–198). Another interesting document is a letter dated February 21, 1522; the Spanish troops had conquered Milan only three months earlier and the French army was still quite close to the city; Gerolamo wrote to Charles to explain that he had given to the soldiers only half of their salary and to inform the emperor about the precarious situation. RAH, *Colección Salazar y Castro*, ms 2903, A-22, f. 233–35.

35. The end of his rival, the wise Ottaviano Fregoso, is shrouded in mystery. After being captured during the siege of Genoa, Ottaviano was brought to Antwerp, and then to Ischia, where he died in prison in 1524, probably poisoned. Bargellini, *Storia popolare*, 552.

36. Kirk, *Genoa and the Sea*, 19.

37. Manuel Herrero Sánchez, "Una república mercantil en la órbita de la Monarquía Católica (1528–1684). Hegemonía y decadencia del agregado hispano-genovés," in *Sardegna, Spagna e Stati italiani nell'età di Carlo V*, ed. Bruno Anatra and Francesco Manconi (Rome: Carocci, 2001), 183–200.

38. "El Duque y la Communidad de Genova an cargado agora un nuevo derecho sopra los que compran y venden los lugares de Sant Jorge que es a cinco sueldos de esta moneda por uno y antes pagavan a diez sueldos por uno y agora pagan a quince . . . y otra forma no ay aqui para aver dineros si no cargando nuevos derechos e ya esta tan cargada esta Communidad que por lo da venir sera travajoso el aver de estas sumas gruessas de dineros y sera necessario que dios y vuestra Magestad lo remeden porque de otra manera no se podra escusar algun alboroto de pueblo con tanta carga y gravezas como se halla esta tierra." RAH, *Colección Salazar y Castro*, ms 4129, A-30, f. 261.

39. On the Genoese constitution, see chapter 2.

40. See Felloni, *Genova e la Storia della finanza*; and Buongiorno, *Il bilancio di uno stato medievale*, 25–30.

41. "A peculiar form of organisation of the public finances had developed in Genoa, which resulted in the majority of tax revenues not going to the commune, but to share-holders in the *compere*. . . . In 1407—during a period of French government, but on the initiative of the administrators of the *compere*, not at the suggestion of the French—all the *compere* were brought together into the Casa di San Giorgio." Shaw, "Genoa," 227.

42. Even the move on the secondary market of public bonds as described by this document seems actually quite implausible: only after the governing bodies of St. George (the *Protettori* and the *Consiglio*) had graciously agreed, Adorno could have managed to raise money in this way.

43. I will return on the specific point of the republican fleet (or better, the lack thereof) below.

44. Unfortunately, the literature on the history of the relations between Savona and Genoa is quite scant. See Giovanni Filippi, *Una contesa tra Genova e Savona nel secolo XV* (Genova: Tip. Sordomuti, 1890); and Enzo Neri, *Savona contro Genova: secolo XIII* (Savona: Stamperia Officina d'arte, 1976).

45. "La dicha Communidad de Genova y los de Saona estan muy diferenti sobre el dominio porque los de Genova quieren el supremo y entero dominio sobre Saona ansi como lo tienen sobre todos los otros lugares que les son subjetos." RAH, *Colección Salazar y Castro*, ms 4129, A-30, f. 261.

46. "Y sobre esto tienen muy estrecha y casi destruida a Saona que no les dexan hazer ningun comercio ni entrar ni sallir ninguna cosa de mercantia ni navios en el Puerto." Ibid., f. 262. Then, with an almost anachronistic and proto-liberist lament, Soria disapprovingly adds:

"y para esto tienen algunos gastos los de esta Communidad, de suerte que los de Saona se destruyen y no ganan nada los de Genova." Ibid.

47. "Y los de Saona no quieren si no que tenga Recurso y apellation a vuestra Cesarea Majestad en caso que fuessen en alguna diferencia con los de Genova y en esto solo difieren porque los de Saona son contentos de observer todos los capitulos y conventiones que tienen con los de Genova y que si esto no abasta que hagan capitulos de Nuevo de todo quanto quisieren y todos los aceptaran, ecepto quiere que en caso que por lo da venir naciesse alguna diferentia inpensada entre ellos que en tal caso sea el juez y puedan apelarsse a vuestra Cesarea Magestad, y esto no quieren los de Genova si no ser ellos los juezes y que no tengan ningun Ricursso a vuestra Cesarea Magestad." Ibid., f. 261–63.

48. For an introduction to the concept of entangled communities in the Atlantic world, see Eliga Gould, "Entangled Histories, Entangled Worlds."

49. RAH, *Colección Salazar y Castro*, ms 4170, A-30, f. 393.

50. "yo no lo se lo que el virrey le a rrespondido, pero este duque y comunidad an estado y estan algo alterados de tal platica aun que tienen por cierto que no lo escuchara el virrey." Ibid.

51. Emphasis added. "no seria servicio de vuestra Majestad que se dicese que andan tales platicas, maxime considerando la calidad de esta ciudad, que es madre de las pasiones y partialidades y revoluciones y creo que no aya dado orecha el dicho virrey a esta platica y hasta a agora no se a entendido." Ibid.

52. See chapter 4.

53. See chapter 3.

54. The *Regulae* of 1413 and 1442 had not altered the fundamental constitutional architecture established in 1363.

55. Francis Hackett, *Francis the First* (New York: Doubleday, Doran & Co., 1937), 277–78.

56. This letter is important not only for the history of Genoa. In the historiography of the Italian Wars, the military expedition of 1524 has at times been presented as the result of a personal initiative by Charles of Bourbon (1490–1527), a French aristocrat who had quarrelled with Francis and, after joining the Imperial cause, had been named commander of the Imperial army in Italy by Charles V. Even recently, Marco Pellegrini has assumed that the invasion of Provence was a hasty, personal decision taken by the French Duke of Bourbon after the victory of Sesia, simply because he wanted to humiliate his former king. Pellegrini, *Le guerre d'Italia*, 168. However, the document that I present here proves how Charles V had wanted and planned an expedition in Provence even before knowing about the battle of the Sesia. And the duke, Charles of Bourbon, as chief commander of Charles V's troops, was surely instructed (probably through a secret, encoded correspondence) to carry out the invasion as soon as the situation on the ground allowed it.

57. "he apretado al dicho duque de Genova paraque armè el y los desta Republica todos los navios que fuere possible." RAH, *Colección Salazar y Castro*, ms 4301, A-31, f. 223.

58. "Y el dize que siempre que sera necessario para hazer la empresa de Prohenza armarà aqui todos quantos navios les fuere possible pero que no lo harà para yr solamente en compania de las galeras de Vuestra Magestad para descurrir la Costa de Prohenza porque desto podria seguirse mucho dano a esta Comunidad." Ibid. All the sections mentioning Provence are encrypted in the original manuscript.

59. It is opportune to stress the fact that this is not a later Genoese source, trying to celebrate the unbroken spirit of autonomy of the Ligurian community; this is a contemporary Spanish source, a diplomatic and secret communication. The secrecy of the document (which itself confirms its trustworthiness) is evident when we consider that large sections of the letter were encrypted, and were only later decoded in Madrid.

60. The republic had only a handful of public galleys, and they were paid exclusively for the defense of the port and of the nearby coast. Even if the doge had wished to help Charles's fleet, it seems quite unlikely that he could have embarked in such military adventure. Bargellini, *Storia popolare*, 557.

61. Ivo Luzzatti, *Andrea Doria* (Milano: Garzanti, 1943); Pierangelo Campodonico, *Andrea Doria* (Genova: Tormena, 1997), first edition 1948; Angelo L. Fiorita, *Andrea Doria* (Genova: Ceretti, 1950); Antonio Perria, *Il corsaro Andrea Doria* (Milano: Longanesi, 1973); Edoardo Grendi, "Andrea Doria: Uomo del Rinascimento," in *La repubblica aristocratica dei genovesi*

(Bologna: Il Mulino, 1987), 139–72; Giorgio Bertone, *Andrea Doria: la nascita di un ammiraglio* (Recco: Le Mani, 2010). On Doria's political reforms, the indispensable reading is Pacini, *I presupposti politici*. See also the article by George Gorse, "Christopher Columbus and Andrea Doria: The Two Worlds of Renaissance Genoa," *Mediterranean Studies (Manchester University Press)* 16 (2007): 120–42.

62. The most important study on Mascardi is Eraldo Bellini, *Agostino Mascardi tra "ars poetica" e "ars historica"* (Milan: Vita e Pensiero, 2002); on the *Congiura*, see in particular 100–111. For a more general introduction see Masca Bettarini, "Agostino Mascardi, scrittore e teorico della storiografia nel Seicento," in *Quaderni di Nova historia*, 10 (Verona, 1953).

63. This book on the Fieschi conspiracy first appeared in 1629, being then published in three different editions. However, in the archives of the Biblioteca Civica Berio (Genoa), there is also a seventeenth-century manuscript copy of this work: Archivio Biblioteca Civica Berio, m.r., VIII.1.12. It is not clear why, by whom, or when this manuscript was written. But Mascardi himself lived in Genoa for some years and he maintained numerous powerful connections in the city; moreover, he had written to the city's authorities in 1627, in order to obtain full access to the documents regarding the Fieschi conspiracy. Bellini, *Agostino Mascardi*, 101. Therefore, the hypothesis that Mascardi penned this manuscript copy as a preview for some prominent Genoese (or as a gift to the republic) cannot be ruled out. The printed edition that is used for reference here is Agostino Mascardi, *La congiura del Conte Gio Luigi de' Fieschi* (Venice: Scaglia, 1637); the previous edition by Scaglia (1629) must be avoided because there the editor had censored several passages. Mascardi's work remains an original and trustworthy reconstruction of the Fieschi revolt. After its publication, this book sparked emotional reactions and a lengthy debate (both for the role attributed to Cardinal Agostino Trivulzio and for the description of King Francis's character). See *Oppositioni e difesa alla "Congiura del Conte Gio Luigi de' Fieschi"* (Venice: Ventura, 1630); and *Lettera di monsignore Agostino Mascardi, circa la censura fatta al suo libro "La congiura di Genova del conte Fieschi,"* printed in *Giornale Ligustico*, 6 (1879). Mascardi's work was translated and published in England as early as 1677; another English edition was printed in 1735. See *History of the Fieschi's Conspiracy Against the State of Genoa* (London: Cooper, 1735); information about the earlier English edition is on iii of the preface.

64. Mascardi, *History of the Fieschi's Conspiracy*, 1–2. For the original, Italian text see Mascardi, *La congiura del Conte Gio Luigi de' Fieschi*, 1–3. Here, as in the following passages, the English edition translated with "common-wealth" the Italian expressions *Imperio della Repubblica* and *Repubblica*, which would be more correctly rendered as "dominion of the Republic," or "republican authority."

65. Mascardi, *History of the Fieschi's Conspiracy*, 2–3. For the original, Italian text see Mascardi, *La congiura del Conte Gio Luigi de' Fieschi*, 4–5.

66. The agreement between Charles V and Andrea Doria has been published in Vicente de Cadenas y Vicent, *El Protectorado de Carlos V en Génova: la "condotta" de Andrea Doria* (Madrid: Hidalguis, 1977), 85–88.

67. Antonio Doria, *Compendio d'Antonio Doria delle cose di sua notitia, et memoria occorse al mondo nel tempo dell'imperatore Carlo Quinto* (Genoa: Bellone, 1571). Interestingly enough, in the Archivio di Stato di Genova there is a manuscript copy of this work. Archivio di Stato di Genova, Ms. Bibl., 183. The bound volume can be dated to the late 1560s and it may be itself a copy of an earlier manuscript version, thus suggesting that Antonio Doria's memoirs were already circulating in the city, before being printed in 1571. This would move the moment of their production even closer to the events narrated by the author.

68. An interesting manuscript describing these events in Antonio's youth is Archivio Biblioteca Civica Berio, m.r., XIV.3.24, c. 137 v.

69. This episode perfectly exemplifies how among the Genoese the lack of both Florentine-style patriotism and monolithic social groups was not caused by (nor itself causing) a strong, counterbalancing sense of kinship. As we have seen in the case of Giovanni da Pontremoli, the overwhelming majority of his employees and business partners were not members of his family (nor were they necessarily members of his original social group); here, we see Antonio Doria taking a decision that makes him at once an enemy of Genoa, of the *nobili*, and of his very family.

70. The life of Antonio Doria is rich of many other fascinating episodes, and it would deserve more attention. Studying Antonio Doria's military career (which was indeed just another form of business for the Genoese) and writings (he wrote several other pamphlets, besides the *Compendio*) would shed more light not just on the political and intellectual history of Genoa, but also on the military impact and the social role of *condottieri* in Renaissance Europe.

71. Doria, *Compendio*, 32–33. In the aforementioned manuscript, A. S. G., Ms. Bibl., 183, 34–36.

72. Bargellini, *Storia popolare*, 567–71.

73. "et egli havendoli pochi anni prima consignato Filiberto Principe d'Orange, e non havendoli mai fatto pagare il riscatto haveva convenuto per la sua taglia di dargli, glieli denegò. E di piu ritrovandosi mal contento del Re, insieme con i cittadini di Genova, per l'occupatione di Savona, facendovi riscotere i Datij, e vendere il sale contra le conventioni, cercò di disporre con tale occasioni, gli animi loro alla unione, et aborrire le partialità, già tant'anni state fra loro, e l'ottenne facilmente." Doria, *Compendio*, 36–37.

74. Ibid., 37.

75. "disceso nella Città con le sue genti, chiamando i cittadini dalle ville dov'erano ritirati per la peste, alla libertà, fu con gran concorso de tutti seguitato, et assediato il Castelletto. . . . il Trivultio disperato del soccorso, assai presto rese il Castelletto. Et a questo modo, quella Repubblica tanto longamente afflitta, con poche forze in tempo pericoloso, con l'esercito nemico vicino, restò ridotta all'antica libertà, con unione e concordia de Cittadini: i quali adunato assai brevemente esercito, la maggior parte della loro natione, e fattone Capitano il Conte Filippino Doria, lo mandarono alla ricuperatione di Savona." Ibid., 38–39.

76. "Et acciò quella Città per la commodità del porto, e sito dov'è posta, non potesse per l'avenire causare gran danno alla Republica, com'era per seguirne, se più longamente fusse stata separata dal suo dominio, perche potendosi portare le mercantie, e'l sale per quella via commodamente in Lombardia, havria levato tanto più il traffico da Genova . . . [i Cittadini] Fecero totalmente riempie il porto, avendo già alcuni ani prima, per le medesime cause, fatto ruinare un bellissimo molo che vi era. Fecero ancora spianare i baloardi, e fortezze fatte per la fortificatione di quella Città, dal Conte Pietro Navarro." Ibid., 39–40.

77. On Sigonio's life and works, see Paolo Prodi, "Storia sacra e controriforma, Nota sulle censure al commento di Carlo Sigonio a Sulpicio Severo," *Annali dell'Istituto storico italo-germanico in Trento* (1977): 75–104; and idem, "Vecchi appunti e nuove riflessioni su Carlo Sigonio," in *Nunc alia tempora, alii mores. Storici e storia in età postridentina*, Atti del Convegno internazionale, Torino (24–27 settembre 2003), ed. M. Firpo (Firenze 2005), 291–310. In English, see William McCuaig, *Carlo Sigonio: The Changing World of the Late Renaissance* (Princeton, NJ: Princeton University Press, 2014).

78. Carlo Sigonio, *Della vita et fatti di Andrea Doria* (Genoa: Pavoni, 1598), 75–108.

79. Emphasis added. "havendo il Rè dato spesse volte speranza al Doria di restituire a Genova la libertà, gli facevano continuamente instanza a che la ristringesse con più dura servitù, e tra l'altre cose li persuasero che fortificasse Savona, levandola dal dominio di Genova, e che fussero imposte alla Città nell'avvenire maggiori gravezze, et a questo effetto mandarono à Genova il Visconte di Turena, a domandare per nome del Rè certa somma di denari; dalle quali cose restò fuor di modo offeso l'animo del Doria." Ibid., 77–78.

80. Ibid., 78–79.

81. George L. Gorse, "A Question of Sovereignty: France and Genoa, 1494–1528," in *Italy and the European Powers*, ed. Shaw, 190.

82. According to Thomas Kirk, Francis did officially replace Savona under Genoese jurisdiction, but the move came too late (July 1528). Kirk, *Genoa and the Sea*, 211, note 32.

83. "Francesco I era arrivato a porre in atto il piano di dividere in due la Liguria. Riservandosi la giurisdizione diretta di Savona, egli aveva cercato di costituire un'alternativa politica, economica e strategico-militare a Genova per il controllo della riviera di Ponente, e per garantirsi un accesso sicuro dal mare all'alta valle Padana." Arturo Pacini, *La Genova di Andrea Doria nell'Impero di Carlo V* (Florence: Olschki, 1999), 40.

84. The economic nature of the growing anti-French sentiment uniting the Genoese businessmen (both nobles and non-nobles) is confirmed by yet another episode, mentioned by the Genoese bishop and humanist Agostino Giustiniani in his *Annali*. According to this text,

Genoese merchants visiting Savona while traveling towards Lyon had been assaulted, and their cloths had been robbed or damaged. These Genoese had sought justice from both the French governor and the king, but to no avail. It was believed that the governor himself had had a share of the stolen merchandise. Agostino Giustiniani, *Annali della Repubblica di Genova* (Genova: Canepa, 1854), v. II, 702. It is reasonable to believe that in the atmosphere of 1527 and 1528 (before Doria's coup) such unpunished crimes were not rare. These events should be added to the list of economic reasons leading the Genoese factions to coalesce around the figure of Doria in order to shake off the transalpine yoke.

85. This incident was recounted just a few years later by Giustiniani. *Annali*, v. II, 695–96. See also Bargellini, *Storia popolare*, 569–70.

86. This is not to say that those five years had been idyllic in absolute terms. On the contrary, plague, famine, and warfare had continued to torment both the city and the *Riviere*. But the Genoese-Hispanic political relations had been relatively good.

87. RAH, *Colección Salazar y Castro*, ms 6065, A-40, f. 432.

88. Dauverd, *Imperial Ambitions*, 35.

89. According to Carlo Taviani, for the first three decades of the sixteenth century "it is possible to document the existence of a series of projects, elaborated to weaken the role of factions in Genoa, and proposed in several occasions, even during the sixteenth-century dogeships of the Adorno and Fregoso." "È possibile infatti documentare l'esistenza di una serie di progetti, elaborati per indebolire il ruolo delle fazioni a Genova, proposti in più occasioni, anche durante i dogati cinquecenteschi degli Adorno e dei Fregoso." Taviani, *Superba discordia*, 239.

90. The page of Giustiniani's *Annali* where the 1527 debates are recounted is extremely revealing, both for the absence of the word state and for this apparently paradoxical—yet typically "Genoese"—statement:

> "And the divine goodness . . . inspired the citizens to do away with all these factions: and to unite the entire people in a body divided in twenty-eight families." (From the original: "E la bontà divina . . . inspirò i cittadini a levar via tutte queste fazioni: e ad unir tutto il popolo in corpo distinto in ventiotto famiglie." Giustiniani, *Annali*, v. II, 699)

The objective was thus to unite the people, by more efficiently fragmenting their allegiances. As we shall see through the eyes of Uberto Foglietta, the Machiavellian dissidents in Genoa believed that this curious understanding of "unity" was an intolerable and reckless legacy of the previous century, which had to be rejected in favor of a militarized and centralized republic.

91. On the economic privileges granted by Charles to Andrea Doria, see Grendi, *La Repubblica aristocratica*, 153.

92. For an introduction to Doria's reforms, see Kirk, *Genoa and the Sea*, 20–28. For a more detailed analysis, besides the already mentioned book by A. Pacini, see Adriana Petracchi, *Norma "costituzionale" e prassi nella Serenissima Repubblica di Genova* (Milan: Giuffrè, 1989).

93. One of the key medieval institutions that survived Doria's reform was the so-called *sindacatori*. I have already talked about this figure when dealing with the *regulae* of 1363. See chapter 3. Interestingly, the importance of the *sindacatori* and their role in limiting the power of the Genoese government did not pass unnoticed by contemporary Spanish. When describing the Republic of Genoa in his 1575 political treatise *Republicas del Mundo*, the Spanish author Hieronymo Roman dedicated a section of the chapter precisely to the powers of the *sindacatori* in Genoa. After describing how the *sindacatori*, or "the supreme five" could judge and punish (*castigar*) the doge, the councilors and other magistrates of the republic, Roman stated: "This is one of the most important laws that can be approved in a republic, . . . because many magistrates, knowing that they will not be punished once they leave office, commit thousands of abuses, because they consider the reward for their crimes more certain than the punishment." From the original: "Es esta una de las mas importantes leyes que se pueden hazer en una republica, . . . porque muchos magistrados sabiendo que no han de ser castigados quando

acaban sus officios hazen mil desafueros, porque tienen mas cierto el premio por sus males que la pena." Hieronymo Roman, *Republicas del Mundo* (Medina del Campo: Francisco del Canto, 1575), 403.

94. Pacini, *La Genova di Andrea Doria*, 87 and 97.

95. I insist in using the term Machiavellian not merely because of the previously mentioned reflections of Machiavelli on France, Ancient Rome, and more in general the territorial state, but also because of Machiavelli's practical applications of such ideas. If it is true that facts speak louder than words, Machiavelli's administrative and organizational efforts between 1505 and 1510, when he was the Florentine secretary of War, would deserve as much attention as his writings, because they can enlighten us on the idea of state actually prescribed by the Florentine intellectual. Since 1505, Machiavelli elaborated a project for a standing army of trained citizens; he recruited these troops among the rural population living in the more peripheral areas of the Florentine republic, and he was eventually able to build a standing force of 20,000 citizen-soldiers, at the orders of the *gonfaloniere* for life, Piero Soderini. Pellegrini, *Le guerre d'Italia*, 135–38. This is not to suggest that Machiavelli's sophisticated idea of republic can be reduced to the presence of a standing army. However, a strong military (at the disposal of a strong executive branch) is undeniably a key component of Machiavellian republicanism—"Machiavellian" not just literarily or theoretically, but also historically, given Machiavelli's personal contribution to the militarization of the Florentine regime. Machiavelli (and Foglietta) wanted this army to be composed of trained and faithful citizen-soldiers; not by chance, the author of *The Prince* bitterly criticized Venice, whose army was large but also led by mercenaries. See Machiavelli, *The Prince*, chapter 12. This form of republicanism was radically different from (and indeed diametrically opposed to) the late medieval and communal republicanism of the Italian city-states—and in particular from the Genoese model. The fact that Machiavelli and other sixteenth-century writers (such as Foglietta) are still using a late medieval or humanist vocabulary does not necessarily mean that they are still prescribing the same kind of republicanism, nor that they are even looking at the same territorial entity as the basis for a viable polity—in fact, they are not, since their reflections and political theories move from the dimension of the city-state to the realm of large states, militarized metropolis dominating several cities, and even kingdoms.

96. Uberto Foglietta, *Delle cose della Repubblica di Genova* (Milan: Antonij, 1575), 5–6.

97. "[nostra Patria] perdesse il dominio di tante terre acquistate in Levante dalla virtù, et fatiche de' nostri maggiori; et insieme col dominio la riputatione anchora del nome, et l'honore appresso." Ibid., 5.

98. "Et quanto alle cose di terra, più facile era à genovesi insignorirsi in Lombardia di una parte di quella, che non fu à Venetiani, percioche in quelli tempi non harebbe truovata unita contra se una potentia di uno stato di Milano, essendo all'hora la Lombardia divisa in tanti stati, quanti erano le città di quella di quella Provincia debole di forze; et da non contrastare una alle recchezze, et forze di Genovesi, se Genovesi in questi acquisti terrestri fossero proceduti con quella virtù, et artificio, col quale procede ogni popolo, il quale acquista Dominio sopra vicini. . . . Ne maggior virtù, ne industria fu gia in fiorentini, ne tante forze avevano all'hora, quando s'insignorirono quasi della maggior parte delle Terre di Toscana, et di Pisa propria, della quale se fussimo noi proceduti nel bene, non è dubbio, che eravamo in quelli tempi antichi di CC anni fa piu atti ad insignorirsi, che Fiorentini. . . . Il quale indubitato acquisto di Pisani harebbe aperta la strada anchora à stendere il nostro imperio in Toscana." Ibid., 86–88.

99. See chapter 1.

100. See chapter 3.

101. "Se questi pericoli tanto importanti soprastano alla Patria, il Principe Doria, il quale è savio, et perciò li doverebbe conoscere, et che è tanto buono, che egli ama più la Patria che la privata grandezza della casa, come si è veduto, perche non vi provide? Essendo in lui tanta autorità, che lo potrebbe fare? Et perche non spoglia li suoi successori delle Galee, et non le dona alla Patria?" Foglietta, *Delle cose della Repubblica*, 139.

102. Niccolò Machiavelli, *The Art of War* (Adelaide: The University of Adelaide Library, 2003), chapter 1. For an introduction to *The Art of War*, see Mikael Hörnqvist, "Machiavelli's military project and the Art of War," in *The Cambridge Companion to Machiavelli*, ed. John M. Najemy (Cambridge: Cambridge University Press, 2010), 112–27.

103. Ibid., 170–72. Although the idea of using the young nobles of the republic to arm the public fleet was probably inspired by the Venetian model, for a Machiavellian thinker this was a fascinating thought also because it represented a step towards a standing force of citizen-soldiers. Needless to say, such thought sounded eerie to many Genoese.

104. "se le discordie Civili ci ridussero spesso à cercare governi Forastieri, erano all'hora certe qualità di tempo, nelle quali era in facoltà de' Cittadini medesimi agevolmente mandarli via ogni volta, che volevano, come sempre, che quelli governi sono loro reusciti, hanno fatto. Mà ora ciascuno vede, che le cose sono talmente cambiate, che non potendosi venire se non in mano de' Principi potentissimi, considerando colui, il quale vi entrasse, di quanta opportunità fosse Genova a' suoi dissegni, e come ella è solità à fastidire, et cambiare spesso li governi forastieri, se ne assicurerebbe in modo, che non potriamo scherzare, et ci ridurrebbe, e con fortezze, et con altri infiniti presidij, in uno stato, e servitù, la quale Dio prohibisca da Noi." Emphasis added. Ibid., 131.

105. Ibid., 162. Foglietta was obviously aware that even during the Italian Wars private armies had repeatedly saved the Genoese republic and overthrown foreign governments. In particular, the 1528 anti-French coup was still fresh in the memory of many of his compatriots; hence, to support his argument Foglietta belittled the role played by Andrea Doria, his galleys and his troops in the events that had led to the liberation of Genoa and the re-conquest of Savona. Ibid., 167–68.

106. On Rome, ibid., 143–46 and 148–61. On Venice, see ibid., 86 and 108. On 161–62, the historical model of Rome and the contemporary example of Venice are interestingly taken together and used to criticize the Genoese Council of the Four Hundred created by Doria. Foglietta believed that such council had to be reformed in order to include all the members of the nobility.

Chapter Six

Beginnings of a "Genoese Atlantic"?

Tracing the Genoese Experience in Sixteenth-Century Spanish America

In the sixteenth century, Genoese businessmen entered—and indeed helped to shape—the Spanish empire in the Americas. As aptly put by Robert S. Lopez, "by the time of Phillip II, the proud empire where the sun never set was almost an economic colony of Genoa."[1] The Genoese could do this not only because of their colonial experience, economic culture, and capital, but also because of their position within Spain at the moment in which the conquest and settlement of the American kingdoms began.[2] This chapter will not attempt a quantitative analysis of the available data; neither will the reader find in the next pages a theorization of the economic impact of the Genoese in the Castilian Americas.[3] Rather, after reflecting on the relation between the events of 1528 and the legal status of the Genoese in the Spanish kingdoms, I shall present sources that open a window on the early presence of the Genoese in the Castilian "New World." These documents show how diverse Genoese careers and businesses were, as well as how Ligurian captains, officials, and entrepreneurs reached almost every corner of the vast and rapidly expanding overseas kingdoms of the Spanish monarchs. That transatlantic Genoese networks existed already in the sixteenth century—as early as the phase of the conquest—does not appear as a surprise, but rather as the consequence of the movement East-West and of the developments in Hispanic-Genoese relations (phenomena and themes that have all been investigated in the previous chapters). These early modern Genoese families, communities, and networks are in turn the cause and the origin of the eighteenth- and nineteenth-century Genoese Atlantic, whose importance and endurance have been recently studied by Catia Brilli.[4]

TOWARDS AN ENTANGLED ATLANTIC: BRIEF CONSIDERATIONS ON THE CONSEQUENCES OF HISPANIC-GENOESE RELATIONS

Andrea Doria's decision to switch sides arguably decided the fate of the Italian Wars. But in 1528, the beginning of a second, more solid Hispanic-Genoese alliance had also other, far-reaching historical consequences. On the other side of the Atlantic, the conquest and pacification of new, vast territories now belonging to the Crown of Castile was under way. In the following century—as colonies were founded and intercontinental businesses started—Genoese capital, colonial techniques, and economic experience became essential ingredients for Spain's empire-building.[5] But what was the legal status of a Genoese entering the Spanish Indies? And, more importantly, is it possible to indicate a link between the Hispanic-Genoese diplomatic relations and the Ligurian presence within the Spanish Atlantic?

Whether the newly discovered lands across the ocean could be visited only by Castilians or also by foreigners—or, more precisely, whether peoples such as Aragonese, Germans, Neapolitan, Lombard, and Genoese were to be considered foreigners—was something unclear even to sixteenth-century imperial bureaucrats. The legislation on the subject continued to change, and even if it had been crystal clear its enforcement would have often been impossible. What we know for sure (and what will be shown in this final chapter) is that since the beginning of the Spanish colonization Genoese sailors, businessmen, and even entire households traveled across the ocean and traded, worked, fought, smuggled, lived, and died in the Americas. Having said this, royal legislation did have an impact on the Genoese presence in the Atlantic, especially in the long term. Whence, it is opportune to briefly take into consideration a few key documents that help us to understand how (and when) the legal position of the Genoese changed, especially between Ottaviano Fregoso's alliance with Francis I (in 1515) and the 1530s.

In 1519, the authorities of the city of Santo Domingo sent a representative to the court of king Charles, holding an official list of requests. Among these *Instrucciones*, there was a specific appeal to allow foreigners to enter the colony and to settle there. Interestingly, the authors of the document clarified that such privilege should not have been conceded to "French and Genoese."[6] This source confirms that the Spanish needed foreign capital and colonists to establish their first overseas communities; but more remarkably, it also suggests that the Genoese in 1519 were discriminated against because of their republic's alliance with France, whose troops were in that very moment fighting against Spain in Italy. In these exceptional circumstances, Genoa was perceived as a political enemy, and this had serious consequences in the Indies.

After the sack of 1522, Genoa switched sides, and even though, as we have seen, one can hardly say that Charles (or even Antoniotto Adorno) was ruling over the city, nonetheless the republic was now officially an ally and, in a sense, part of the imperial system. But did such change have an impact on the status of Genoese settlers in the Americas? A partial answer to this question may come from a *cédula* penned at Charles's court in 1525. This document stated that "those foreigners who are subjects of His Majesty and natives, *both of the empire and Genoese*, can populate and trade in the Indies like the natives of Castile and Leòn."[7] The following year, another document confirmed this policy, once again explicitly mentioning the Genoese:

> We give license and permission to all our subjects and to the inhabitants of all our Kingdoms and Dominions as well as to all the other subjects and inhabitants of the Empire, both Genoese and all the others, to go to the said Indies and to stay there and to trade according to the rules and ways and conditions in which the inhabitants of our Kingdoms and Dominions of Castile and Leòn do and are allowed to do.[8]

While these brief reflections are in no way exhaustive, the chronological correspondence between the political events in Genoa and the fluctuating legal position of Ligurians in Spanish documents dealing with foreigners seems striking. It is not far-fetched to hypothesize that the Hispanic-Genoese relations did indeed have an impact on the Ligurian presence within the Spanish kingdoms. Therefore, in 1528, Andrea Doria's alliance with Charles V strengthened the Genoese economic penetration in the Castilian kingdoms and represented the indispensable political premise for the existence (in the following centuries) of Ligurian networks within the Spanish Atlantic. Furthermore, in the case of Doria's regime one could even argue that the bettering of the Genoese merchants' status in the Americas was not merely an accidental or indirect consequence, but rather the result of a deliberate and carefully thought agenda. According to Claudio Sigonio, since the very beginning of the secret negotiations between Doria and Charles (carried out through the imperial captains who were Andrea's captives), the Genoese admiral expressly asked "that all the Genoese in the states of the Emperor would be treated as if they were their natural-born subjects."[9] Revealingly enough, the Genoese, who had been expressly mentioned in the documents allowing foreigners to do business in the Americas, would not be named in the laws that in 1538 reversed the 1525/26 *cédulas* and forbade foreign sailors and travelers to reach the Indies.[10] By then, Genoa's port, Genoese bankers, and Doria's fleet were key pieces of the Spanish political puzzle in the Mediterranean. Moreover, by the 1530s, the Genoese had already begun to use old strategies—hispanization of their surnames, naturalization, and marriages with Spanish women—in order to definitively legalize their status within the rapidly evolving legal and political framework of the Atlantic empire. In addition, even those who were still considered as *genoveses* could easily enter the Indies, upon obtaining royal licenses.

The evolution of the diplomatic relations between Genoa and Castile during the Italian Wars is thus fundamental to understand the attitude of Spanish monarchs and officials towards those Genoese businessmen who wanted to journey across the Atlantic. However, we also have to consider cultural aspects, such as the way in which the Genoese polity was perceived by Spanish kings, ministers, and bureaucrats. If (as I have argued here) the Republic of Genoa had been able to maintain its medieval constitutional architecture and its skepticism towards public military endeavors, then it should not come as a surprise that the Spanish never perceived as a threat the Genoese entering the still scarcely settled American territories. In this chapter, we will follow some of these Genoese adventurers, as they crossed the ocean and deployed their diverse talents to embark upon a remarkable number of activities and careers.

VERSATILE AND INDISPENSABLE: GENOESE CONQUISTADORS FROM PERU TO CHILE

The history of the conquest of Chile does not resemble Hernán Cortés' sensational encounter with the Aztec empire; neither does it echo the legendary wealth found in Peru by the Pizarro brothers. Instead, the Spanish penetration in the lands that lay south of Peru was characterized by long wars against the indigenous populations (which in fact would continue even after the end of the colonial period), poverty, and periodic hunger.[11] Yet, due to the resoluteness of Pedro de Valdivia (1497–1553), an experienced soldier from Extremadura, the Spaniards were eventually able to conquer and populate a strip of land in the most remote corner of the known world.[12] But besides the merits and the shortcomings of his personality, there are at least two reasons if Valdivia succeeded where another veteran conquistador, Diego de Almagro, had failed just ten years earlier. The first reason is that Valdivia—unlike Almagro—enthusiastically embarked in the conquest of Chile, while he could have stayed in Peru, where he had received from Francisco Pizarro a large *encomienda* and a mine.[13] And the second reason, which will be the subject of the next pages, bears the name of Giovanni Battista Pastene (1507–1580), a Genoese adventurer who became indispensable for Valdivia's colonies, saving them several times from starvation and at least once from civil war.

After reaching northern Chile and founding the town of Santiago in February 1541, Valdivia and his fellow colonists were constantly engaged in warfare. For about four years, from 1541 to 1545, Valdivia had to fight simply in order to defend his position, commanding only a handful of starving Spaniards.[14] Crops had to be sown and then guarded day and night; horses had to be fed better than men, since the defense of the settlement depended on them.[15] However, a small Spanish posse fighting against large indigenous armies was not something unseen in those days of expeditions into the unknown. What rendered the situation of the first colonial outposts in Chile truly exceptional was actually something else: their utter, prolonged, and tragic isolation. This isolation—which could spell doom for Valdivia and his besieged settlers in Santiago—is the key to understanding that the importance of Pastene's arrival and of his subsequent enterprises in the service of Valdivia can hardly be overestimated. The only two land routes connecting Chile with Peru passed through the perennial snow of the Andes and the sun-baked Atacama Desert. In 1535, Almagro's expedition had been decimated by the freezing temperatures during his passage across the mountains. Moreover, the situation was worsened by the bad reputation that the lands south of Peru had since the return of Almagro and of those who had survived his disastrous expedition.[16] Given the risks versus the potential return, it was becoming increasingly unlikely that a merchant would arrive in Santiago from Peru or that other Spaniards would join the colony. This was so much the case that even communication became a problem, and Valdivia learned of the assassination of Francisco Pizzarro only indirectly, through the words of captured indigenous enemies.[17] As Ida Stevenson Weldon Vernon put it,

> It was soon clear to Valdivia that the best efforts of his small force would not be enough to save his colony unless help could be obtained from the outside. He was in desperate need of more men, more horses, more ammunition, to say nothing of clothing and food.[18]

Valdivia had first attempted to open a line of communication with the construction of a ship, but as this was burned by indigenous warriors he decided to send six men across the desert, in a hazardous attempt to have news about Francisco Pizzarro and to obtain help. Valdivia was troubled by the rumor about Francisco Pizarro's death, not merely because of their old friendship, but also because the legitimacy of his position in Chile depended on a grant signed precisely by the conqueror of Peru. If Pizarro had really been assassinated, then Valdivia needed to strengthen his legitimacy as governor of Chile either by petitioning the new governor of Peru (whoever that might be) or by writing directly to the emperor.[19] Almost two years of silence and continuous isolation followed. In the meantime, four of the six men sent by Valdivia died crossing the desert, killed by indigenous people who kept the remaining two Spaniards as captives for several months. After they escaped and reached Cuzco, the new governor Cristóbal Vaca de Castro promised to raise funds among the colonists and send some ships to the Chilean outposts.[20] In September 1543, the two colonists returned to Santiago, with new recruits, horses, and supplies; at the same time, also a ship reached Valparaiso. After that, yet another nine months passed without any communication with Peru, and the situation become once again critical. Until, in the summer of 1544, a Genoese navigator came with his ship to visit Valdivia's colony.[21] This Ligurian captain would soon break Chile's isolation, thus making it possible for the Spanish to finally secure the settlement of Santiago and start a military expansion in the surrounding territories.

Giovanni Battista Pastene was born in Genoa, in 1507. He probably lived in Spain for a few years, before going to the Indies in 1526, officially becoming a resident of Peru in 1537.[22] It is noteworthy that Pastene undertook the passage to America in the year 1526, because, as we have seen, two cédulas in 1525 and 1526 authorized the Genoese to settle and trade in the Indies. In the meantime in Genoa, Antoniotto Adorno was doge, and the first Hispanic-Genoese alliance had been in existence for four years. In his third letter to the king, Valdivia recounts:

> While I was thus busied, in July of this year 1544, there arrived at the said harbor of Valparaiso the Captain Juan Bautista de Pastene, a Genoese, pilot-general in this South Sea for the lords of the Real Audiencia at Panama, with a ship of his own, which, to serve Your Majesty and through the action of the Governor Vaca de Castro, he and a servant of his loaded with goods to come to the help of this land.[23]

After a few lines, the missive continues explaining the reasons that induced Valdivia to make use of Pastene's talents, naming him his *teniente general en la mar*:[24]

> In the following September of this year 1544, knowing the good will with which the captain-pilot Juan Bautista de Pastene had come, and offered himself to me to serve Your Majesty and me in your imperial name, and his fame as a pilot, and his skill and experience in navigating this sea, and exploring new lands, and all his other attainments needed for Your Majesty's service and the weal of all your vassals and of this land—I made him my lieutenant-general by sea, sending him at once to explore for me one hundred and fifty to two hundred leagues of coast as far as the Strait of Magellan, and to bring me interpreters from it all, and so put him to work. And at the end of this month he had gone and come back on the commission I entrusted him with on Your Majesty's behalf.[25]

Therefore, in 1544 Pastene had already made a name for himself, since Valdivia stated that he was aware of "his fame as a pilot." It seems clear that Pastene possessed a unique set of skills and a remarkable experience; yet, he was not only a merchant and a talented navigator. To be sure, he had come to the Americas as a businessman, and with his ship, the *San Pedro*, he had been one of the first captains to navigate the difficult waters of the Pacific, linking New Spain with Panama and Peru.[26] But Pastene was more than a shipowner entrusted by the Audiencia of Panama with the exploration of strategic sea routes and the logistic support of the Spaniards fighting in Peru: he was himself a conquistador.

According to Giovanni Bonfiglio, before joining Valdivia, Pastene "was also in Lima, where he participated in the struggle between conquistadors and was a witness to Francisco Pizarro's death."[27] Contrary to this opinion, neither Roa y Ursua nor Miguel Donoso Rodríguez believes that the Genoese captain had a role in the conquest and settlement of Peru.[28] Unfortunately, Bonfiglio does not support his claim with any primary source, curiously ignoring Valdivia's letters. However, it is exactly there that one can find significant hints suggesting that in fact Pastene had fought in Peru before 1544. In several of his missives, Valdivia stated that, besides being employed by the Audiencia of Panama, and before being asked by the governor Vaca de Castro to sail for Chile, Pastene had served Francisco Pizarro. For example, in his first missive to the king, Valdivia wrote:

> Juan Bautista Pastene, from Genoa, a man highly skilled in bearings and things relating to navigation, one of those that best understand this craft of all that sail this southern sea, a man of much honour, faith, and truth, and that has been of great service to Your Majesty in the provinces of Peru, and to D. Francisco Pizarro, and after his death, in their recovery under the commission of the governor Vaca de Castro.[29]

In a letter to Hernando Pizarro, the conqueror of Chile called Pastene "a servant of the Marquis," *criado del Marqués* (Francisco Pizarro), and went on saying: "and as we already know the captain," *y como nos conocíamos el capitan.*[30] Furthermore, in a message penned by Valdivia for his representatives at the Spanish court, the description of Pastene includes the following sentence:

> and I knew him as a man of valour and of prudence and of experience in the war with the Indians and new discoveries.[31]

Finally, Alonso de Ovalle (1603–1651), who as we shall see was himself a great-grandson of Pastene, explicitly talked of conquest when portraying his ancestor:

> noble of the very ancient and greatly distinguished House of the Pastene from Genoa, of whom there is no other memory in that republic (due to the death of all the members of this family) than what can be found in its archives, where one sees many of his forefathers, not only written in the books of the nobility, but also among the senators and councilors. . . . He went to the conquests of that New World with the desire, among others, to gain glory and wealth for his House.[32]

Therefore, some brief, key passages in various sources seem to indicate that Pastene was already a conquistador before joining Valdivia. Besides being one of the best available navigators of the "South Sea," it would appear that the Genoese nobleman had actively taken part in different phases of the conquest of Peru, not only furnishing transport and supplies, but also serving the Pizarro brothers, fighting against the Indians, being involved in the civil wars (in particular, "in the recovery of the Provinces of Peru"), and probably meeting Valdivia in Lima before the latter's expedition to Chile.

In 1544, after being named *teniente general*, Pastene received a banner (with the coats of the imperial arms and of Valdivia's House) and took an oath;[33] by September 4, his ship was unloaded and ready to sail, so the Genoese captain left the port of Valparaiso, heading South, towards uncharted waters. His exploration was fast and successful. Pastene reached the river Biobío, explored several natural harbors, and took formal possession of new territories.[34] After his return, on September 30, Valdivia decided that it was time to expand his colony.

> Having heard the report given me by the captain and those who went with him of their voyage, and of what they took possession of, and of the wealth of the land, the abundance of men and cattle, and the reports given me by the interpreters he brought, I set about putting in the mines the Anaconcilla and Indian women in our service that we had brought from Peru, and to help us they went with good will. It was no small a task, for there were five hundred of them; and we carried them their food with our horses from the town, which is twelve leagues away, sharing equally with them what we had for the support of our children and our slaves, and which we had sown and gathered by our own hands and toil.[35]

It was thus as a result of Pastene's exploration and report that Valdivia decided to organize a military expedition to the lands situated between Santiago and the river Biobío. As the letter goes on to explain, Valdivia put indigenous people to work in the recently discovered mines precisely in order to finance such enterprise.[36] Ten months later, when an adequate amount of gold had been obtained, Pastene sailed for Peru, with the task of enlisting more men and purchasing weapons and horses. In February 1546, Valdivia led a small force by land to see for himself where he could found new towns once Pastene brought him reinforcements, ammunitions, and supplies. Reaching the river Biobío, Valdivia tested for the first time the impressive military power of the Mapuche.[37] With his men afraid of being surrounded by more indigenous warriors and finding themselves trapped there, Valdivia retreated to Santiago, hoping to see Pastene's ship arriving soon. Yet, this time the Ligurian *teniente* would disappear for a total of twenty-seven months.

As soon as he arrived in Lima, Giovanni Battista learned that Gonzalo Pizarro was leading a rebellion of outraged *encomenderos*, who did not intend to accept the New Laws protecting the Indians.[38] Peru was in turmoil.[39] The *San Pedro* was confiscated by the rebels, Valdivia's gold was taken, and Pastene was forbidden to leave the city "under pain of death."[40] Antonio de Ulloa, the captain to whom Valdivia had entrusted some important missives with the task of continuing the voyage to Spain, publicly and scornfully destroyed the documents, joining the rebellion. In this delicate and dangerous situation, Pastene demonstrated that he was a faithful and cool-headed servant of Valdivia (and of the emperor). He did not join Gonzalo Pizarro's rebellious fleet but, knowing that he could be killed at any time on trumped up charges, he waited quietly in Lima, without showing his support for the viceroy. Then, when an opportunity presented itself, Pastene carefully took advantage of it. After the battle of Añaquito (January 18, 1546)—where Pizarro had obtained a victory against the royal army, killing the viceroy Blasco Núñez Vela—Gonzalo's right-hand man, Francisco de Carvajal arrived in Lima. Because Carvajal was a long-time friend of both Pastene and Valdivia (with whom he had also fought in Italy at the battle of Pavia),[41] Pastene approached him and asked for help. From this conversation, Pastene learned that Ulloa, with the support of his cousin Lorenzo de Aldana, had lied to Gonzalo Pizarro, claiming to be a loyal friend of Valdivia and obtaining the permission to use his gold to organize an expedition to bring supplies and men to Chile. Nevertheless, Carvajal knew that Ulloa's real intention was to murder Valdivia and replace him as governor of Chile, so he gave Pastene official permission to leave Lima and visit Gonzalo Pizarro, in Quito.[42] Following Carvajal's suggestion, Pastene did not try to convince Gonzalo that Ulloa had lied to him and was carrying out a conspiracy; instead, the Genoese captain pretended to sympathize with the rebellion and simply asked for permission to purchase a ship and join the expedition to Chile. Gonzalo agreed, and although Aldana and Ulloa tried their best to hinder him, Pastene was able to purchase a little vessel ("a ship that was no more than a hull")[43] and find enough men to weigh anchor. When Pastene left Peru, Ulloa (with the stolen *San Pedro* and another ship) had already sailed; but the Ligurian *teniente* was able to overtake him, avoid an assassination attempt, and escape, thanks to his superior seafaring experience. Seeing that Pastene was going to reach Valdivia before them, thus warning him of the plot, the conspirators abandoned their plan and returned to Peru.

Pastene had saved Valdivia's life, or at the very least he had avoided a civil war in the Chilean territories conquered by the Spaniards. With the few men and scarce resources that he had, Valdivia quickly organized an expedition to help the royal army in Peru. Thus, Valdivia decided to remain faithful to the king, even though he had a longstanding friendship with the Pizarro brothers (to whom he owed the permission to conquer Chile). Valdivia reached the troops led by the new viceroy, Pedro de la Gasca, and was named colonel of the infantry, participating in the campaign against Gonzalo Pizarro. It is not clear what role was played by Pastene during the civil war, but after the defeat of the rebellious *encomenderos*, he went back to Chile with Valdivia, who had been finally named by La Gasca governor of those lands (New Extremadura).[44] Pastene continued to be Valdivia's indispensible "lieutenant-general by sea," supporting his expansion in the South, and guaranteeing that the Chilean colonists would be in contact with Peru. In 1550, the governor reached once more the river Biobío, this time founding the city of Concepción, on a site first sighted by his Genoese captain during the exploration of 1544. The year 1550 is also when Pastene received from Pedro de Valdivia the most typical prize assigned to the best (and luckiest) conquistadors: an *encomienda*.[45]

Giovanni Battista Pastene represents by himself a remarkable case study, which can help scholars to trace the beginnings of the Genoese presence in the Spanish Americas as well as the maritime tradition and cosmopolitan culture brought by the Genoese into the Atlantic. The Genoese that entered, settled, and traded in the Spanish Indies constituted a sort of mimetic empire: a group of individuals who did not share any "Ligurian" political agenda (thus not constituting a threat for the king), but who did share a certain economic culture, a useful array of colonial techniques, and seafaring expertise. Between 1525 and the 1590s, in the limitless, socially fluid, and rapidly expanding world of the Spanish Indies, opportunities never lacked for those willing to use their talents and risk their lives. Pastene was surely one of these men. But one could say that his exceptional career was also due to the fact that he was able at times to leave his "Genoeseness" behind, in order to achieve what a true Castilian hidalgo would desire: a stable and prestigious social position in the new colonial society. For this reason, before briefly presenting some other cases of Genoese adventurers in sixteenth-century Spanish America, a few pages should be dedicated to some of the numerous manuscripts produced by Giovanni's descendants and still preserved in the Spanish archives. These documents constitute an invaluable opportunity to consider how—and to what extent—the second and third generations of Genoese conquistadors tried to fully integrate into the Spanish empire.

In 1646, José Pastene Justiniano, one of Giovanni Battista Pastene's grandsons, wrote a report (*Informaciones de oficio y parte*) for the emperor.[46] The reason why this kind of letter was written was usually to inform the imperial government of some services that a family or an individual had allegedly done for the benefit of the king; these "reports" were accompanied by the request for a reward, in the form of either money or titles. José introduced himself as "Captain," and in the first lines of the document he declared that he was still waiting for the council of the Indies to decide about a compensation for the services of his grandfathers and of his father, who had been among the very first "conquerors and settlers" (*conquistadores y pobladores*) of the Kingdom of Chile.[47] The document continues with José briefly mentioning the deeds of his paternal grandfather, Giovanni Battista; then, a few lines are dedicated to the author's maternal grandfather, the captain Vicencio Pascual, who had served very well "in the war of this said Kingdom," and who had done so using his own money, for which the royal treasury was "indebted with his sons and heirs."[48] Vincenzo Pasquale was a Genoese merchant who arrived in Chile in 1569, establishing his business along the route connecting Callao and Valparaiso.[49] Thanks to two other documents preserved in the same file, one that bears the signature of José Pastene and one penned by his mother, Catalina Justiniano, it is possible to ascertain that Vincenzo had married a woman named Jerónima Justiniano, whose father, Ambrosio Giustiniano, was also a Genoese businessman living in Chile.[50]

José Pastene's petition to the king continues with an interesting description of the career of Francisco Pastene—who was the author's father and one of Giovanni Battista Pastene's sons:

> and following the services of my aforementioned grandfathers they were continued by the lawyer Francisco Pastene, my father, in the offices of attorney of the royal audiencia of Los Reyes and of the audiencia of this city [Santiago], where he [also] held the offices of your prosecutor in its founding and of judge of the province and of the goods of the departed with great rectitude and Christianity, having held before the office of lieutenant general and chief justice in this said kingdom . . . having also held for the clergy the office of vicar-general of this bishopric and the office of mayor of this said city and of *regidor* several times.[51]

José then proceeded to introduce himself more in detail, explaining that he had studied since his childhood (*desde mi niñez*) to obtain his degree, and recalling the offices that he had held for the king: *theniente general* of the province of Omasuyos; and governor of the Villa de San Juan de Sahagún.[52] The military careers of two of the writer's brothers are also mentioned in the document:

> And similarly the captains don Francisco Pastene and don Joan Negron, my legitimate brothers, in the war of this kingdom have served your royal person since their tender age, and for their services they have deserved the posts of military officers, which the said captain don Francisco held as captain of the Spanish infantry, captain of the cavalry, and second general in the said kingdom . . . and the said captain don Joan Negron, having gone, offered himself, and served your royal person, was named captain of the Spanish infantry in the state of Arauco and then was named second general of the kingdom as well.[53]

This investigation into the career and life of Giovanni Battista Pastene and some of his heirs is not exhaustive, but rather deliberately exemplificative—aiming to uncover the historical roles, social strategies, and economic networks of the Genoese in the Spanish Atlantic. Nevertheless, considering both what has been presented in the previous pages and the specific objectives of this book, a few conclusive observations can be made about Giovanni Battista Pastene, his family, and other Genoese in the Indies. When the Ligurian captain crossed the Atlantic in 1526, he started a business doing what a Genoese did best: navigating. Moving to the westernmost area of what constituted the Atlantic world at that time, he made a name for himself as shipowner and explorer of new routes in the Pacific.[54] In the early 1530s, he probably began to transport people from Mexico and Panama to Peru;[55] he also traded goods, connecting the Spanish ports along the coast.[56] It is not surprising that a man of his talents would have soon been befriended by the Pizarro brothers and employed by the Audiencia of Panama. Giovanni Battista thereby started to juxtapose a career in the Spanish imperial ranks to his career as a merchant. He became progressively more involved in the conquest and settlement of new territories, not just in Peru, where the land was rich yet the *encomiendas* were already all assigned, but also in Chile, where serving the governor Valdivia he reached both the apogee of his military career (becoming *teniente general*) and the socioeconomic position desired by every Castilian conquistador (that of *encomendero*).[57] Giovanni Pastene married a Spanish woman, Ginebra de Seixais, and his heirs continued this process of assimilation. His son Tomás inherited the *encomienda* and married a Spanish woman, Augustina Lantadilla; the chronicler Alonso de Ovalle was one of their grandsons.[58] Similarly, Tomás' sister Ana María married a Spanish *encomendero*; his brother Pedro became a conquistador himself, fighting in the war of Arauco; and another brother, Juan Francisco, joined the Franciscans living at the convent in the town of Valdivia.[59] Nevertheless, while it is undeniable that the Pastenes were adapting to the colonial society, they were also partly maintaining their Genoese identity, making alliances with other Genoese families living along the Pacific coast of the Castilian Americas. This is evident when one considers Francisco, the youngest son of Giovanni Battista. As we have seen, Francisco Pastene studied law and held prestigious offices in the royal administration, while also working for the Church. However, he did not marry a Castilian woman, but rather Catalina Justiniano, who was herself the daughter of two Genoese who married in the Americas—Vicencio Pascual and Jeronima Justiniano. The fact that a Genoese family who had reached the status of *encomendero* and had placed several brothers in key political, ecclesiastical, and bureaucratic positions would decide to make an alliance with Genoese businessmen who had not been willing (or able) to integrate as successfully into the colonial elite can be explained with the typically Ligurian desire to carry on a multiplicity of simultaneous businesses and careers within the same family, but also recalling that Giovanni Battista died poor.[60] When the members of the family found themselves in a bad financial situation, they turned to other Genoese families living in Chile that had continued their trading business. These families, the Justiniano and the Pascual (and perhaps the Negron), were wealthy, but they lacked both the social status and the political power of the Pastenes (which is presumably the reason why they left scantier archival traces). Hence, the marriage between Francisco and Catalina Justiniano strengthened both parties, while expanding the Ligurian network in the kingdom that since 1544 Genoese colonists had helped to explore, conquer, settle, defend, and administer.

ADAPTABILITY AND DIVERSIFICATION OF CAREERS: AN OVERVIEW OF THE SIXTEENTH-CENTURY "GENOESE ATLANTIC"

The case of Giovanni Battista Pastene and his heirs is significant, because the archival documents and other primary sources that have been produced (both by members of this family and by contemporary Spaniards) show how a Genoese family was able to participate in the phase of conquest and settlement of the Americas while also building socioeconomic networks and integrating into the colonial elite. Some other Genoese captains (e.g., Giustiniani, Pascual) who arrived in Peru and Chile in the same decades but for whom we possess very little documentation have already been mentioned. In the next pages, I shall briefly present an array of examples of Ligurian men and women who traveled and settled across the Spanish Atlantic. These cases show that the Genoese presence in the Castilian Americas was significant and widespread already at the dawn of the Habsburg transatlantic empire. Furthermore, the activities in which these Genoese were involved confirm the adaptability of their economic praxis, as well as the fact that their employment in the ranks of the imperial bureaucracy was not casual or extemporaneous.[61]

Numerous members of the Cattaneo family entered the Spanish Indies since as early as the 1530s. Their surname in the documents is written in the hispanized form Cataño, and even though they probably belonged to different branches of the family, their diversification of economic investments and activities is impressive.[62] In 1535, the Spanish queen signed a *cédula*, or licence, granting Juan Cataño, *genovés*, the right to trade with the Americas, or—more precisely—"to go to our Indies, islands and mainland of the Ocean Sea with certain merchandise."[63] In 1537, a royal *cédula* gave to another Cataño, named Jerónimo, the right to transport seventy-six slaves to the Indies.[64] This permission was not granted as a result of a request made by

Jerónimo. Instead, the Genoese businessman had already invested some capital in the newly open transatlantic economy, and was receiving this *cédula* only as a form of compensation, after 220,000 maravedíes that he had transported to Seville in two vessels had been stopped and sequestrated by the royal treasury upon their arrival.[65] It is not certain in what kind of business Jerónimo was involved prior to this episode, although it seems that he was a merchant selling goods to the American colonies.[66] But what the archival records demonstrate is that he quickly adapted to what we may call the "forced *asiento*," becoming in a few years a professional slave trader. In 1541, he obtained two *cédulas*, allowing him to transport a total of 350 slaves.[67] At the same time, he continued to trade merchandise, sometimes managing to leave the port without waiting for the fleet, and thus reaching the Americas before the other merchants.[68] In December 1547, more than ten years after the first, "forced" *asiento*, Jerónimo was still a slave trader, preparing to purchase and transport to the Indies 180 slaves.[69]

Yet, while the documents on Juan and Jerónimo prove that Ligurian traders were investing capital in the commerce with the Indies as early as the 1530s, other Genoese bearing the surname Cataño chose different careers within the empire. For example, Gabriel Cataño de Sandoval became a bureaucrat and an administrator in the imperial ranks. But contrary to Giovanni Battista Pastene, Gabriel did not have to patiently and laboriously toil in the Americas in order to obtain an office: he did not have a talent for navigation and war, but he evidently did possess other important skills, in the field of social relations and politics. So, when he sailed from Spain, he was already the beneficiary of two official appointments from the metropolis. A *real provision* (royal decree) dated April 1538 made him *regidor* of the second town to be founded in Florida by the conquistador Hernando de Soto; while with a second manuscript, penned only two months later, the king named him *regidor* of the second town to be peopled in the province of Cartagena, in New Granada.[70] Considering the dangers of Soto's expedition into the unknown,[71] it is not surprising that Gabriel chose to settle in Cartagena.[72] Later in the sixteenth century, the Cataño family continued to hold offices in the royal administration.[73] In 1580, Luis Cataño de Casana (in some documents spelled Cassaria), obtained a post as *factor real* of Cuzco and a licence to cross the ocean.[74] Indeed, he went to Cuzco and worked there for the royal treasury, as proved by a voluminous account book for the fiscal years 1591–1594.[75] The *factor real* was a key figure in the imperial bureaucracy, representing the king during the collection of fiscal revenues, gathering all merchandises and goods destined to the Crown, and working with other colonial authorities to take cohesive fiscal decisions (also beyond his territorial jurisdiction).[76] Moreover, during the sixteenth century the office of *factor* had taken over the prerogatives of the suppressed office of *veedor*;[77] and in 1563, a *real provision* ordered to leave the posts of *factor* vacant in all the

American provinces, with the exception of the wealthiest ones.[78] Therefore, by the time Luis obtained the office in Cuzco, the *factores* had become less numerous and more powerful. Unsurprisingly, in the second half of the century the *factor* became the officer who was constantly informing the metropolis, maintaining regular correspondence with the Casa de Contratación in Seville.[79] That a Genoese could purchase this appointment shows that Ligurian immigrants were able to go beyond the roles of banker[80] and merchant, seizing opportunities to join the Spanish elite in the Americas, thus permanently entering the colonial society.[81] The Crown needed to use a talented Genoese for this position also because Spanish rulers refused to allow the creation (or immigration) of a nobility in the Americas. Even the class of *encomenderos*, seen as a necessary evil during the conquest and settlement of the new kingdoms, was going to be disempowered and replaced with royal officials.[82] It is not possible to know whether Luis was in contact with any of his relatives already living in the Americas; but for sure, he was not going to be the only member of the Cattaneo family to be a resident of Peru. By 1570, at least one other Cataño, named Juan Díaz, had already settled there. Francisco de Toledo, the viceroy of Peru, penned a licence with the intention of protecting him as he went to Panama to take his family. More specifically, the viceroy ordered all colonial authorities to let Juan travel,

> so that he can freely come and take from the said kingdom of *Tierra firme* the said Constanza de Quirós his wife with his possessions and his children that he may have to these kingdoms and provinces of Peru on the ship that he will wish or will come with.[83]

Toledo's protection and intervention seems to suggest that Juan Díaz Cataño had been a resident in Peru for several years, and that he was part of (or at least had access to) the political elite of the kingdom. But he had also lived for some time in Panama, before moving South, because the viceroy stated clearly in the document that Juan had married his wife in Panama.[84] In the 1550s, yet another Cataño, Luis de Barrios had become a resident of one of the colonial towns in the Americas, as shown by a royal *cédula* written in Seville in 1562, which allowed him to bring his wife and three nephews to be with him on the other side of the Ocean.[85]

The Cattaneos were not the only Genoese family trading with the American colonies in the 1530s. At this early stage, Ligurian merchants, with their capital and their expertise, were needed to furnish the Spanish outposts on the other side of the ocean with all sorts of goods and supplies.[86] At times, Genoese merchants would establish companies with other countrymen, just as they had done for centuries in the Mediterranean and in the Black Sea. For example, the Genoese Gregorio Lercaro (from the Lercaro family) was in business with the Centuriones, who were also part of the Ligurian community in Spain. In a document dated 1542, the Crown ordered the *oidores* and the other officials of the Audiencia of *Tierra firme* to collect the possessions left by Gregorio, who had died there.[87] This royal *cédula* was the result of a request penned by Gregorio's associate, Andrés Centurión. Andrés believed that, at the moment of his death, his countryman was in possession of "silver and gold and other things."[88] Therefore, he had asked the king to intervene, ordering the colonial authorities to investigate the matter, collect all valuable possessions, search for a will, and send everything to the Casa de Contratación in Seville. Unfortunately, the manuscript does not specify the nature of the business in which Gregorio Lercaro and Andrés Centurión were involved (Andrés had simply declared that he had a certain company with Gregorio).[89] For sure, more members of the Lercaro family replicated the model of a company established with the participation of other Ligurian businessmen. For instance, in the same years a man called Cristóbal Lercaro was selling slaves in the Americas with the help of Leonardo Lomelín and Nicolás Marín. In 1544, these three Genoese slave traders obtained a licence to transport 200 black slaves from Portugal or the islands of Cape Verde or Guinea to the Indies.[90] These documents are significant because they exemplify the Genoese presence and activities in the Spanish Atlantic in the second quarter of the sixteenth-century. They also prove that the Lercaros first entered the Indies as merchants; yet, this family later became part of the imperial bureaucracy and colonial elite.[91] Thus, the Lercaros followed the same pattern already seen with the Pastenes and the Cataños.

At this early stage, Genoese adventurers and businessmen settled also in Mexico. Juan Agustín Justiniano was living in Mexico City when he died in 1583. He had become quite wealthy in the Spanish colonies; so much so that his mother, who still lived in Genoa, sent a grandson named Jerónimo Salvo to Seville, to claim Juan Agustín's inheritance.[92] Jerónimo went to Seville to ask for permission to travel to Mexico City, stating that his uncle, "having lived for more than twenty-five years in the City of Mexico, married with a woman from the Canary Islands, died without leaving any legitimate son."[93] This means that as early as the 1550s Genoese immigrants were engaged in economic activities in the capital of the kingdom of New Spain.[94] But was Juan Agustín the only Genoese living in Mexico at the time? And in what kind of economic activities was he involved? A document written in the same month as Jerónimo Salvo's petition (June, 1584) and summarizing the testimonies of men who knew Juan Agustín suggests that the deceased Genoese had crossed the Atlantic even earlier than what imagined by his relatives, because he had not immediately settled down in Mexico City, living instead for about five years somewhere else in New Spain. Hence, in total "he lived and stayed in this kingdom and in the said provinces as subject and resident of these kingdoms for more than thirty years."[95] Moreover, according to one witness, Juan Agustín had lived in the Canary Islands for several years, and before reaching Mexico he had stopped for an indefinite amount of time in the island of Santo Domingo.[96] Most importantly, all the witnesses stated that Juan Agustín's *hacienda* in Mexico was nothing less than "mines and slaves" and that he had extracted silver and conducted other businesses in the region for decades.[97] In the following pages of the manuscript, the author(s) recorded how the witnesses declared that they were shocked by the news that Juan Agustín was a Genoese, since he had always presented himself as a Castilian.[98] Yet, this Ligurian mining entrepreneur had not cut all relationships with his countrymen once he had reached the other side of the ocean. Instead, he had befriended another Genoese living in Mexico, Agustín Espinola, who at some point traveled all the way to the Canary Islands, to take his sister Damiana Spinola to Mexico to marry the wealthy Justiniano.[99] Uncovering yet another facet of the Genoese activities in the New World, Juan Agustín's story exemplifies how diversified the Genoese economic activities in the New World were, very early on.[100] A man born in Genoa and whose family was still in Liguria was among the first immigrants to settle in Mexico; initially a merchant,[101] he quickly seized the economic opportunities that he found in New Spain, buying a mine and extracting silver from it for about three decades; but, like Francisco Pastene, he maintained links with other Genoese men living in the Americas, eventually deciding to marry a woman of Ligurian descent who lived in the Canary Islands, but whose family he had befriended in Mexico City.

With regard to the Spinolas, it is worth mentioning that at the beginning of the seventeenth century one of them became archdeacon of the Cathedral of Quito.[102] Gaspar Centurión Espinola, who had already been priest in the parish of San Sebástian, in Lima, received promotion to this higher clerical office by the king, in 1607.[103] In 1609, two officials of the Audiencia of *Tierra firme* accused the Genoese clergyman of concealing some property that should have been declared (and probably taxed). This seems to suggest that Gaspar was taking advantage of his ecclesiastical and political position to smuggle some goods into the American kingdoms. The document penned by the officials in Panama reads:

> doctor don Gaspar Centurion Espinola, chaplain of Your Majesty and archdeacon of the Cathedral of Quito arrived in this kingdom, and hearing that he had brought a large quantity of property without registering it, we proceeded against him, and in thirty-two cases labelled as clothing and books. . . . As well as the books and clothing, we discovered a quantity of merchandise.[104]

Gaspar did not accept the decision and appealed against the officers. For sure, Gaspar was not happy about his economic situation. In the subsequent years, he asked the king to grant him a better prebend (the portion of the cathedral revenue assigned to him as his stipend),[105] but how had he been able to reach such a high ecclesiastical position in the Indies in the first place? In a letter written in 1618, Gaspar mentioned the name of his father, Phelippe Centurión, recalling that he had served the king in several places in Spain, Granada, and the Flanders.[106] The name Felipe Centurión is indeed present among a list of bankers (many of whom bearing Genoese surnames) who had anticipated money for the Crown in 1590.[107] But Felipe was not just a banker. Since the early 1580s, he had started to trade with the Indies.[108] So, in two generations of Genoese, we can find a banker who was also a merchant and a doctor in theology who had embarked in an ecclesiastical career in the Indies while allegedly continuing to (illegally) bring merchandise from the metropolis.

THE IMMEASURABILITY OF IDEAS AND CULTURES: GENOESE MIMESIS AND MENTAL CAPITAL

Since the methodological framework of my work rests upon the study of the relationship between human action, civic culture, and political as well as colonial institutions, this chapter has offered an overview of the beginnings of the early modern Genoese presence in the Spanish Atlantic, with the intention to exemplify—not to quantify—the career(s) and the socioeconomic behavior(s) of the first Ligurian men and women who peopled the Americas.[109] The cases presented are relevant for they show how, by the end of the sixteenth century, the Genoese adapted to the economic challenges created by the discovery and conquest of new kingdoms in the Americas. The strategies used by Ligurian economic actors to create for themselves a legitimate political and social space in the Castilian Indies, or even to enter the colonial elite, were strikingly diverse. They entered the Spanish Atlantic not only as merchants and bankers, but also as conquistadores and mining entrepreneurs; and while it seems that they often purchased important offices in the imperial administration, at least some families among them never ceased to trade slaves, silver, or other goods.

The conclusion to draw is that the Genoese were part of the Castilian colonies since a very early stage, at a time when all other foreigners were forbidden to enter. The documents that I presented suggest that the Genoese entered the Spanish Indies practicing a vast array of professions and occupations, from sailor to *factor*, from merchant to *encomendero*. Crucially, these careers were not mutually excluding, but rather often simultaneous. The Genoese used the institutional instruments of the Castilian world and often tried to integrate into the colonial society. As we have seen, Pastene obtained an *encomienda*, and his sons (even if troubled by financial constraints) were part of the colonial elite. Yet, in a sense these men remained Genoese, just like the Ligurian merchants trading, living, and at times holding public offices in fourteenth-century English city ports.[110] The history of this multiform mental capital, this entrepreneurial and adaptable economic culture—fostering (and fostered by) a unique series of notarial, financial, and communal institutions—has been delineated in this book seeking its late medieval origins and its politico-intellectual underpinnings. But the history of peoples, cultures, and economic processes defies periodizations, easily overflowing the scope of monographs. That a "Genoese Atlantic" (within the Spanish Atlantic) existed as such is in fact confirmed, more unquestionably and spectacularly, by the resilience of Ligurian networks and communities in the subsequent centuries. Even after the Spanish-American Wars of Independence, the history of these Genoese communities and transatlantic networks would continue, as they would survive the collapse of the shell that they had contributed to build.

NOTES

1. Lopez, "Market Expansion: The Case of Genoa," 461–62.
2. On the economic, social, and intellectual role of the Genoese in Spain between the fifteenth and the sixteenth centuries, see Igual Luis and Navarro Espinach, "Los genoveses en España."
3. For a recent collection of essays, many of which using quantitative and mathematical methods, see *Génova y la monarquía hispánica*, ed. by Herrero Sanchez. For a brilliant critique of quantitative history, or "quantohistory," see Gertrude Himmelfarb, *The New History and the Old* (Cambridge: Harvard University Press, 1987), especially 41–46. A more lengthy treatment of the debate on quantitative economic history is in the introduction, on xxi–xxiv.
4. Brilli, "Da Cadice a Buenos Aires"; idem, "The Genoese response to the collapse"; and idem, "Il Rio de la Plata, nuova frontiera."
5. The Genoese also transferred to the Spanish Atlantic the legal language, the rites of political legitimization and the contractual framework of some of their medieval colonies. "The various types of colonial concessions that existed in the Genoese possessions in the Levant were handed on to the Iberian nations and merged with the feudal forms inherited from the medieval past of those countries. . . . In this way Mediterranean colonial practices were transplanted to the Atlantic zone." Verlinden, *The Beginnings of Modern Colonization*, 13.
6. *Colección de documentos inéditos: relativos al descubrimiento, conquista y organización de las antiguas posesiones españolas de América*, ed. Joaquín Francisco Pacheco, Francisco de Cárdenas, Luis Torres de Mendoza (Madrid: Ministerio de Ultramar, 1865), v. 1, 362.
7. Emphasis added. "Extranjeros puedan poblar y tratar en Indias que sean sùbditos de su Majestad y naturales, y del imperio y genoveses como los naturales de Castilla y Leòn." Ibid., v. 21, 91.
8. "Damos licencia y facultad a todos los nuestros sùbditos y naturales de todos los nuestros Reinos y Señoríos y asimismo a todos los sùbditos y naturales del Imperio así genoveses como todos los otros, para que puedan pasar a las dichas Indias y estar y contratar en ellas segùn y de la forma y maneras y con las condiciones que lo hacen y pueden hacer los naturales destos nuestros Reinos y Señoríos de Castilla y Leòn." Archivo General de Indias, Indiferente, 421, 11, f. 336.
9. "che tutti i Genovesi nelli stati dell'Imperatore fussero tenuti per naturali d'essi." Sigonio, *Della vita et fatti di Andrea Doria*, 96.
10. *Colección de documentos inéditos*, v. X, 448.

11. For a treatment of the ethnohistory of the indigenous populations of Chile, see Guillaume Boccara, *Los vencedores: historia del pueblo Mapuche en la epoca colonial* (San Pedro de Atacama: Universidad Católica del Norte, 2007).

12. The best introduction to Valdivia remains Ida Stevenson Weldon Vernon, *Pedro de Valdivia, Conquistador of Chile* (Austin: University of Texas Press, 1946). Another useful, yet dated, work is R. B. Cunninghame Graham, *Pedro de Valdivia, Conqueror of Chile* (London: Heinemann, 1929), which includes the English translation of the five letters written by Valdivia to Charles V. A new biography of Valdivia is much needed, and the only (relatively) recent pieces of scholarship on the subject are the first chapter in Ricardo Ferrando Keun, *Y así nació la frontera: Conquista, guerra, ocupación, pacificación, 1550–1900* (Santiago: Editorial Antártica, 1986), especially 40–68, and two chapters in Hugh Thomas's book *The Golden Empire* (New York: Random House, 2010), 331–54. For a recent study on the war of conquest from the perspective of the Mapuche, see José Bengoa, *Historia de los antiguos mapuches del sur* (Santiago de Chile: Catalonia, 2004). Valdivia's writings have been studied, from a literary point of view, in two excellent articles: Lucia Invernizzi, "Los trabajos de la guerra y los trabajos del hambre: dos ejes del discurso narrativo de la conquista de Chile (Valdivia, Vivar, Góngora Marmolejo)," *Revista Chilena de Literatura* 36 (1990): 7–15; and Sarissa Carneiro, "Tiempo dorado en la tierra vidriosa: el relato de los primeros años de la conquista de Chile," in *Anales de literatura Chilena* 10 (2008): 25–36.

13. In his third letter to the Emperor, Valdivia briefly remembers these possessions that he had to abandon when leaving Peru. "And in Peru I also left food behind, as the Marquis had it, and that was the valley of Canela in Charcas, which was given to three *conquistadores* (being Diego Centeno, Lope de Mendoza, and Bobadilla), and a silver mine, which since has been worth over two hundred thousand *castellanos*, without having any profit of it, nor did the Marquis give me such towards the expedition." Letter of Valdivia to Charles V, October 15, 1550. Graham, *Pedro de Valdivia*, 156–57.

14. "many of the Christians had to go sometimes to dig up roots for food . . . and there was no meat, and the Christian who got fifty grains of maize a day thought himself well off; and he who had a handful of wheat did not grind it to take away the husks." Ibid., 133–34.

15. See letter of Valdivia to Charles V, September 4, 1445. Ibid., 132.

16. See the letter written by Valdivia to his representatives at the Spanish court, where he explains that Chile had become "la tierra más mal infamada de cuantas hay en las Indias." "Valdivia a sus apoderados en la corte," October 15, 1550, in *Cartas de Pedro de Valdivia*, ed. José Toribio Medina (Seville: Carmona, 1929), 99 (the letter begins on 95). On the circulation of glum stories about the road to Chile among the Spanish in Peru, see also Alejandra Vega, "Experiencias de cordillera, ecos de frio: relatos cruzados entre Chile y Quito en el siglo XVI," *Revista Chilena de Literatura* 80 (2011): 223–42, in particular 231–34. Ricardo Ferrando Keun summarizes this situation writing that, after the return of Almagro, "the assessment of a Chile that was poor, bellicose, lacking gold and silver, cold, and rainy—all negative characteristics—is the image that spreads in Peru." "La apreciación de un Chile pobre, belicoso, escaso de oro y plata, frío y lluvioso—solo aspectos negativos—es la imagen que se difunde en el Perú." Ferrando Keun, *Y así nació la frontera*, 40.

17. Letter of Valdivia to Charles V, September 4, 1445. Graham, *Pedro de Valdivia*, 129–30. On the murder of Pizarro, see John Hemming, *The Conquest of the Incas* (London: Macmillan, 1993), 252–53.

18. Stevenson Weldon Vernon, *Pedro de Valdivia*, 96.

19. The situation was complicated by the plots of Sancho de Hoz, a conquistador who claimed to be the legitimate leader of any expedition south of Peru. On de Hoz, see Thomas, *The Golden Empire*, 332–36.

20. Graham, *Pedro de Valdivia*, 34–36. See also the letter of Valdivia to Charles V, September 4, 1445, ibid., 134–37. In addition, the story of the six men's misadventure is recounted with some more details by the chronicler Alonso de Góngora Marmolejo (1523–1565), in his *Historia de Todas las Cosas que han Acaecido en el Reino de Chile y de los que lo han gobernado* (Madrid: Iberoamericana, 2010), chapter V, 110–17.

21. Graham, *Pedro de Valdivia*, 39–40.

22. Luis de Roa y Ursua, *El reyno de Chile, 1535–1810: estudio histórico, genealógico y biográfico* (Valladolid: Talleres, 1954), 3.
23. Letter of Valdivia to Charles V, October 15, 1550. Graham, *Pedro de Valdivia*, 159.
24. "Lieutenant-general of the sea": This is the title written by Valdivia in Spanish. *Cartas de Pedro de Valdivia*, 153.
25. Letter of Valdivia to Charles V, October 15, 1550. Graham, *Pedro de Valdivia*, 159.
26. The name of Pastene's ship is mentioned in numerous documents, such as the first letter of Valdivia to Charles V, Graham, *Pedro de Valdivia*, 138. The establishment of sea routes along the Pacific coast had been fast, but also problematic (due to a lack of vessels and ocean currents that made a round trip painstakingly long). See Woodrow Wilson Borah, *Early Colonial Trade and Navigation between Mexico and Peru* (Berkeley: University of California Press, 1954), in particular 1–7. If as early as 1544 Pastene had already a long and prosperous career, it is not far-fetched to imagine that he had been among the first captains to explore (and trade along) the Pacific sea route connecting Mexico and Peru.
27. Giovanni Bonfiglio, *Gli italiani nella società peruviana. Una visione storica* (Torino: Fondazione Agnelli, 1999), 4.
28. See the brief biographical notes on Pastene by Miguel Donoso Rodríguez's "Glosario de personajes históricos," in Góngora Marmolejo, *Historia*, 586; and Roa y Ursua, *El reyno de Chile, 1535–1810*, 3.
29. Letter of Valdivia to Charles V, September 4, 1445. Graham, *Pedro de Valdivia*, 138.
30. "Valdivia a Hernando Pizarro," September 4, 1545, in *Cartas de Pedro de Valdivia*, 64 (the letter begins on 51).
31. "y le conoscí por hombre de valor y de prudencia y espiriencia de guerra de indios e nuevos descubrimientos." "Valdivia a sus apoderados en la corte," October 15, 1550, in *Cartas de Pedro de Valdivia*, 109 (the letter begins on 94).
32. "caballero de la antiquísima y muy ilustre casa de los Pastenes de Génova, de que no hay ya en aquella república más memoria (por haberse muerto todos los de esta familia) que la que se halla en sus archivos, donde se ven muchos de sus antepasados, no sólo escritos en los libros de la nobleza, sino entre los senadores y ancianos. . . . Pasó a las conquistas de aquel Nuevo Mundo con el deseo, que otros, de la gloria y aumentos de su casa." Alonso de Ovalle, *Histórica relacion del reyno de Chile* (Santiago: Istituto de Literatura Chilena, 1969), 194. First edition, 1646.
33. "Poder que Valdivia dió a Pastene," in *Colección de documentos inéditos para la historia de Chile desde el viaje de Magallanes hasta la batalla de Maipo, 1518–1818*, ed. José Toribio Medina (Santiago; Ercilla, 1888–1902), vol. VIII, 71.
34. "Auto de posesión de Pedro de Valdivia: Chile," Archivo General de Indias, PATRONATO, 29.
35. Letter of Valdivia to Charles V, October 15, 1550. Graham, *Pedro de Valdivia*, 159–60.
36. Ibid., 160.
37. Stevenson Weldon Vernon, *Pedro de Valdivia*, 114–15.
38. The *encomienda* was a grant of labor force used in Spain and in the Americas mainly to reward subjects who had fought in the conquest. The *encomendero* received tithes and tributes, which constituted a kind of royal pension. One of the best books on this institution remains Silvio Arturo Zavala, *La encomienda Indiana* (Madrid: Centro de Estudios Historicos, 1935); see also Robert G. Keith, *Conquest and Agrarian Change* (Cambridge: Harvard University Press, 1976); and Carlos Sempat Assadourian, "La renta de la encomienda en la decada de 1550," *Revista de Indias* 48 (1988): 109–46. About the rebellion, see Rosa Arciniega, *Dos rebeldes españoles en el Perú: Gonzalo Pizarro ('El gran rebelde') y Lope de Aguirre ('El cruel tirano')* (Buenos Aires: Editorial Sudamericana, 1946), 17–267; James Lockhart, *Spanish Peru 1532–1560: a Colonial Society* (Madison: University of Wisconsin Press, 1968), 5 and 29–30; David Anthony Brading, *The First America* (Cambridge: Cambridge University Press, 1991), 267–68; and Hemming, *The Conquest of the Incas*, 258–62.
39. The story of Pastene's actions in Peru can be found in the Letter of Valdivia to Charles V, October 15, 1550. Graham, *Pedro de Valdivia*, 164–70.
40. Ibid., 165.

41. The fact that when Carvajal and Valdivia were still fighting against the French in Northern Italy (in the 1520s) Pastene had already crossed the Atlantic exemplifies how early the Genoese penetration in the Spanish Americas began. On Valdivia's role during the Italian Wars, see how he recalled that service to the king at the beginning of the letter (where he also affirms that he came to the Indies in 1535, almost ten years after the Genoese captain). Ibid., 156.

42. It is worth noting that in this conversation between Pastene and Carvajal, as we find it reported in Valdivia's letter, there is another confirmation of the fact that the Genoese was "an old servant" of the Pizarro brothers. Ibid., 167.

43. Ibid., 164.

44. Thomas, *The Golden Empire*, 349.

45. Toribio Medina, *Colección de documentos*, vol. VIII, 445. However, Giovanni Battista had financial problems later in his life, and died poor. See footnote 481.

46. Studying this manuscript, together with other legal papers preserved in the same file, it is possible to partly retrace the Pastene family tree, at least with regard to the children and grandchildren of Giovanni Battista. Roa y Ursua has also furnished a precise family tree of the family; however, he has not used José's *Informaciones*, and therefore he does not mention any detail about his career or those of his brothers Francisco and Joan. Roa y Ursua, *El reyno de Chile, 1535–1810*, 4–5.

47. Archivo General de Indias, "Informaciones: José Pastene Justiniano," CHILE, 45, m. 5, n. 1, f. 2 r.

48. Ibid.

49. Bonfiglio, *Gli italiani nella società peruviana*, 5.

50. The two documents are in Archivo General de Indias, "Informaciones: José Pastene Justiniano," CHILE, 45, m.5, n. 2, f. 2 r.; and ibid., f. 3 r.–4. v. In the second document, Jeronima records also her mother's name, Juana Gutierrez de Torquemada.

51. "y en continuación de los serbicios de los dichos mi abuelos los continuo el licenciado Francisco Pastene mi padre en los oficios de abogado de la real audiencia de los reyes y de la de esta ciudad donde exercio el oficio de buestro fiscal en su fundacion y el de juez de provincial y de bienes de difuntos con toda rectitud y cristianidad habiendo exercido antes el oficio de theniente general y Justicia mayor en este dicho reyno . . . habiendo tambien exercido por lo eclesiastico el oficio de probisor y bicario general de este obispado y el de alcalde ordinario de esta dicha ciudad y de regidor varias veces." Archivo General de Indias, "Informaciones: José Pastene Justiniano," CHILE, 45, m. 5, n. 1, f. 2 r.

52. Ibid., f. 2 v.

53. "Y por la misma continuidad los capitanes don Francisco Pastene y don Joan Negron mis hermanos legitimos en la guerra de este dicho reyno an serbido a buestra real persona desde sus tiernos años y por sus serbicios an merecido los puestos de alferez que dicho capitan don Francisco exercio el de capitan de ynfanteria española el de capitan de cavallos y el de alferez general entre dicho reyno . . . y el dicho capitan don Joan Negron habiendo ido, ofrecido y servido a vuestra real persona fue nombrado por capitan de ynfanteria española en el estado de Arauco y despues fue nombrado por alferez general asimismo." Ibid.

54. It may be opportune to remember at this point that the Atlantic world is a relational concept, not a geographic area.

55. "In the Audiencia of Mexico, circumstances were unusually favorable for migration to Peru. By 1530 it was clear that there were far more conquerors than encomiendas, and there emerged a rather numerous group of unprovided-for conquerors." Borah, *Early Colonial Trade*, 8.

56. As we have seen, the governor, Vaca de Castro, contacted Pastene because he was a shipowner and a merchant, who could be interested in "helping" the Spanish outpost in Chile. Letter of Valdivia to Charles V, October 15, 1550. Graham, *Pedro de Valdivia*, 159.

57. If the fact that Pastene became an *encomendero* embodies the adaptability and the readiness with which the Genoese capitalized on the new opportunities and social processes characterizing the colonial society and the imperial frontier, his service as captain and his military career exemplify the historical continuity of a long tradition, as Ligurian admirals were given key positions in the fleets fighting for the Castilian king since as early as the thirteenth

century. See Lopez, "Alfonso el Sabio y el primer almirante"; and Luigi Tommaso Belgrano, "Un ammiraglio di Castiglia," in *Archivio Storico Italiano* (1884), 42–53.

58. Archivo General de Indias, CHILE, 41, m. 12.

59. Roa y Ursua, *El reyno de Chile, 1535–1810*, 4–5.

60. Besides the already mentioned Joan Negron, José Pastene had at least another brother who chose to adopt Negron as surname, namely the doctor and cleric Diego Pastene Negron, whose *Informaciones* are in Archivo General de Indias, CHILE, 44, m. 20. This seems to suggest that the Pastene and Pascual families had at some point made an alliance also with this other Genoese family, although nothing in the surviving records shows when and who exactly married a Negron. The manuscript penned by Diego Pastene Negron is important because it states that Giovanni Battista Pastene "died poor," *murio pobre*, an information that could partly explain the amount of petitions sent by his heirs to the king, as well as the reason why some of them chose to use other surnames (Justiniano, Negron), either in combination with or instead of Pastene. Ibid., f. 2 v. See also Donoso Rodríguez's "Glosario de personajes históricos," in Góngora Marmolejo, *Historia*, 586.

61. Interestingly, also Céline Dauverd, while writing about the Ligurian presence in southern Italy, has recently stressed the adaptability of the early modern Genoese. In particular, she argues that "the Spanish chose the Genoese as their symbiotic partners because only they took steps to adapt culturally to their new environment." Dauverd, *Imperial Ambitions*, 6.

62. The surname was first (partly) hispanized as Cataneo in the Genoese communities in Spain during the fifteenth century. Igual Luis and Navarro Espinach, "Los genoveses en España," 312.

63. "yr a las nuestra yndias yslas et tierra firme del mar oceano con ciertas mercaderias." Archivo General de Indias, INDIFERENTE, 422, m. 16, f. 209 r.–209 v.; the quote is from ibid., f. 209 r.

64. Archivo General de Indias, INDIFERENTE, 423, m. 18, f. 2 r.–3 r.

65. The *cédula* points out that the sum considered is in fact 220,000 maravedíes plus 6,400 maravedíes of interests. Ibid., f. 2 r. Moreover, Jeronimo is gaining something from this forced purchase, because the tax for each slave is 8 ducats, therefore the Crown is rounding off the number of slaves that the Genoese is allowed to transport. Ibid., f. 2 v. The document also specifies that he can take the slaves not only from Spain, but also from other markets, such as Portugal or Guinea. Ibid.

66. See his licence to sail with a ship carrying merchandise, in Archivo General de Indias, INDIFERENTE, 1962, l. 5, f. 290 r.–290 v.

67. Archivo General de Indias, INDIFERENTE, 423, l.19, f. 480 v.–482 r.; and Archivo General de Indias, INDIFERENTE, 423, l. 20, f. 511 r.–512 v. In both cases, one third of the slaves must be female, and the Genoese could buy them in Spain, Portugal, Cape Verde, or Guinea.

68. On this, see the reaction of the other merchants and the decision to officially forbid Jeronimo from leaving the port before the rest of the fleet. Archivo General de Indias, INDIFERENTE, 1963, l. 8, f. 215 r.–216 v.; and ibid., f. 237 v.–238 r.

69. Archivo General de Indias, INDIFERENTE, 424, l. 21, f. 88 v.–90 r.

70. "Título de regidor en la Florida: Gabriel Cataño de Sandoval," Archivo General de Indias, PATRONATO, 19, r. 2; and Archivo General de Indias, PATRONATO, 277, n. 4, r. 83.

71. On Hernando de Soto's expedition, see *The Hernando de Soto expedition: history, historiography, and "discovery" in the Southeast*, ed. Patricia Galloway (Lincoln : University of Nebraska Press, 2005).

72. A permission to travel across the province of Cartagena, written for Gabriel Cataño de Sandoval, is in Archivo General de Indias, SANTA FE, 987, l. 2, f. 55 v.

73. The Cattaneos worked as imperial officers also later, in the seventeenth century. For example, a man called Luis de Mendoza Cataño was fiscal of the Audiencia of Mexico in the 1650s. Archivo General de Indias, FILIPINAS, 330, l.5, f. 28 r.–29 v.

74. Archivo General de Indias, CONTRATACION, 5229, n. 1, r. 14.

75. This account book is not preserved in Spain, but in Chicago. "Account book of taxes paid to the Royal Treasury in Cuzco for the year 1591 [manuscript] 1591 Feb. 4–1595 Jan. 12," Newberry Library, Special Collections, Ayer, ms. 1878.

76. According to John J. TePaske and Herbert S. Klein, "[a] factor served as fiscal agent or business manager for each treasury, carried on negotiations with other factors in other *cajas* in the Indies, and protected the arms, munitions, and supplies stored in the royal warehouses of the *caja* district." John J. TePaske and Herbert S. Klein, *The Royal Treasuries of the Spanish Empire in America* (Durham, NC: Duke University Press, 1982), viii.

77. Ismael Sanchez-Bella, *La organisación financiera de las Indias (siglo XVI)* (Seville: Escuela de Estudios Hispano-Americanos, 1968), 28–29.

78. Archivo General de Indias, INDIFERENTE, 427, l. 30. f. 127 v.–129 r. See also Carlos R. Salinas Araneda, "Los oficiales reales de Indieas en el siglo XVII," in *Poder y presion fiscal en la America española* (Valladolid: Universidad de Valladolid, 1986), 364–65.

79. Sanchez-Bella, *La organisación financiera*, 109. On the activities of the *factor*, see also ibid., 143–44. On the Casa de Contratación, the royal institution attempting to control transatlantic trade and migration, see Carlos Álvarez Nogal, "Instituciones y desarrollo económico: la Casa de Contratación y la Carrera de Indias (1503–1790)," in *La Casa de la Contratación y la navegación entre España y las Indias*, ed. Antonio Acosta Rodríguez, Adolfo Luis González Rodríguez, Enriqueta Vila Vilar (Seville: Univesidad de Sevilla, 2004), 21–51, in particular 26–30.

80. On the Genoese banking companies in Spain between the fifteenth and the sixteenth centuries, see Giuseppe Felloni, "Asientos, juros y Ferias de Cambio Desde El Observatorio Genovés (1541–1675)," in *Dinero y Crédito (siglos XVI al XIX)*, ed. Alfonso Otazu (Madrid: Moneda y Crédito, 1978), 335–59; and Carlos Álvarez Nogal, "Las compañías bancarias genovesas en Madrid a comienzos del siglo XVII," in *Hispania*, 65 (2005), 67–90.

81. Already during the Middle Ages, Genoese businessmen in Castile had ceased to be mere merchants and bankers to hold public offices and collect taxes. Consequently, once again, the presence of Genoese businessmen, families, and networks within the Spanish Atlantic appears to be based on historical continuity rather than novelty. The late medieval Genoese economic praxis characterized by private entrepreneurship, simultaneity of careers, and diversification of investments continued in the age of discoveries and empire-building. On this important point, see Charles Verlinden, "Italian Influence," in particular 201–2.

82. About the reasons why the Crown initially opted for the *encomienda*, see Timothy J. Yeager, "Encomienda or Slavery?," *The Journal of Economic History* 4 (1995), 842–59.

83. "Para que libremente pueda venir y traer del dicho Reino de Tierra firme a la dicha Constanza de Quirós su mujer con su casa y hijos que tubiece a estos rreinos y provincias del Piru en el navio que quisiere o viniere." Archivo General de Indias, PANAMA, 13, r. 10, n. 34.

84. Ibid.

85. Archivo General de Indias, INDIFERENTE, 1966, l. 14, f. 152 v. This royal *cédula* is really nothing more than a couple of lines in the register for the year 1562; unfortunately, it does not state where Luis had settled, but being a document prepared for the Casa de Contratación there is no doubt that the Genoese man was living in the Indies. The nephews that he brought with him were probably the sons of a brother living in Seville, who entrusted them to Luis so that they could see the Indies and learn the art of trade.

86. One of the first studies in English on the economic importance of the Genoese for the Spanish Atlantic is Pike, *Enterprise and Adventure*.

87. Archivo General de Indias, PANAMA, 235, l.8, f. 14 r.–14 v.

88. "or y plata y otras cosa." Ibid., f. 14 r.

89. "Gregorio Lercaro, con quien el tenía cierta compañía falecio en esa ciudad del Nombre de Dios." Ibid.

90. Archivo General de Indias, INDIFERENTE, 423, l.20, f. 799 v.–800 v.

91. In 1632, a man named Pedro Lercaro was appointed as fiscal of the Audiencia of Guadalajara. Archivo General de Indias, CONTRATACION, 5414, n.92. And in 1663, Juan Francisco Lercaro, who since two years earlier was *escribano* in La Trinidad (Buenos Aires), obtained a licence to bring to the Americas his son, Miguel Ruiz de Lercaro. Archivo General de Indias, BUENOS AIRES, 2, l. 7. f. 26 r.–28 v.; and Archivo General de Indias, CONTRATACION, 5433, n. 3, r. 7.

92. Archivo General de Indias, INDIFERENTE, 740, n. 264.

93. "haviendo bivido mas de veynte y cinco años en la ciudad de Mexico casado con una muyer natural de las yslas de Canaria fallecio sin dexar hijos ligitimos." Ibid.

94. The woman who Juan Agustín had married is not named in this source, but another document confirms that she was a Genoese, Damiana Spinola. In 1569, she had obtained a license to move from the Canary Islands to Mexico, because her husband had called for her. Damiana had brought with her across the ocean not only her three daughters, but also her mother. Archivo General de Indias, INDIFERENTE, 2052, n. 3.

95. "bivio y residio en estos reynos y en las dichas provincias como vecino y natural de estos Reynos por tiempo de mas de treynta años." Archivo General de Indias, INDIFERENTE, 2061, n. 171.

96. See the testimony of Agustín Garcia Loçano, on the sixth page of the file. Ibid.

97. This is repeated throughout the file. At the bottom of the first page, the author writes also the mine's location: "the said Juan Agustín Justiniano had a business of mines and slaves in the mines of Tasco that is twenty leagues from Mexico City." "el dicho Juan Agustin Justiniano tubo una hacienda de minas y esclavos en las minas de Tasco que es veynte leguas de la ciudad de Mexico." Ibid.

98. On the second page of the file, a hint is given to the reason why Juan Agustín Justiniano might have wanted to hide his Genoese origins: he was afraid that somebody "would not allow him to keep the business that he had with mines and slaves in the said mines of Tasco." "no le dexaran tener la hacienda que tenia de minas y esclavos en las dichas minas de Tasco." Ibid.

99. Ibid.

100. Juan Agustín Justiniano was not the only Genoese owning a mine in the American kingdoms in the sixteenth century. Since the 1590s, Pedro Espinola de Luna had owned a mine in Potosí; in 1614, he complained that some unauthorized men had seized his mine while he was busy carrying out military tasks for the king. Archivo General de Indias, CHARCAS, 418, l. 3, f. 148 r.–148 v.

101. Agustín Garcia Locano briefly mentioned that Juan Agustín had first gone to Santo Domingo carrying some "merchandise." On the sixth page of the file, Archivo General de Indias, INDIFERENTE, 2061, n. 171.

102. Archivo General de Indias, CONTRATACION, 5301, n. 2, 69 r.

103. He went to Spain to receive the official appointment; then he embarked for the return voyage with a servant. Ibid., r. 70.

104. "vino a este rreyno el doctor don Gaspar Centurion Espinola capellan que dejia ser de Vuestra Majestad y arcidiano de la cathedral de Quito y haviendo tenido noticia que traya mucha cantidad de hacienda sin registro procedimos contra el y en trenta y dos baules que traya a titulo de sus bestidos y libros . . . y le allamos demas de libros y bestidos cantidad de mercaderia." Archivo General de Indias, PANAMA, 34A, n. 5.

105. Archivo General de Indias, QUITO, 29, n. 12.

106. See the first page of the second letter in Archivo General de Indias, QUITO, 80, n. 46.

107. See the *real cédula* of 1592 in Archivo General de Indias, INDIFERENTE, 541, l. 1 DESP, f. 169–169 v.

108. Archivo General de Indias, JUSTICIA, 940, n. 4.

109. A precise quantification of the Genoese presence in the Americas is arguably impossible. This seems clear if one considers the several cases in which we know about Genoese living in the Indies only accidentally, thanks to documents that indirectly mention them. For example, in 1592, a Spanish woman called Ana de Ojeda obtained a license to move to Cuba with her children. In the manuscript, the officials acknowledged that she had a good reason to cross the ocean, since her husband, Antonio Genovés, was a resident of San Cristóbal de la Habana. Archivo General de Indias, INDIFERENTE, 2066, n. 69.

110. The late medieval Genoese colonies in England, Tunisia, and the Black Sea have been treated in chapter 1.

Conclusion

A new picture of apparently unrelated issues such as medieval entrepreneurship, republicanism, and Atlantic imperialism, emerges from this book. Genoa has been the protagonist of my work insofar as it represents an intellectual cradle—the place where a historically relevant economic and civic culture took shape. While it could be argued that, in the long run, the "Machiavellian" idea of *stato* won the ideological clash with the civic philosophy embodied by late medieval and early modern Genoa, the story of the latter is still worth studying. The value of studying Genoese history from this angle becomes evident when considering the mutual influence, the inextricable relation that existed between the Genoese republican model—based on private arms and division of power—and Genoa's role in the history of colonization and economic development. Although Genoese ideas of *libertà* and sovereignty may have eventually faded from the main stage of world history—to the point of being forgotten and conflated by many scholars into the category of a monolithically Tuscan "Renaissance republicanism"—my research suggests that Genoa's value system sparked the creation of original institutions and mental capital. That these crucial phenomena took place within the framework of a late medieval polity whose government was lacking almost any fiscal and military power is a fact obviously destined to challenge narratives of the rise of modernity and economic progress that assign an essential role to the "Machiavellian," centralized, modern state. Contrary to such narratives, institutions protecting property rights and favoring the accumulation of capital (e.g., budgetary laws, communal constitutions, private banks) were first devised in pre-modern, specifically medieval political environments. These findings are meaningful, as they help to answer one of the biggest questions ever asked in the study of human history: why was it in Europe that some communities first achieved per capita economic growth over a long period of time? It is important for political, intellectual, and economic historians to address this problem, without focusing exclusively on early modern, Northwestern Europe. Through the study of a particularly significant medieval city republic, its people's entrepreneurship, institutional history, and Mediterranean as well as Atlantic endeavors, this book has therefore tried to propose a reorientation of the field of history towards the bigger questions that once it dared to ask and debate with more consistency.

Among the main conclusions reached by my study, the first one deals with the history of the Genoese late medieval economic network. This history is difficult to write, because the Ligurian colonies were not the result of a planned military expansion. The Genoese businessmen and merchants who established financial links, set up colonial outposts, and devised notarial institutions across the Mediterranean (and beyond) did so without following a coordinated political strategy, and usually without the diplomatic support of their mother country. When the commune of Genoa signed international agreements or treaties with exotic rulers or distant polities, it often did so in the aftermath of an already successful Genoese economic penetration—not before it. Evidently, not all the maritime cities and kingdoms of the Mediterranean basin lived the commercial revolution in the same way. Nevertheless, it was precisely Genoa's model of private, unplanned, and relatively unhampered market expansion—not the Venetian one—that would survive the disintegration of the *Pax Mongolica*, the fall of Constantinople, and the loss of Levantine markets. Therefore, two of the most compelling conclusions to be drawn from the primary sources presented in the first two chapters of this book are that in the cosmopolitan and geographically distant markets shaped and connected by anonymous Genoese navigators and businessmen at the end of the Middle Ages there were spontaneous orders, resulting from the interaction of many people, but which had not been deliberately created by anyone; and that such orders were not static, as if depending on unrepeatable geographical or geopolitical circumstances: on the contrary they were the fruit of an economic culture (navigational and mercantile techniques, legal and banking institutions, and, ultimately, entrepreneurial values) that was constantly evolving and able to become entangled with other markets and different political entities. In particular, the business letters written by Giovanni da Pontremoli show how economic calculation, risk-taking, the connection of distant commercial hubs through representatives, and capital supply were all key factors in the development of a movement East-West, after the fall of Constantinople and the loss of the Black Sea colonies.

Writing the late medieval and early modern constitutional and intellectual history of Genoa is similarly and particularly challenging if one tries to illuminate the republican institutions and the unsung civic culture that, beneath factional clashes and political upheavals, consistently characterized the Ligurian polity (at least well into the sixteenth century). However, this book (and in particular chapters 2 and 3) indicates that tracing the ideological premises and the institutional originality of Genoa is possible, through the study of legal documents, literary works, archival sources, and key institutions. Among the institutions playing a decisive role, we find some that, like the *sindacatori*, are enshrined in Genoa's constitutional order and seem similar (though not identical) to late medieval offices that were present in other Italian city-states. Yet, we also find non-governmental institutions like the Bank of St. George, born as an association of creditors and representing a relatively large, cross-class group of entrepreneurs, professionals and bankers (among whom Giovanni da Pontremoli). St. George became progressively involved not only with the financing of the commune (therefore tying the hands of the doge and of any foreign governor) but also with the day-to-day administration of the colonies, the selection of consuls and castellans, and the collection of taxes. It should therefore be clear that it is impossible to assess Genoa's institutional and political history without taking into consideration St. George. This peculiar form of republicanism (or better, of republican conservatism) undermines both the Florentine-centric view of Renaissance republicanism and the entrenched conviction (dating back to Machiavelli himself) that the dramatic events taking place from 1494 (with the invasion of French armies and the beginning of the Italian Wars) could be (or had to be) met necessarily with a process of territorialization, centralization, and militarization that would mimic the rise of nation states in other parts of Europe.

Another important subject on which this book has shed light is the coexistence within the Habsburg Empire of multiform, partly contradictory and even conflicting ideas of sovereignty, authority, and political legitimacy. In the crucial years between the sack of 1522 and Doria's coup in 1528, the Genoese people came to progressively understand that Charles V's polycentric empire was potentially less authoritative and predatory than France. Crucially, Francis I did not appreciate the threat posed by private arms to whatever regime coercively imposed to the Genoese polity: the French monarch simply did not believe that Genoa could indeed reassert its territorial claims and defend itself for long, without having a standing army and a public fleet. Charles, on the other hand, had a better understanding of the internal tensions and the importance of private arms in Genoa: he never attempted to back Genoa's potential rival, Savona, and he supported a reform of the Genoese institutions that left the republican government weak—surely unable to take possession of any Ligurian private asset without the approval of a large part of the city's commercial and financial elite. This is not to say that Charles did not take advantage of his alliance with Genoa; yet, he did so discretely, through private means, namely hiring Doria's fleet and concluding vital loans with Genoese bankers. Charles was willing to do anything that was necessary to bring Genoa to the Habsburg side because Genoese resources were needed not only to win the Italian Wars, but also to face the growing Ottoman threat in the Mediterranean.[1] For all these reasons, it was acceptable and indeed reasonable for both parties (Habsburg Spain and Doria's Genoa) to leave questions of sovereignty and political status open. The importance of this progressive, mutual understanding that occurred in the period 1522–1528 (and that my work has described through a variety of sources) is hard to overestimate. At the French court, an accurate, politically acute perception of the Genoese polity never developed. Even more than a decade after irreparably losing Liguria and his best admiral, Francis continued to demonstrate a complete lack of knowledge with regard to Genoa's political and economic culture, as he unsuccessfully asked the Genoese republic for a conspicuous loan. The Genoese government, baffled by such request, hastened to respond that in Genoa the state had little money, and that if the monarch wanted to obtain a loan, he could do so in the capital market, contacting and bargaining with one of the many Genoese bankers and private moneylenders—just as Charles V was doing.[2]

Finally, although more research on this is surely needed, I have reached some tentative conclusions with regard to the Genoese political and economic contributions to the creation (and expansion) of the sixteenth-century Spanish Atlantic. The existence of Genoese networks within the Spanish Americas was made possible by at least three factors: Genoese mental capital and colonial techniques; developments in Hispanic-Genoese diplomatic relations (whose historical origins stretched back to the policies of Ferdinand the Catholic, as shown in chapter 4); and Castile's necessities linked to the enormous task of building and administering an empire on the other side of the ocean. Chapter 6 has opened a window on the lives, careers, and businesses of Genoese colonists in the New World, showing that they were present since the phase of the conquest and in different areas of the Americas, and that that they were not merely involved in trade and money-lending. Three centuries later, this Hispanic-Genoese Atlantic—which was at least in part the historical heir of the Genoese Mediterranean—survived to the disintegration of the Spanish Empire exactly because of its mimetic, adaptable and economically diverse nature.

As my work has endeavored to show, the story of the Ligurian immigrants who have entered the Atlantic world until the beginning of the past century, and of the numerous Genoese communities existing to this day across Latin America, started with pragmatic ideas of freedom and republican self-government. These ideas, born among the restless sailors, merchants, and bankers of a medieval city-port and its cosmopolitan colonies, inspired institutions and value systems that—protecting property rights and enfranchising private profit—stimulated innovation, economic calculation, and market expansion, while preventing (or at least delaying) the militarization and territorialization of the state. As shown in this book, the anonymous, wealthy, "dispersed" Genoese venturing the sea and living far from home assumed a central place in late medieval and early modern Genoese identity and self-perception. The results of this study, therefore, confirm that the history of economic development can, without doubt, benefit from being viewed through a broad chronological lens, able to illuminate the medieval origins of "modern" institutions and mindsets. Cosmopolitanism, which has become such a crucial term in the study of the Atlantic, finds itself impeccably embodied in the actions and historical legacies of Genoa's industrious and ubiquitous entrepreneurs.

NOTES

1. Dauverd, *Imperial Ambitions*, 31–35. See also Aurelio Espinosa, "The Grand Strategy of Charles V (1500–1558): Castile, War, and Dynastic Priority in the Mediterranean," *Journal of Early Modern History*, 9 (2005): 239–83.
2. The curious, telling episode is recounted in Pacini, *La Genova di Andrea Doria*, 458–59.

Bibliography

MANUSCRIPTS

Archivio di Stato di Genova:

Antico Comune, II–MCCCXXXX (*Massaria*).
Leges Genuenses, ms 133, cc. 96 r.–100 v.
Litterarum Comunis Ianue (Archivio Segreto), 24 A/1800, c. 78 r.–v.
Manoscritti di San Giorgio, IV (*Diversor. Negotior.*), 1453–1480, LX v.
Manoscritti, n. 707—*miscellanea Pallavicini.*
Manoscritti Bibl., 168.
Manoscritti Bibl., 183—"Compendio d'Antonio Doria delle cose di sua notitia, et memoria occorse al mondo nel tempo dell'imperatore Carlo Quinto."
Membranacei di San Giorgio, ms. IV (*Regule Comperarum Capituli*), cc. CLXXXVII r.–CLXXXXVIII v.
Missive Off. Caffe, 1464–1475, folio 11 v.
Ordini Religiosi, n. 672 (1423–1543).

Biblioteca Civica Berio (Genova):

Manoscritto 1.3.14, cc. 1v–12r.
M.r., VIII.1.12—"Congiura del conte Fiesco."
M.r., XIV.3.24, c. 137 v.

Biblioteca Universitaria di Genova:

Ricordi, ms. B.VIII.26.

Archivio di Stato di Milano:

Potenze Estere (Missive), 1464–1465, ms. 67, c. 34–r. 36.
Registri Ducali, 50.

Archivo General de Indias:

BUENOS AIRES, 2, l. 7. f. 26 r.–28 v.
CHARCAS, 418, l. 3, f. 148 r.–148 v.
CHILE, 45, m. 5, n. 1—"Informaciones: José Pastene Justiniano."
CHILE, 41, m. 12.
CONTRATACION, 5229, n. 1, r. 14.
CONTRATACION, 5301, n. 2, 69 r.–70 r.
CONTRATACION, 5414, n. 92.
FILIPINAS, 330, l.5, f. 28 r.–29 v.
INDIFERENTE, 421, 11, f. 336.
INDIFERENTE, 422, m. 16, f. 209 r.–209 v.
INDIFERENTE, 423, m. 18, f. 2 r.–3 r.
INDIFERENTE, 423, l.19, f. 480 v.–482 r.
INDIFERENTE, 423, l. 20, f. 511 r.–512 v. and f. 799 v.–800 v.
INDIFERENTE, 424, l. 21, f. 88 v.–90 r.
INDIFERENTE, 427, l. 30. f. 127 v.–129 r.
INDIFERENTE, 541, l. 1 DESP, f. 169–169 v.
INDIFERENTE, 740, n. 264.
INDIFERENTE, 1962, l. 5, f. 290 r.–290 v.
INDIFERENTE, 1963, l. 8, f. 215 r.–216 v. and f. 237 v.–238 r.
INDIFERENTE, 1966, l. 14, f. 152 v.
INDIFERENTE, 2052, n. 3.
INDIFERENTE, 2061, n. 171.
INDIFERENTE, 2066, n. 69.
JUSTICIA, 940, n. 4.
PATRONATO, 19, r. 2.
PATRONATO, 29—"Auto de posesión de Pedro de Valdivia: Chile."
PATRONATO, 277, n. 4, r. 83.
PANAMA, 13, r.10, n. 34.
PANAMA, 34A, n. 5.
PANAMA, 235, l.8, f. 14 r.–14 v.
QUITO, 29, n. 12.
QUITO, 80, n. 46.
SANTA FE, 987, l. 2, f. 55 v.

Biblioteca Vaticana:

Reginensi latini, ms 1393, cc. 115 v.–116 v.

British Library:

Libertas Londonienis, MS Additional 14252, fos. 104v–105v.

The National Archives (UK):

Special Collections (Petitions), SC 8/216/10773.
Special Collections (Petitions), SC 8/232/11560.
Special Collections (Petitions), SC 8/230/11465.
Special Collections (Petitions), SC 8/22/1098.

Newberry Library (Chicago):

Special Collections, Ayer, ms. 1878—"Account book of taxes paid to the Royal Treasury in Cuzco for the year 1591 [manuscript] 1591 Feb. 4–1595 Jan. 12."

Real Academia de la Historia (Madrid):

Colección Salazar y Castro, ms 2668, A-21, f. 138–142.
Colección Salazar y Castro, ms 2686, A-21, f. 197–198.
Colección Salazar y Castro, ms 2903, A-22, f. 233–235.
Colección Salazar y Castro, ms 4129, A-30, f. 261.
Colección Salazar y Castro, ms 4170, A-30, f. 393.
Colección Salazar y Castro, ms 4301, A-31, f. 223.
Colección Salazar y Castro, ms 6065, A-40, f. 432.

OTHER PRIMARY SOURCES

Atti della Società Ligure di Storia Patria, nuova serie, volume XI, 2. Genoa: SLSP, 1971.
Atti Rogati a Chilia da Antonio di Ponzò (1288–1289), ed. by Geo Pistarino. Genova: Università di Genova, 1971.
Atti Rogati a Tunisi da Pietro Battifoglio (1288–1289), ed. by Geo Pistarino. Genova: Università di Genova, 1986.
Bell, James Stanislaus. *Journal of a Residence in Circassia During the Years 1837, 1838, 1839*. London: Moxon, 1840.
Bembo, Pietro. *Opere in Volgare*. Firenze: Sansoni, 1961.
Cartas de Pedro de Valdivia, ed. by José Toribio Medina. Seville: Carmona, 1929.
Castiglione, Baldassarre. *Il Cortegiano*. Firenze: Sansoni, 1894.
Colección de documentos inéditos para la historia de Chile desde el viaje de Magallanes hasta la batalla de Maipo, 1518–1818, ed. by José Toribio Medina. Santiago; Ercilla, 1888–1902.
Contribuzioni alla storia di Genova specialmente nella poesia. Genova: ASLSP, 1888.
Descriptio adventus Ludovici XII Francorum Regis in Urbem Genuam, Anno MDII, authore Benedicto Portuensi Reipublicae Genuensis Cancellario, in Atti della Società Ligure di Storia Patria, volume XII, fasc.V. Genova: Tipografia del R.I. de'Sordo-muti, 1884.
Desimoni, Cornelio, ed. *Quatre titres des propriétés des Génois à Acre et à Tyr*. Archives de l'Orient latin, 2 (1884).
Dolfin, Giorgio. *Cronicha dela nobil cità de Venetia et dela sua provintia et distretto*. Venice: Cicogna, 2007.
Doria, Antonio. *Compendio d'Antonio Doria delle cose di sua notitia, et memoria occorse al mondo nel tempo dell'imperatore Carlo Quinto*. Genoa: Bellone, 1571.
Ferretto, A., ed. *Codice Diplomatico delle Relazioni fra la Liguria, la Toscana e la Lunigiana ai Tempi di Dante*. Genoa: ASLSP, 1901–1903.
Foglietta, Uberto. *Delle cose della Repubblica di Genova*. Milan: Antonij, 1575.
Gallo, Antonio. *Commentarius de Genuensium maritima classe in Barchinonenses expedita*. Città di Castello: Lapi, 1910.
Gioffre, Domenico, ed. *Lettere di Giovanni da Pontremoli, mercante Genovese: 1453–1459*. Genova: Università di Genova, 1982.
Giustiniani, Agostino. *Annali della Repubblica di Genova*. Genova: Canepa, 1854.
Góngora Marmolejo, Alonso de. *Historia de Todas las Cosas que han Acaecido en el Reino de Chile y de los que lo han gobernado*. Madrid: Iberoamericana, 2010.
Gray Birch, Walter de, ed. *Historical Charters and Constitutional Documents of the City of London*. London: Whiting, 1887.
Guicciardini, Francesco. *Istoria d'Italia*. London: Dove, 1822.
———. *Ricordi politici e civili*. Milano: Rizzoli, 1977.
Guidi, Jacopo d'Albizzotto. *El sommo della condizione di Vinegia*. Rome: Zauli, 1995.

Hommaire de Hell, Xavier. *Travels in the steppes of the Caspian Sea, the Crimea, the Caucasus, &c.* London: Chapman and Hall, 1847.
Jarry, Eugène, ed. *Les origines de la domination française à Gênes, 1392–1402*. Paris: Picard, 1896.
Letter written by Leo the Great to the bishops of Campania, Picene and Tuscany, dated October 443.
Liebermann, Felix, ed. *Die Gesetze der Angelsachsen*. Halle, 1903.
Machiavelli, Niccolò. *Istorie Fiorentine*. Firenze: Barbera, 1883.
———. *The Discourses*. London: Penguin, 2003.
———. *The Art of War*. Adelaide: The University of Adelaide Library, 2003.
———. *The Prince*. Adelaide: The University of Adelaide Library, 2008.
Il manuale di mercatura di Saminiato de' Ricci. Genova: Di Stefano, 1963.
Mascardi, Agostino. *Oppositioni e difesa alla 'Congiura del Conte Gio Luigi de' Fieschi'*. Venice: Ventura, 1630.
———. *La congiura del Conte Gio Luigi de' Fieschi*. Venice: Scaglia, 1637.
———. *History of the Fieschi's Conspiracy Against the State of Genoa*. London: Cooper, 1735.
———. *Lettera di monsignore Agostino Mascardi, circa la censura fatta al suo libro 'La congiura di Genova del conte Fieschi'*, in *Giornale Ligustico*, 6 (1879).
Morosini, Antonio. *Morosini Codex*. Ghezzo&Melville-Jones: Padua, 1999.
Nuova serie di documenti sulle relazioni di Genova coll'Impero Bizantino raccolti dal cav. Angelo Sanguineti e pubblicati con molte aggiunte dal prof. Gerolamo Bertolotto. Genova: ASLI, 1898.
Ovalle, Alonso de. *Histórica relacion del reyno de Chile*. Santiago: Istituto de Literatura Chilena, 1969.
Pacheco, Joaquín Francisco, and de Cárdenas, Francisco, and Mendoza, Luis Torres de, eds. *Colección de documentos inéditos: relativos al descubrimiento, conquista y organización de las antiguas posesiones españolas de América*. Madrid: Ministerio de Ultramar, 1865.
Piccolomini, Enea Silvio. "Description of Genoa," published in *Der Briefwechsel des Eneas Silvius Piccolomini*. In *Fontes rerum austriacarum*, edited by Rudolf Wolkan, (1909) LXI, letter 6.
Regulae Communis Ianuae anno MCCCLXIII, tempore ducatus domini Gabrielis Adurni conditae, in *Historiae Patriae Monumenta*, v. XVIII. Torino: Bocca, 1901, c. 243–388.
Roman, Hieronymo. *Republicas del Mundo*. Medina del Campo: Francisco del Canto, 1575.
Rovere, Antonella, ed. "Documenti della Maona di Chio (secc. XIV–XVI)," in *Atti della Società Ligure di Storia Patria, nuova serie*, volume XIX, 2. Genoa: SLSP, 1979.
Sabellico, Antonio. *Historie Vinitiane*. Venice, 1544.
Sigonio, Carlo. *Della vita et fatti di Andrea Doria*. Genoa: Pavoni, 1598.
Simonetta, Giovanni. *Le memorabili e magnanime imprese di Francesco Sforza*. Rubbettino, 2009.
The Statutes of the Realm. London: George Eyre and Andrew Strahan, 1810.
Tacitus, Cornelius. *Annals*. The University of Adelaide Library, 2008.
Tafur, Pero. *Andanças é viajes de Pero Tafur por diversas partes del mundo avidos: 1435–1439*. Madrid: Miguel Ginesta, 1874.
Torre, Antonio de la, ed. *Documentos sobre relaciones internacionales de los Reyes Católicos*. Barcelona: CSIC, 1949–1966.
Trattati e Negoziazioni Politiche della Repubblica di Genova (958–1797). Genova: ASLSP, 1960.
Vigna, Amedeo. "Codice diplomatico delle colonie tauro-liguri durante la signoria dell'Ufficio di S. Giorgio," in *Atti della Società Ligure di Storia Patria*, volume VI. Genova: Tipografia del R.I. de'Sordo-muti, 1868.
———. "Codice diplomatico delle colonie tauro-liguri durante la signoria dell'Ufficio di S. Giorgio," in *Atti della Società Ligure di Storia Patria*, volume VII, 1. Genova: Tipografia del R.I. de'Sordo-muti, 1871.

———. "Codice diplomatico delle colonie tauro-liguri durante la signoria dell'Ufficio di S. Giorgio," in *Atti della Società Ligure di Storia Patria*, volume VII, 2. Genova: Tipografia del R.I. de'Sordo-muti, 1879.

Villeneuve, Guillaume de. *Mémoires, 1494–97; contenant la conqueste du royaume de Naples par Charles VIII, et la manière dont les François en furent chasses*, in *Collection complète des mémoires relatifs à l'histoire de France*. Paris, 1826.

Walsingham, Thomas of. *Historia Anglicana*. Wiesbaden: Kraus, 1965.

SECONDARY SOURCES

Abulafia, David. "L'Attività Commerciale Genovese nell'Africa Normanna: la Città di Tripoli." In *Atti del Congresso Internazionale di Studi sulla Sicilia Normanna*, 395–402. Palermo: 1973.

———. *The French descent into Renaissance Italy, 1494–95: antecedents and effects*. Aldershot: Ashgate, 1995.

Alcalá Galve, Angel. "¿Un rey contra su reino? antiforalismo del rey Fernando en la imposición de la Inquisición a su Aragón." In *Ferdinandus Rex Hispaniarum, príncipe del renacimiento*, 309–318. Zaragoza, Palacio de la Aljafería, Cortes de Aragón, 6 de octubre de 2006 a 7 de enero de 2007.

Álvarez Nogal, Carlos. "Instituciones y desarrollo económico: la Casa de Contratación y la Carrera de Indias (1503–1790)." In *La Casa de la Contratación y la navegación entre España y las Indias*, edited by Antonio Acosta Rodríguez, Adolfo Luis González Rodríguez and Enriqueta Vila Vilar, 21–51. Seville: Univesidad de Sevilla, 2004.

———. "Las compañías bancarias genovesas en Madrid a comienzos del siglo XVII." *Hispania*, 65 (2005): 67–90.

Arciniega, Rosa. *Dos rebeldes españoles en el Perú: Gonzalo Pizarro ('El gran rebelde') y Lope de Aguirre ('El cruel tirano')*. Buenos Aires: Editorial Sudamericana, 1946.

Ardito, Alissa M. *Machiavelli and the Modern State: The Prince, the Discourses on Livy, and the Extended Territorial Republic*. Cambridge: Cambridge University Press, 2015.

Argenti, Philip P. *The occupation of Chios by the Genoese and their administration of the island, 1346–1566*. Cambridge: Cambridge University Press, 1958.

Ashtor, Eliyahu. *Levant Trade in the Later Middle Ages*. Princeton, NJ: Princeton University Press, 1983.

Assereto, Giovanni. *Le metamorfosi della Repubblica*. Savona: Ferraris, 1999.

Avramescu, Catalin. "Machiavelli and the Theory of Exemplary Constitutions." In *Niccolò Machiavelli: History, Power, and Virtue*, edited by Leonidas Donskis, 67–76. Amsterdam: Rodopi, 2011.

Balard, Michael. "Les Gènois dans l'ouest de la Mer Noire au XIV siècle." In *Actes du XIV Congrès International des ètudes byzantines (1971)*. Bucarest: 1975.

———. *La Romanie génoise (XIIe -début du XVe siècle)*. Rome: École française de Rome; 1978.

———. "Il Sistema Portuale Genovese d'Oltremare (secc. XIII–XV)." In *Il Sistema Portuale della Repubblica di Genova*. Genova: Universita' degli Studi di Genova, 1988.

———. "Genoese Naval Forces in the Mediterranean during the Fifteenth and Sixteenth Centuries," in *War at Sea*, edited by John B. Hattendorf and Richard W. Unger, 137–150. Suffolk: Boydell Press, 2003.

Banchero, Giuseppe. *Genova e le due Riviere*. Genova: Pellas, 1846.

Barbacetto, Stefano. *"La più gelosa delle pubbliche regalie"*. Venezia: Istituto veneto di scienze, lettere ed arti, 2008.

Bargellini, Mariano *Storia popolare di Genova*. Genova: Monni, 1836.

Bassani, Luigi Marco, and Lottieri, Carlo. "The Problem of Security; Historicity of the State and 'European Realism.'" In *The Myth of National Defense*, edited by Hans-Hermann Hoppe, 21–64. Auburn, AL: The Ludwig von Mises Institute, 2003.

Belgrano, Luigi Tommaso. "Un ammiraglio di Castiglia." *Archivio Storico Italiano* (1884): 42–53.

Bellini, Eraldo. *Agostino Mascardi tra "ars poetica" e "ars historica."* Milan: Vita e Pensiero, 2002.
Belloni, Cristina. "Ludovico il Moro, il protonotario Obietto Fieschi ed il cardinale Paolo Fregoso." In *La Storia dei genovesi*, XI, 193–218 (Genova, 1991).
Bengoa, José. *Historia de los antiguos mapuches del sur*. Santiago de Chile: Catalonia, 2004.
Bent, Theodore. *Genoa: How the Republic Rose and Fell*. London: Kegan Paul, 1881.
Bertone, Giorgio. *Andrea Doria: la nascita di un ammiraglio*. Recco: Le Mani, 2010.
Bettarini, Masca. "Agostino Mascardi, scrittore e teorico della storiografia nel Seicento." In *Quaderni di Nova historia*, 10 (Verona, 1953): 1–20.
Bettin Lattes, Gianfranco. *Un caso d'amour fou nella società aristocratica Genovese del secolo XVI*. Firenze, Firenze University Press, 2011.
Bisson, Thomas N. *The Medieval Crown of Aragon*. Oxford: Clarendon, 2000.
Bitossi, Carlo. *Il governo dei magnifici. Patriziato e politica a Genova fra Cinque e Seicento*. Genova: ECIG, 1990.
Boccara, Guillaume. *Los vencedores: historia del pueblo Mapuche en la epoca colonial*. San Pedro de Atacama: Universidad Católica del Norte, 2007.
Bonfiglio, Giovanni. *Gli italiani nella società peruviana. Una visione storica*. Torino: Fondazione Agnelli, 1999.
Borah, Woodrow Wilson. *Early colonial trade and navigation between Mexico and Peru*. Berkeley: University of California Press, 1954.
Borsari, Silvano. *Il dominio veneziano a Creta nel XIII secolo*. Napoli: Fiorentino, 1963.
Borucki, Alex, "Trans-imperial History in the Making of the Slave Trade to Venezuela, 1526–1811." *Itinerario*, 2 (2012): 29–54.
Boscassi, Angelo. "Le spese della Repubblica di Genova nel 1349." In *Gazzetta di Genova*, 2 (1915).
Boschetto, Luca. *Leon Battista Alberti e Firenze: Biografia, Storia, Letteratura*. Florence: Olschki, 2000.
Brading, David Anthony. *The First America*. Cambridge: Cambridge University Press, 1991.
Bratianu, Georges I. *Recherches sur le commerce genois dans la mer Noire au XIIIe siècle*. Paris: Geuthner, 1929.
———. *La mer noire; des origines à la conquête ottoman*. Munich: Societas academica Dacoromana, 1969.
Braudel, Fernand. *The Wheels of Commerce: Civilization and Capitalism 15th–18th Century*. New York: Harper and Row, 1982.
Braun, Harald E., and Vollendorf, Lisa, eds. *Theorising the Ibero-American Atlantic*. Boston: Brill, 2013.
Brilli, Catia. "Da Cadice a Buenos Aires: crisi e rinascita del commercio ligure nella nuova configurazione dell'Atlantico iberico (1797–1837)." *Annali della Fondazione Luigi Einaudi*, XLIII (2009): 99–125.
———. "The Genoese response to the collapse of the Spanish Empire in America." *Jahrbuch für Geschichte Lateinamerikas/Anuario de Historia de América Latina (JbLA)*, 47 (2010): 247–72.
———. "Il Rio de la Plata, nuova frontiera del commercio ligure (1750–1810)." In *Génova y la monarquía hispánica (1528–1713)*, edited by Manuel Herrero Sánchez, 933–964. Genova: SLSP, 2011.
Brucker, Gene. "The Italian Renaissance." In *A Companion to the Worlds of the Renaissance*, edited by Guido Ruggiero, 21–38. Oxford: Blackwell, 2002.
Buongiorno, Mario. *Il bilancio di uno stato medievale: Genova, 1340–1529*. Genova: Università di Genova, 1973.
Cabezuelo Pliego, José Vicente. "Diplomacia y Guerra en el Mediterráneo medieval. La liga véneto-aragonesa contra Génova de 1351." *Anuario de estudios medievales*, 36 (2006): 253–94.
Cadenas y Vicent, Vicente de. *El Protectorado de Carlos V en Génova: la "condotta" de Andrea Doria*. Madrid: Hidalguis, 1977.
Caferro, William. "City and Countryside in Siena in the Second Half of the Fourteenth Century." *Journal of Economic History*, 54 (1994): 85–103.

Campodonico, Pierangelo. *Andrea Doria*. Genova: Tormena, 1997.
Canale, Michele Giuseppe. *Nuova Istoria della Repubblica di Genova*. Firenze: LeMonnier, 1860.
Cañizares-Esguerra, Jorge, *Puritan Conquistadors: Iberianizing the Atlantic, 1550–1700*. Stanford: Stanford University Press, 2006.
———, ed. *The Atlantic in Global History, 1500–2000*. Upper Saddle River: Pearson Prentice Hall, 2007.
———. "Entangled Histories: Borderland Historiographies in New Clothes?" *American Historical Review* 112 (2007): 787–99.
Canny, Nicholas. "Writing Atlantic History; or, Reconfiguring the History of Colonial British America." *Journal of American History*, 3 (1999): 1093–114.
Canny, Nicholas, and Pagden, Anthony. *Colonial Identity in the Atlantic World, 1500–1800*. Princeton, NJ: Princeton University Press, 1989.
Canosa, Romano. *Banchieri genovesi e sovrani spagnoli tra Cinquecento e Seicento*. Sapere: Roma, 2000.
Carande, Ramón. *Carlos V y sus banqueros*. Barcelona: Critica, 1977.
Carneiro, Sarissa. "Tiempo dorado en la tierra vidriosa: el relato de los primeros años de la conquista de Chile." *Anales de literatura Chilena*, 10 (2008): 25–36.
Carnino, Cecilia. "Luxury and Consumption in Eighteenth-Century Italy: Intellectual History, Methodological Ideas and Interdisciplinary Research Practice." *History of European Ideas*, 40 (2014): 495–515.
Casado Alonso, Hilario. *Castilla y Europa: Comercio y mercaderes en los siglos XIV, XV y XVI*. Burgos: Diputación Provincial de Burgos, 1995.
Catalano, Franco. *La politica dell'equilibrio nell'Italia del Quattrocento*. Milano: La Goliardica, 1970.
Cervelli, Innocenzo. *Machiavelli e la crisi dello stato veneziano*. Napoli: Guida, 1974.
Chahin, Mack. *The Kingdom of Armenia*. London: Croom Helm, 1987.
Chambers, David S. *The Imperial Age of Venice, 1380–1580*. London: Thames and Hudson, 1970.
Chatziioannou, Maria Christina. "Mediterranean Pathways of Greek Merchants to Victorian England." In *Historical Review*, 7 (2010): 213–35.
Chojnacki, Stanley. "Political Adulthood in Fifteenth-Century Venice." *American Historical Review*, 91 (1986): 791–810.
Cochrane, Eric W. *Historians and Historiography in the Italian Renaissance*. Chicago: The University of Chicago Press, 1981.
Codinach, Guadalupe J. "Veracruz, almacén de plata en el Atlántico: la Casa Gordon y Murphy, 1805 1824." *Historia Mexicana*, 2 (1988): 325–53.
Coles, Paul. "The Crisis of Renaissance Society Genoa 1488–1507." *Past & Present*, 11 (1957): 17–47.
Costantini, Claudio. *La repubblica di Genova nell'età moderna*. Torino: UTET, 1991.
Cunninghame Graham, R. B. *Pedro de Valdivia, Conqueror of Chile*. London: Heinemann, 1929.
Dauverd, Céline. *Imperial Ambitions in the Early Modern Mediterranean*. New York: Cambridge University Press, 2015.
Davis, Robert C. *The War of the Fists: Popular Culture and Public Violence in Late Renaissance Venice*. New York, 1994.
Deletant, Dennis. "Genoese, Tartars and Rumanians at the Mouth of the Danube in the Fourteenth Century." *Slavonic and East European Review*, 4 (1984): 511–30.
Del Treppo, Mario. *I mercanti catalani e l'espansione della Corona d'Aragona nel secolo XV*. Napoli: L'Arte Tipografica, 1972.
Desimoni, Cornelio. *Nuovi Studi sull'Atlante Luxoro*. Genova: ASLSP, 1868.
Doehaerd, Renée. *Les relations commerciales entre gênes, la Belgique et l'outremont d'après les archives notariales génois es aux XIII et XIV siècles*. Bruxelles and Rome: Academia Belgica, 1941.

Dotson, John. "Venice, Genoa and Control of the Seas in the Thirteenth and Fourteenth Centuries." In *War at Sea in the Middle Ages and the Renaissance*, edited by John B. Hattendorf and Richard W. Hunger, 119–135. Woodbidge, Suffolk: Boydell Press, 2003.

Elliott, J. H. *Imperial Spain, 1469–1716*. Harmondsworth: Pelican, 1970.

———. "A Europe of Composite Monarchies." *Past & Present*, 137 (1992): 48–71.

———. *Empires of the Atlantic World: Britain and Spain in America 1492–1830*. New Haven: Yale University Press, 2006.

Epstein, Steven A. *Genoa and the Genoese, 958–1528*. Chapel Hill: University of North Carolina Press, 1996.

Espinosa, Aurelio. "The Grand Strategy of Charles V (1500–1558): Castile, War, and Dynastic Priority in the Mediterranean." *Journal of Early Modern History*, 9 (2005): 239–83.

Fasano Guarini, Elena. "Machiavelli and the Crisis of the Italian Republics." In *Machiavelli and Republicanism*, edited by Gisela Bock, Quentin Skinner, and Maurizio Viroli, 17–40. Cambridge: Cambridge University Press, 1991.

Felloni, Giuseppe. "Asientos, juros y Ferias de Cambio Desde El Observatorio Genovés (1541–1675)." In *Dinero y Crédito (siglos XVI al XIX)*, edited by Alfonso Otazu, 335–59. Madrid: Moneda y Crédito, 1978.

———. *Genova e la Storia della finanza: una serie di primati?* Genova: Tormena, 2005.

Fernández-Armesto, Felipe. *Ferdinand and Isabella*. London: Weidenfeld and Nicolson, 1975.

———. *Before Columbus*. London: Macmillan, 1987.

Ferrando Keun, Ricardo. *Y así nació la frontera: Conquista, guerra, ocupación, pacificación, 1550–1900.* Santiago: Editorial Antártica, 1986.

Ferrante, Riccardo. "Legge e Repubblica: l'esperienza genovese tra XIV e XVI secolo." In *Politica e cultura nelle repubbliche italiane dal Medioevo all'Età moderna*, edited by Simonetta Adorni Braccesi and Mario Ascheri, 237–65. Roma: Istituto Storico Italiano per l'Età Moderna e Contemporanea, 2001.

Ferrer Mallol, María Teresa. *Corsarios castellanos y vascos en el Mediterráneo medieval*. Barcelona: CSIC, 2000.

Filippi, Giovanni. *Una contesa tra Genova e Savona nel secolo XV*. Genova: Tip. Sordomuti, 1890.

Fiorita, Angelo L. *Andrea Doria*. Genova: Ceretti, 1950.

Galanti, Livio. "La Lunigiana nella Divina Commedia." In *Corriere Apuano* (22 March 1980).

Gallina, Mario. *Una società coloniale del Trecento: Creta fra Venezia e Bisanzio*. Venezia: Deputazione editrice, 1989.

Galloway, Patricia, ed. *The Hernando de Soto Expedition: History, Historiography, and "Discovery" in the Southeast*. Lincoln: University of Nebraska Press, 2005.

Gatti, L. *Un Catalogo dei Mestieri*. Genova: Centro Studi Storia Tecnica, 1980.

Geanakoplos, Deno J. *Emperor Michael Paleologus and the West, 1258–1282*. Cambridge: Harvard Press, 1959.

Gioffre, Domenico. *Il Mercato degli Schiavi a Genova nel Secolo XV*. Genova: Bozzi, 1971.

Giurescu, Constantin C. "The Genoese and the Lower Danube in the XIIIth and XIVth centuries." *Journal of European Economic History*, 5 (1976): 587–600.

Gli Sforza a Milano e in Lombardia e i loro rapporti con gli Stati italiani ed europei (1450–1535). Milan: Cisalpino-Goliardica, 1982.

González Arce, José Damián. "El Consulado Genovés de Sevilla (siglos XIII–XV)." *Studia Historica. Historia Medieval*, 28 (2010): 179–206.

González Cruz, David, ed. *Extranjeros y enemigos en Iberoamérica: la visión del otro: del Imperio español a la Guerra de la Independencia*. Madrid: Sílex, 2010.

Gorse, George. "Christopher Columbus and Andrea Doria: The Two Worlds of Renaissance Genoa." *Mediterranean Studies (Manchester University Press)*, 16 (2007): 120–42.

Gould, Eliga. "Entangled Histories, Entangled Worlds: The English-Speaking Atlantic as a Spanish Periphery." *American Historical Review*, 3 (2007): 764–86.

Grendi, Edoardo. "Andrea Doria: Uomo del Rinascimento." In *La repubblica aristocratica dei genovesi*. Bologna: Il Mulino, 1987.

———. *La repubblica aristocratica dei genovesi*. Bologna: Il Mulino, 1987.

Hackett, Francis. *Francis the First*. New York: Doubleday, Doran & Co., 1937.

Hemming, John. *The Conquest of the Incas*. London: Macmillan, 1993.
Herrero Sánchez, Manuel. "Una república mercantil en la órbita de la Monarquía Católica (1528–1684). Hegemonía y decadencia del agregado hispano-genovés." In *Sardegna, Spagna e Stati italiani nell'età di Carlo V*, edited by Bruno Anatra and Francesco Manconi, 183–200. Rome: Carocci, 2001.
———, ed. *Génova y la monarquía hispánica*. Genova: SLSP, 2011.
Himmelfarb, Gertrude. *The New History and the Old*. Cambridge: Harvard University Press, 1987.
Holmes, G. A. "Florentine Merchants in England, 1346–1436." *The Economic History Review*, 13 (1960): 193–208.
Hörnqvist, Mikael. "Machiavelli's military project and the Art of War." In *The Cambridge Companion to Machiavelli*, edited by John M. Najemy, 112–27. Cambridge: Cambridge University Press, 2010.
Hoskins, G. *Provincial England*. London: Macmillan, 1963.
Hudson, Pat. *History by Numbers*. Arnold: London, 2000.
Ibarra y Rodríguez, Eduardo. *El problema cerealista en España durante el reinado de los Reyes Católicos (1475–1516)*. Madrid: Instituto Sancho de Moncada de Economía, 1944.
Igual Luis, David. "¿Crisis? ¿Qué crisis? El comercio internacional en los reinos hispánicos de la Baja Edad Media." *Edad Media*, 8 (2007): 203–23.
Igual Luis, David and Germán Navarro Espinach. "Los genoveses en España en el tránsito del siglo XV al XVI." *Historia. Instituciones. Documentos*, 24 (1997): 261–332.
Invernizzi, Lucia. "Los trabajos de la guerra y los trabajos del hambre: dos ejes del discurso narrativo de la conquista de Chile (Valdivia, Vivar, Góngora Marmolejo)." *Revista Chilena de Literatura*, 36 (1990): 7–15.
Jones, Eric L. *The European Miracle: Environments, Economies, and Geopolitics in the History of Europe and Asia*. Cambridge: Cambridge University Press, 1987.
Jurdjevic, Mark. "Machiavelli's Hybrid Republicanism." *The English Historical Review* 122 (2007): 1228–257.
Keith, Robert G. *Conquest and Agrarian Change*. Cambridge: Harvard University Press, 1976.
King, Charles. *The Black Sea*. Oxford: Oxford University Press, 2004.
Kirk, Thomas A. *Genoa and the Sea*. London: Hopkins University Press, 2005.
Knapton, Michael. "Venezia e Treviso nel Trecento. Proposte per una ricerca sul primo dominio veneziano a Treviso." In *Tomaso da Modena e il suo tempo*, edited by Amelio Tagliaferri, 41–78. Treviso: 1981.
———. "Venice and the Terraferma." In *The Italian Renaissance State*, edited by Andrea Gamberini and Isabella Lazzarini, 132–55. Cambridge: Cambridge University Press, 2012.
Krueger, H. C. "Genoese Trade with North-West Africa in the Twelfth Century." *Speculum*, VIII (1933): 377–95.
———. "Early Genoese Trade with Atlantic Marocco." *Medievalia et Humanistica*, III (1945): 3–15.
La Corona d'Arargona in Italia (sec. XIII–XVIII), XIV Congresso di storia della Corona d'Aragona. Sassari: Delfino, 1993.
Ladero Quesada, Miguel Angel. "La esclavitud por guerra a fines del siglo XV: el caso de Malaga." In *Hispania*, 27 (1967), pp. 63–88.
Le Mesurier, E. A. *Genoa: Her History as Written in her Buildings*. Genoa: Donath, 1889.
Leoni, Bruno. *Freedom and the Law*. Indianapolis: Liberty Fund, 1991.
———. "Two Views of Liberty, Occidental and Oriental(?)." *Libertarian Papers* 1 (2009): 1–16.
Levati, Luigi Maria. *Dogi perpetui di Genova (1339–1528)*. Genova: Certosa, Marchese & Campora, 1928.
Llopis, Enrique, and Comín, Francisco, and Hernández, Mauro. *Historia económica de España, siglos X–XX*. Barcelona: Critica, 2002.
Lockhart, James. *Spanish Peru 1532–1560: a Colonial Society*. Madison: University of Wisconsin Press, 1968.
Lopez, Robert Sabatino. "Il predominio economico dei genovesi nella monarchia spagnola." *Giornale storico e letterario della Liguria*, 2 (1936): 65–74.

———. *Storia delle colonie genovesi nel Mediterraneo*. Bologna: Zanichelli, 1938.
———. "Alfonso el Sabio y el primer almirante genovés de Castilla." *Quadernos de Historia de España*, 14 (1950): 5–16.
———. "Majorcans and Genoese on the North Sea Route in the Thirteenth Century." *Revue Belge de Philologie et d'Histoire*, 29 (1951): 1163–179.
———. *Naissance de l'Europe*. Paris: Colin, 1962.
———. "Market Expansion: The Case of Genoa." *The Journal of Economic History*, 4 (1964): 445–64.
———. *The Commercial Revolution of the Middle Ages, 950–1350*. Cambridge; New York: Cambridge University Press, 1998.
Luzzatti, Ivo. *Andrea Doria*. Milano: Garzanti, 1943.
Macfarlane, Alan. *The Riddle of the Modern World: Of Liberty, Wealth and Equality*. London: Macmillan, 2002.
Mack Smith, Denis. *A History of Sicily, Medieval Sicily: 800–1713*. London: Chatto&Windus, 1968.
Madden, Thomas F. *Enrico Dandolo and the Rise of Venice*. Baltimore: John Hopkins University Press, 2007.
Mallet, Michael E. "La conquista della Terraferma," in *Storia di Venezia*, edited by Alberto Tenenti and Ugo Tucci, 181–244. Rome: Istituto della Enciclopedia italiana, 1996.
Mallet, Michael E., and Hale, J. R. *The Military Organization of a Renaissance State: Venice, c. 1400 to 1617*. New York: Cambridge University Press, 1984.
Malnate, Natale. *Della storia del porto di Genova dalle origini all'anno 1892*. Genova: Istituto sordo-muti, 1892.
Marin, Manuela and El Hour, Rachid. "Captives, Children and Conversion." *Journal of Economic and Social History of the Orient*, 4 (1998): 453–73.
Marino, John A. "Economic Encounters and the First Stages of a World Economy." In *A Companion to the Worlds of the Renaissance*, Guido Ruggiero, 279–95. Oxford: Blackwell, 2002.
McCloskey, Deirdre N. *The Treasured Bourgeoisie: How Markets and Innovation Became Ethical, 1600–1848, and Then Suspect*. Chicago: Chicago University Press, 2015.
McCuaig, William. *Carlo Sigonio: The Changing World of the Late Renaissance*. Princeton, NJ: Princeton University Press, 2014.
McKee, Sally. "The Revolt of St. Tito." *Mediterranean Historical Review*, 9 (1994): 173–204.
———. *Uncommon Dominion: Venetian Crete and the Myth of Ethnic Purity*. Philadelphia, 2002.
Miller, William. *The Latins in the Levant, a History of Frankish Greece*. New York: Dutton, 1908.
———. *Trebizond: The Last Greek Empire*. Amsterdam: Hakkert, 1968.
Mitler, Luis. "The Genoese in Galata: 1453–1682." *International Journal of Middle East Studies*, 10 (1979): 71–91.
Morison, Samuel E. *The Great Explorers*. New York: Oxford University Press, 1978.
Muir, Edward. *Civic Ritual in Renaissance Venice*. Princeton, NJ: Princeton University Press, 1986.
Musso, Riccardo. "Lo stato cappellazzo. Genova tra Adorno e Fregoso (1436–1464)." *Studi di storia medievale e diplomatica*, 17 (1998): 223–88.
Nader, Helen. "Desperate Men, Questionable Acts: The Moral Dilemma of Italian Merchants in the Spanish Slave Trade." *The Sixteenth Century Journal*, 33 (2002): 401–22.
Neri, Enzo. *Savona contro Genova: secolo XIII*. Savona: Stamperia Officina d'arte, 1976.
North, Douglass C. "Institutions." *The Journal of Economic Perspectives*, 5 (1991) 97–112.
Norwich, John J. *A History of Venice*. Harmondsworth: Penguin, 1983.
O'Connell, Monique. "The Venetian Patriciate in the Mediterranean: Legal Identity and Lineage in Fifteenth-Century Venetian Crete." *Renaissance Quarterly*, 57 (2004) 466–93.
Ortalli, Gherardo. "Venezia e Creta. Fortune e contraccolpi di una conquista." In *Venezia e Creta*, edited by Idem, 9–32. Venezia: Istituto veneto di scienze, lettere ed arti, 1998.
Owen Hughes, Diane. "Urban Growth and Family Structure in Medieval Genoa." *Past & Present*, 66 (1975): 3–28.

Pacini, Arturo. *I presupposti politici del secolo dei genovesi: la riforma del 1528*. Genova: SLSP, 1990.
———. *La tirannia delle fazioni e la repubblica dei ceti: vita politica e istituzioni a Genova tra Quattro e Cinquecento*. Bologna: Il Mulino, 1992.
———. *La Genova di Andrea Doria nell'Impero di Carlo V*. Florence: Olschki, 1999.
———. "Ideali repubblicani, lotta politica e gestione del potere a Genova." In *Politica e cultura nelle repubbliche italiane dal Medioevo all'Età moderna*, edited by Simonetta Adorni Braccesi e Mario Ascheri, 189–236. Roma: Istituto Storico Italiano per l'Età Moderna e Contemporanea, 2001.
Pandiani, Emilio. *Vita privata genovese nel Rinascimento*. Genova: Tipografia Nazionale di L. Sambolino, 1915.
Papagno, Giuseppe. *I Portoghesi d'Oro*. Reggio Emilia: Diabasis, 2006.
Pavlovic Karpov, Sergej. *L'Impero di Trebisonda, Venezia, Genova e Roma: 1204–1461*. Roma: Il Veltro, 1986.
Pellegrini, Marco. *Le guerre d'Italia: 1494–1530*. Bologna: Il Mulino, 2009.
Perria, Antonio. *Il corsaro Andrea Doria*. Milano: Longanesi, 1973.
Petracchi, Adriana. *Norma "costituzionale" e prassi nella Serenissima Repubblica di Genova*. Milan: Giuffrè, 1989.
Petti Balbi, Giovanna. *Le relazioni tra Genova e la Corona d'Aragona dal 1468 al 1478*. Bordighera: Istituto Internazionale Studi Liguri, 1974.
———. *Simon Boccanegra e la Genova del '300*. Genova: Marietti, 1991.
———. "Tra dogato e principato: il Tre e Quattrocento." *Storia di Genova: Mediterraneo Europa Atlantico*, ed. Dino Puncuch. Genova: SLSP, 2003: 233–324.
———. *Governare la città. Pratiche sociali e linguaggi politici a Genova in età medievale* Firenze: Firenze University Press, 2007.
Peyronnet, Georges. *Il Ducato di Milano sotto Francesco Sforza, 1450–1466*. Firenze: Olschki, 1958.
Phillips, J. R. S. *The Medieval Expansion of Europe*. Oxford: Oxford University Press, 1988.
Phillips, William D., and Phillips, Carla Rahn. *The Worlds of Christopher Columbus*. Cambridge: Cambridge University Press, 1992.
Pieri, Piero. *Il Rinascimento e la crisi militare italiana*. Torino: Einaudi, 1952.
Pike, Ruth. *Enterprise and Adventure: The Genoese in Seville and the Opening of the New World*. Ithaca, NY: Cornell University Press, 1966.
Pistarino, Geo. "La spesa ordinaria della Repubblica di Genova nella crisi del 1461–1462." In *Miscellanea di Storia Ligure in memoria di Giorgio Falco*, 239–63. Genova: Università di Genova, 1966.
———. "Chio dei Genovesi." *Studi medievali*, 10 (1969): 3–68.
Podestà, Francesco. *L'acquedotto di Genova: 1071–1879*. Genova: Istituto sordo-muti, 1879.
———. *Il porto di Genova: dalle origini fino alla caduta della repubblica Genovese*. Genova: Spiotti, 1913.
Poloni, Alma. "La mobilità sociale nelle città comunali italiane nel Trecento." In *I comuni di Jean-Claude Maire Vigueur. Percorsi storiografici*, edited by Maria Teresa Caciorgna, Sandro Carocci, and Andrea Zorzi, 281–304. Rome: Viella, 2014.
Pontieri, Ernesto. *Per la storia del regno di Ferrante I d'Aragona re di Napoli*. Napoli: 1969.
Pozza, Marco. *I patti con l'impero latino di Costantinopoli, 1205–1231*. Rome: Viella, 2004.
Prodi, Paolo. "Storia sacra e controriforma, Nota sulle censure al commento di Carlo Sigonio a Sulpicio Severo," *Annali dell'Istituto storico italo-germanico in Trento* (1977): 75–104.
———. "Vecchi appunti e nuove riflessioni su Carlo Sigonio," in *Nunc alia tempora, alii mores. Storici e storia in età postridentina*, Atti del Convegno internazionale, Torino (24–27 settembre 2003), ed. M. Firpo (Firenze 2005), 291–310.
Queller, Donald E., ed. *The Latin Conquest of Constantinople*. New York: Wiley, 1973.
Raggio, Osvaldo. *Faide e parentele: lo stato genovese visto dalla Fontanabuona*. Torino: Einaudi, 1990.
Raico, Ralph. "The Theory of Economic Development and the 'European Miracle.'" In *The Collapse of Development Planning*, edited by Peter J. Boettke, 37–58. New York: NYU Press, 1994.

Reynolds, Robert L. "In Search of a Business Class in Thirteenth-Century Genoa." *The Journal of Economic History*, 5 (1945): 1–19.

Ricciardelli, Fabrizio: *The Myth of Republicanism in Renaissance Italy*. Turnhout: Brepols, 2015.

Riley-Smith, Jonathan. *The Feudal Nobility and the Kingdom of Jerusalem*. London: Macmillan, 1973.

Roa y Ursua, Luis de. *El reyno de Chile, 1535–1810: estudio histórico, genealógico y biográfico*. Valladolid: Talleres, 1954.

Ronco Valenti, Maria Luigia. "Un angolo di Liguria nel cuore di Trastevere." *Storia*, 4 (2004): 70–79.

Roover, Raymond de. "The Organization of Trade." In *The Cambridge Economic History of Europe*, edited by M. M. Postan, E. E. Rich, and E. Miller, 42–118. Cambridge: Cambridge University Press, 1963.

Rota, Maria Pia. "Insediamenti genovesi e corsi nella Corsica del Cinquecento." In *Atti del Congresso internazionale di studi storici Rapporti Genova-Mediterraneo-Atlantico nell'eta' moderna—1982*, edited by Raffaele Belvederi, 65–79. Genova: Università di Genova, 1983.

Rothbard, Murray N. *A History of Money and Banking in the United States: The Colonial Era to World War II*. Auburn, AL: Ludwig von Mises Institute, 2002.

Ruddock, Alwyn A. "Alien Merchants in Southampton in the Later Middle Ages." *The English Historical Review*, 61 (1946): 1–17.

Ruggiero, Guido. *The Boundaries of Eros: Sex Crime and Sexuality in Renaissance Venice*. Oxford: Oxford University Press, 1985.

Salavert y Roca, Vincente. "El problema estratégico del Mediterraneo occidental y la política aragonesa (siglos XIV y XV)." In *Actas y comunicaciones del IV congreso de historia de la Corona d'Aragón*, 201–21. Palma de Mallorca: Gráficas Miramar, 1959.

Salinas Araneda, Carlos R. "Los oficiales reales de Indieas en el siglo XVII." in *Poder y presion fiscal en la America española*, 363–90. Valladolid: Universidad de Valladolid, 1986.

Sanchez-Bella, Ismael. *La organisación financiera de las Indias (siglo XVI)*. Seville: Escuela de Estudios Hispano-Americanos, 1968.

Savelli, Rodolfo. *La repubblica oligarchica: legislazioni, istituzioni e ceti a Genova nel Cinquecento*. Milano: Giuffrè, 1981.

———. *Dalle confraternite allo stato: il sistema assistenziale genovese nel Cinquecento*. Genova: Società Ligure di Storia Patria, 1984.

———. "'Capitula,' 'Regulae,' e pratiche del diritto a Genova tra XIV e XV secolo." In *Statuti città territori in Italia e Germania tra Medioevo ed Età moderna*, edited by G. Chittolini and D. Willoweit, 447–502. Bologna: Il Mulino, 1991.

———. "Il rovescio e il diritto. Immagini e problemi della storia di Genova in età moderna." In *El siglo de los genoveses*, edited by Piero Boccardo and Clario Di Fabio, 15–21. Milano: 1999.

Scott, Tom. *The City-State in Europe, 1000–1600*. Oxford: Oxford University Press, 2012.

Sempat Assadourian, Carlos. "La renta de la encomienda en la decada de 1550." *Revista de Indias*, 48 (1988): 109–46.

Sestan, Ernesto. "Le origini delle signorie cittadine: un problema storico esaurito?" in *Italia Medievale*, edited by idem, 193–223. Napoli: Edizioni Scientifiche Italiane, 1968.

Sforza, Giovanni. *Storia di Pontremoli dalle origini al 1500*. Firenze: Franceschini, 1904.

Shaw, Christine, ed. *Italy and the European Powers. The Impact of War, 1500–1530*. Boston: Brill, 2006.

Shaw, Christine, "Concepts of *Libertà* in Renaissance Genoa." In *Communes and Despots in Medieval and Renaissance Italy*, edited by John E. Law and Bernadette Paton, pp. 177–92. Burlington: Ashgate, 2010.

———. "Genoa." In *The Renaissance State*, edited by Andrea Gamberini and Isabella Lazzarini, 220–36. Cambridge: Cambridge University Press, 2012.

Sidbury, Jim and Cañizares-Esguerra, Jorge. "Mapping Ethnogenesis in the Early Modern Atlantic." *William and Mary Quarterly*, 68 (2011): 181–208.

Sieveking, Heinrich. *Studio sulle finanze genovesi nel medioevo e in particolare sulla Casa di San Giorgio*. Genova: ASLSP, 1905–1906.

Solano Costa, Fernando. "El reino de Aragon durante el gobierno de Fernando el Catolico." *Cuadernos de historia Jerónimo Zurita*, 16–18 (1963–1965): 221–46.

Stevenson Weldon Vernon, Ida. *Pedro de Valdivia, Conquistador of Chile*. Austin: University of Texas Press, 1946.

Stinger, Charles L. *The Renaissance in Rome*. Bloomington: Indiana University Press, 1998.

Studnicki-Gizbert, Daviken. *A nation upon the ocean sea: Portugal's Atlantic diaspora and the crisis of the Spanish Empire, 1492–1640*. New York and Oxford: Oxford University Press, 2007.

Taviani, Carlo. *Superba discordia: guerra, rivolta e pacificazione nella Genova di primo Cinquecento*. Roma: Viella, 2008.

TePaske, John J., and Klein, Herbert S. *The Royal Treasuries of the Spanish Empire in America*. Durham, NC: Duke University Press, 1982.

Thomas, Hugh. *The Golden Empire*. New York: Random House, 2010.

Thornton, John. *Africa and Africans in the Making of the Atlantic World*. Cambridge: Cambridge University Press, 1998.

Toffolo, Sandra. *Depicting the City, Depicting the State. Fifteenth-Century Representations of Venice and the Venetian Terraferma*. PhD diss., European University Institute, 2013.

———. "Constructing a Mainland State in Literature: Perceptions of Venice and its *Terraferma* in Marin Sanudo's Geographical Descriptions." *Renaissance and Reformation* 37 (2014): 5–30.

Tognetti, Sergio. "Attività industriali e commercio di manufatti nelle città toscane del tardo Medioevo (1250 ca.–1530 ca.)." *Archivio storico italiano*, 159 (2001): 423–79.

Vanzetti, Carlo. *Due secoli di storia dell'agricoltura veronese*. Verona: Giuliari, 1965.

Varela, Consuelo. "El entorno florentino de Cristòbal Colòn." In *Colloquia sulla presenza italiana in Andalusia nel basso medioevo*, edited by Alberto Boscolo and Bibiano Torres, 125–34. Rome: Cappelli, 1984.

Vega, Alejandra. "Experiencias de cordillera, ecos de frio: relatos cruzados entre Chile y Quito en el siglo XVI." *Revista Chilena de Literatura*, 80 (2011): 223–42.

Verlinden, Charles. "The Rise of Spanish Trade in the Middle Ages." *The Economic History Review*, 10 (1940) 44–59.

———. "Italian Influence in Iberian Colonization" *The Hispanic American Historical Review*, 33 (1953): 199–211.

———. *The Beginnings of Modern Colonization*. Ithaca, NY: Cornell University Press, 1970.

Vermeersch, Arthur. "Usury." In *The Catholic Encyclopaedia*. New York: Robert Appleton, 1912, v. 15, 235.

Vicent Vives, Jaime. *An Economic History of Spain*. Princeton, NJ: Princeton University Press, 1969.

Viroli, Maurizio. *From Politics to Reason of State*. Cambridge: Cambridge University Press, 2005.

Yeager, Timothy J. "Encomienda or Slavery?," *The Journal of Economic History*, 4 (1995): 842–59.

Zavala, Silvio Arturo. *La encomienda Indiana*. Madrid: Centro de Estudios Historicos, 1935.

Zevakin, E. S. and Pencko, N. A. "Ricerche sulla Storia delle Colonie Genovesi nel Caucaso Occidentale nei Secoli XIII–XV." In *Miscellanea di Studi Storici* (Genova: Bozzi, 1969).

Zorzi, Andrea. "The Popolo." In *Italy in the Age of the Renaissance: 1300–1550*, edited by John M. Najemy, 145–64. Oxford: Oxford University Press, 2006.

Index

About the Author

Dr. Matteo Salonia is currently adjunct lecturer at the University of Liverpool. He has also taught at Manchester Metropolitan University.

www.ingramcontent.com/pod-product-compliance
Lightning Source LLC
Chambersburg PA
CBHW071251180926
51613CB00001B/12
9781498534215